A Trag

How a Good vs. Evil Mentality

Destroyed the Bush Presidency

A Tragic Legacy

GLENN GREENWALD

CROWN PUBLISHERS NEW YORK

Library of Congress Cataloging-in-Publication Data
Greenwald, Glenn.
A tragic legacy : how a good vs. evil mentality destroyed the Bush presidency /
Glenn Greenwald.—1st ed.
p. cm.
1. Bush, George W. (George Walker), 1946– —Political and social views.
2. Bush, George W. (George Walker), 1946– —Ethics.   3. Bush, George W.
(George Walker), 1946– —Influence.   4. United States—Politics and government—
2001—Decision making.   5. Good and evil—Political aspects—United States—Case
studies.   6. Political leadership—United States—Case studies.   7. Character—
Case studies.   8. Presidents—United States—Biography.   I. Title.
E903.3.G74   2007
973.931092—dc22   2007010813

ISBN 978-0-307-35419-8

Printed in the United States of America

DESIGN BY BARBARA STURMAN

10 9 8 7 6 5 4 3

First Edition

CONTENTS

PREFACE   ix

CHAPTER ONE   *Bush Agonistes*   I

CHAPTER TWO   *The Manichean Warrior*   39

CHAPTER THREE   *The Manichean Road to Baghdad*   97

CHAPTER FOUR   *Iran: The Next War?*   153

CHAPTER FIVE   *The Manichean Paradox:*
                   Moral Certitude Tramples Moral Constraints   229

CHAPTER SIX   *The Tragic Legacy of George W. Bush*   265

ACKNOWLEDGMENTS   285

INDEX   287

PREFACE

Let me just first tell you that I've never been more convinced that the decisions I made are the right decisions.

—GEORGE W. BUSH, September 12, 2006,
speaking to a group of right-wing pundits in the White House

I do not think much of a man who is not wiser today than he was yesterday.

—ABRAHAM LINCOLN

The attacks of September 11 presented George Bush with a rare opportunity of historic proportions. Virtually overnight, he led a suddenly unified and purposeful citizenry that was prepared—even eager—to set aside the petty though intense partisan wars which had plagued the country for the prior two decades, and once again focus on the nation's core values and shared political principles, the ones which transcend ideological differences and which make America so worth defending.

The president's principled and eloquent post-9/11 rhetoric solidified this unity and ensured that the vast bulk of Americans—Republicans, Democrats, and Independents—would loyally support both him and his policies over the course of the next two years. There are very few periods in American presidential history, if there are any, that compare to the widespread popularity and unchallenged power George Bush amassed—not only in the immediate aftermath of the terrorist attacks but also up to, including, and for some time following the March 2003 invasion of Iraq. Few presidents have soared as high or commanded such unthwarted power as did the post-9/11 George W. Bush.

And yet, as the end of his presidency approached, historians and political figures from across the ideological spectrum—including many of his previously most fervent supporters—were speaking of the Bush legacy as one of colossal failure. As President Bush entered his lame-duck term, few presidents in American history had ever been as isolated or as unpopular for such a sustained duration. Democrats and Independents intensely and irreversibly disapproved of his presidency, and droves of previously loyal Republicans—both political leaders and rank-and-file—abandoned him as well.

The sheer scope of the collapse of the Bush presidency is most dramatically illustrated by comparing the two midterm elections that took place during his tenure. In 2002, the Republican Party was able to ride President Bush's potent personal popularity to a truly historic victory in the midterm elections, as it seized control of the Senate and increased substantially its control of the House—an extremely rare feat for a sitting president's party. Yet the 2006 midterm election produced the precisely opposite outcome for Republicans: a crashing and shattering defeat, universally attributed to the country's deep dislike of the president and his signature, legacy policy—the invasion and ongoing occupation of Iraq. The heights to which George Bush ascended in the first few years of his presidency were matched only by the severe depths to which he plunged.

How and why did the Bush administration squander its deep-seated and seemingly intractable popularity? How and why did the president tragically waste the opportunity to restore at least some enduring unity in the American populace and rejuvenate a shared sense of national identity and purpose? This book explores these questions by examining the Bush legacy—a legacy of profound failure, chaos, and incalculable, perhaps unprecedented, damage to the country.

The Bush legacy is tragic because its outcome was far from inevitable. Historical circumstances created an opportunity for lasting achievement, but the president's chosen Manichean worldview, accompanied by his suffocatingly rigid conviction in his own Rightness, steered the country on a course of disaster and literally prevented him from modifying that course, let alone choosing another, even as inescapable evidence of his own failures mounted.

The steep and powerful rise of the Bush presidency, and its abrupt and cataclysmic collapse, are examined and documented in chapter 1. As that chapter demonstrates, it is genuinely difficult to overstate the extent to which the country has repudiated George Bush.

Following the resounding 2006 midterm defeat, the president's approval ratings neared the level of Richard Nixon's when he was forced from office in disgrace. President Bush's isolation and abandonment became so severe that even red-state Republican officeholders facing reelection were forced to offer their constituents proof that they vigorously opposed Bush and his policies, and even more tellingly, the movement that was most responsible for Bush's twice being elected as president and that chose him as its standard-bearer—political conservatism—undertook a full-blown effort to disassociate George Bush from their ideology by suddenly claiming that, all along, Bush was never a "real conservative."

Elite political pundits who had supported both the president and his war literally began denying having done so. President Bush became such a radioactive commodity—such a clear consensus had arisen that he was one of the worst presidents, if not the single worst president, in American history—that disassociating oneself from him became a matter of political survival and a prerequisite for preserving any remnants of credibility.

The core principles and decision-making patterns that drove George Bush and engendered the collapse of his presidency are examined in chapter 2. Despite the continuous and enthusiastic embrace of Bush by the vast bulk of political conservatives, it has long been vividly clear that the president (just as was true for Ronald Reagan) simply does not govern in accordance with the claimed principles of political conservatism as they exist in their "pure," abstract form. George Bush has presided over massive increases in domestic spending, the conversion of a multibillion-dollar surplus into an even larger deficit, the creation of vast new bureaucratic fiefdoms, an unprecedented expansion of the power of the federal government, governmental intrusions into multiple areas previously preserved for the states or off-limits altogether, and a wanton disregard for the rule of law. Whatever political philosophy has propelled George Bush's governance, it is not the abstract tenets of Goldwater/small-government conservatism.

Instead, what lies at the heart of the Bush presidency is an absolutist worldview capable of understanding all issues and challenges only in the moralistic, overly simplistic, and often inapplicable terms of "Good vs. Evil." The president is driven by his core conviction that he has found the Good, that he is a crusader for it, that anything is justified in pursuit of it, and that anything which impedes his decision-making is, by definition, a deliberate or unwitting ally of Evil. This mentality has single-handedly prevented him from governing, changing course, and even engaging realities that deviate from those convictions. The president's description of himself as "the Decider" is accurate. His mind-set has dominated the American political landscape throughout his presidency, and virtually all significant events of the Bush Era are a by-product of his core Manichean mentality.

Chapter 3 examines how this mind-set led the United States into disaster in Iraq and subsequently ensured a brutal, entirely counterproductive and seemingly endless occupation. Chapter 4 details how precisely this same mind-set, clung to as tenaciously as ever before by the president, has also placed the country on a potentially even more disastrous, and seemingly inevitable, collision course with Iran.

As those two chapters demonstrate, the president became convinced, by a variety of disparate factions which influenced him, that those countries and their leaders were literally the embodiment of "ultimate Evil"— the equivalent of Adolf Hitler—and that full-scale destruction of the "enemies" via unrelenting war was and is the only viable option. That single-minded conviction remained—and continues to remain—in place even as its obvious failures became glaringly evident and even as constraints of resources and other realities rendered pursuit of that militaristic course plainly disastrous. The discussion in these chapters includes an examination of how the country's key political institutions—led by the national media—came to enable and even embrace the president's moralistic mentality, thereby precluding any meaningful debate or rational examination for the courses he chose.

Chapter 5 examines the ultimate tragic irony of George Bush's Manichean morality—namely, that embracing a core, unshakable conviction of one's own rightness legitimizes, and even renders inevitable, some of the most amoral and ethically monstrous policies, justified as necessary means to achieve a morally imperative end. The Bush presidency, awash in moralistic rhetoric, has ushered in some of the most extremist, previously unthinkable and profoundly un-American practices—from indefinite, lawless detentions, to the use of torture, to bloody preventive wars of choice, to the abduction of innocent people literally off the street or from their homes, to radical new theories designed to vest in the president the power to break the law.

These measures were pursued not despite the moralistic roots of the president's agenda, but *because* of them. Those who believe that they are on the path of righteousness, who are crusaders for the objective Good, will frequently become convinced that there can be no limitations on the weapons used to achieve their ends. The moral imperative of their agenda justifies—even requires—all steps undertaken to fulfill it. As the president ceaselessly proclaimed the Goodness at the heart of America's destiny and its role in the world, his actions have resulted in an almost full-scale destruction of America's moral credibility in almost every country and on every continent. The same president who has insisted that core moralism drives him has brought America to its lowest moral standing in history.

The final chapter, chapter 6, places the Bush legacy in historical context, and finds that only one modern president can remotely be compared to Bush in terms of how isolated, weakened, and unpopular Bush has become: the Vietnam-plagued Lyndon Johnson. But whereas Johnson had a string of widely admired and long-lasting domestic achievements, Bush has virtually none.

The damage of Johnson's one-term presidency was contained by his decision not to seek reelection, a decision mandated by intense opposition from every sector of the country, including Johnson's own party. Bush, however, will have wielded power for eight long, highly eventful years—fueled by a Congress controlled by loyalists in his party, a generally docile press, and a political movement that rarely opposed any decision he made. For that reason, and in stark contrast to the far more contained impact of the Johnson administration, the Bush presidency has transformed the national character of the United States and fundamentally altered how the world perceives our country.

It is always crucial for a nation that has endured—and allowed—such radical change to understand why it has occurred. And, in every case, the value of understanding what drives an American presidency is self-evident. But in the case of the Bush presidency—undoubtedly one of the most consequential presidencies in American history—the task of examining its dynamics and its legacy is vital for an entirely separate reason.

George W. Bush is a single individual, who will permanently leave the American political stage on January 20, 2009. But the political movement that transformed Bush into an icon—and which loyally supported, glorified, and sustained him—is not going anywhere. Bush is but a by-product and a perfect reflection of that movement, one which has been weakened and diminished by Bush's staggering unpopularity but is far from dead. It intends to rejuvenate itself by finding a new leader, one who appears cosmetically different from the deeply unpopular Bush, but who, in reality, shares Bush's fundamental beliefs about the world (which are the core beliefs of that movement) and who intends to follow the same disastrous course Bush has chosen for this country.

To understand Bush and his presidency, then, is not merely a matter of historical interest. Examining the dynamic driving his presidency is also vital for understanding the right-wing political movement that has dominated our political landscape since the mid-1990s—a movement that calls itself "conservative" but which, as many traditional conservatives have themselves complained, has no actual allegiance to the political principles for which conservatism claims to stand. That is the movement that George Bush has come to embody, and the attributes of the Bush presidency, the ones which have spawned such a tragic legacy for our country, are the same attributes driving the movement that created, supported, and sustained that presidency.

The values and principles on which America was founded are far greater than any single president. American ideals—those to which the country has long aspired (if not always perfectly followed)—transcend the damage that any one presidency can inflict, even in eight years. But a thorough understanding of the Bush era is indispensable in attempting to reverse and repair the damage wrought by the legacy of George W. Bush's tragic presidency, to re-affirm the defining values of our country, and to restore America's strength and credibility in the world.

A Tragic Legacy

CHAPTER ONE

Bush Agonistes

86 • 66 • 59 • 48 • 39 • 32

Those numbers designate the percentages of Americans who approved of George W. Bush's performance as president in late 2001, 2002, 2003, 2004, 2005, and 2006, respectively. This data, from *Washington Post*–ABC News polls, demonstrate that every year George Bush has remained in office, fewer and fewer Americans have approved of the job he has done, and more and more Americans have become dissatisfied with his presidency.

And it is not merely the quantity but also the intensity of the disapproval that has steadily increased. The percentages of Americans who "strongly disapprove" have risen dramatically from the end of 2001 to the end of 2006: 6, 20, 29, 38, 47, 53. And the group consisting of the president's most enthusiastic supporters—those who "strongly approve" of his performance—has shrunk year after year: 64, 45, 39, 27, 20, *18*.

The dramatic shift in the public's perceptions of George Bush is unsurprising in light of what a consequential presidency this has been.

Among admirers and opponents of George Bush, there are exceedingly few grounds for agreement. But few Americans, regardless of their political leanings, would dispute that the impact of the Bush presidency on America will be both profound and long lasting.

During Bush's tenure, the United States suffered the first major foreign terrorist attack on its soil. The U.S. invaded two sovereign nations—one which had an integral connection to that attack and one which had none—followed by a violent and protracted occupation of both countries with no end in sight. Beyond Iraq, the Bush administration has been directing increasingly threatening rhetoric toward yet more countries, particularly Iran, the most powerful Middle Eastern nation other than Israel. Yet by the end of 2006, all of the demands on America's armed forces had resulted in a military that was stretched so thin that new missions were and remain all but unthinkable. Prominent politicians in both parties were calling for a significant expansion of the U.S. military based on the expectation that far more missions lie ahead.

Subsequent to 9/11, the Bush administration constructed a super-maximum security prison in Guantánamo Bay, Cuba, which it declared beyond the reach of any law, and the image of its orange-clad, bowed, and shackled prisoners became a symbol of anti-American resentment around the world. The president's lawyers engaged in a series of legal battles to defend unprecedented theories of virtually limitless presidential power, which the president applied not only to foreign nationals but also to American citizens, including those on U.S. soil. Immediately prior to being voted out of office, the Republicans who controlled Congress enacted a law vesting in the president sweeping new powers of indefinite detention and coercive interrogation.

Throughout the Bush tenure, the U.S. military and intelligence agencies sent terrorist suspects to secret prisons, so-called black sites, throughout Eastern Europe. They abducted citizens off the streets of other nations—including those of America's own allies—and sent them for interrogation to countries notorious for the use of torture. World opinion toward America underwent a fundamental shift as anti-American sentiment reached an all-time high, spreading throughout most countries and on every continent.

Multiple bombing campaigns and other U.S. military assaults have undoubtedly killed scores of Al Qaeda members, along with tens of thousands, if not hundreds of thousands, of innocents. Al Qaeda's ability to operate freely in Afghanistan has surely been impeded, and—other than the now-forgotten though still-unsolved series of deadly anthrax attacks in 2001 aimed at political leaders and prominent journalists—there have been no further terrorist attacks on U.S. soil, nor any convincing evidence of a serious, formidable plot to perpetrate one. However, the leader of Al Qaeda at the time of the 9/11 attacks, Osama bin Laden, has been neither apprehended nor killed, at least to the administration's knowledge. By all accounts, Al Qaeda's Taliban allies are resurgent, and Al Qaeda has exploited the chaos caused by the removal of Iraq's government to operate within a portion of Western Iraq. As the president entered lame-duck status, his vows to prosecute the "war"—encompassing not only Iraq but a whole host of other nations and groups—transformed into threats to escalate it further still.

Even without further increases in military spending, and even though the United States is the world's sole superpower, military spending has skyrocketed under the Bush presidency. In early 2007, the Bush Pentagon sent to Congress a request for a $622 billion defense budget, only $141 billion of which was to be devoted to Iraq and Afghanistan. Even with inflation adjustments, and as the U.S. continues to swelter under massive budget deficits, that proposed amount for defense spending is the highest since World War II. The amount of "peacetime" defense spending, and the overall expenditures for defense, has increased every year during the Bush administration. The U.S., by itself, accounts for more than 50 percent of *total* worldwide military spending. The U.S. military budget is larger than the total spending of the next twenty largest spenders combined, and its military budget under Bush is six times larger than that of China, the country with the second-highest defense budget. The seemingly endless expansion of American military spending reflects an intent not merely to defend America from attacks but also to occupy and rule large parts of the world—particularly the Middle East—as an imperial power.

It is difficult to argue with the conclusion of Bush admirer John Podhoretz, who contended—in his 2004 literary homage to Bush's greatness entitled *Bush Country: How Dubya Became a Great President While*

Driving Liberals Insane—that the president has "constructed one of the most consequential presidencies in the nation's history." In an article highly critical of the president's governance, former Reagan and Bush 41 speechwriter Peggy Noonan observed in a September 2006 *Wall Street Journal* column that Americans generally agree that the president either "is a great man or a catastrophe," but nothing in the middle, and she added:

> The one thing I think America agrees on is that George Bush and his presidency have been enormously consequential. He has made decisions that will shape the future we'll inhabit. It's never "We must do this" with Mr. Bush. It's always "the concentrated work of generations." He doesn't declare, he commits; and when you back him, you're never making a discrete and specific decision, you're always making a long-term investment.

Thomas Mann, senior fellow of governance studies at the Brookings Institution, observed that "George Bush will go down in history as one of the most consequential presidents in American history." For better or for worse, the Bush presidency will have long-lasting effects for America. The legacy of George W. Bush will be the legacy of the United States for some time to come.

THE ARC OF ICARUS

The Bush presidency, perhaps more than any other in American history, has been shaped by a single event. The September 11 attacks presented an opportunity for leadership and for renewing America's unity and sense of purpose greater than any event since the Japanese attack on Pearl Harbor. And even the president's most virulent critics would likely agree that this was an opportunity which the president seized—decisively and aggressively. In the aftermath of those attacks, a president who was elected with three million fewer votes than his opponent and who presided over a deeply divided electorate, commanded one of the most unified and resolute American citizenries in history. In the wake of 9/11, support for President Bush spanned the political spectrum and was abundant and enthusiastic in both political parties.

Support for the president suffered a slow, natural erosion from the 90 percent level he enjoyed in the immediate aftermath of the 9/11 attacks. A portion of that early support was a fleeting, ephemeral by-product of a traumatized and angry nation. But the bulk was solid and sustained, resulting in an intense desire on the part of most Americans for the president to succeed. Most of the post-9/11 support for President Bush and his policies was both genuine and committed.

Thus, over the course of the next two years—through the March 2003 invasion of Iraq and for at least six months thereafter—the president's approval ratings never fell below 60 percent, and generally remained in the 66 percent range; fully two-thirds of the American public continued to endorse his job performance. Manifestly, Americans of many political stripes remained joined in common cause, standing behind their president through this period.

And the profound depth and breadth of that support, of that national coming together, enabled him to take any action, request any legislation, obtain any new executive powers with no meaningful opposition. Throughout late 2001 and 2002, true bipartisanship (for better or worse) reigned in Congress, engendering a near total absence of controversy and the enactment of laws bestowing on the president broad new powers. Criticism of the president was negligible in the political mainstream. Most opposition came from factions that were successfully stigmatized and relegated to the relatively inconsequential fringes.

Beginning in mid-2002 and continuing for the rest of the year, the president devoted himself almost exclusively to insisting that Saddam Hussein's Iraq constituted a grave threat to the United States and must be confronted. Standing on his broad-based support, he campaigned to persuade Americans of the wisdom and necessity of invading Iraq, notwithstanding that Iraq had not attacked, had not threatened to attack, and lacked the capability to attack the United States.

The audacity of preemptively invading another country was no match for George Bush's popularity. The trust and faith placed by Americans in the president assured that the outcome of the "debate" over going to war against Iraq was preordained. As had been true with virtually every issue, large and small, foreign and domestic, since the 9/11 attacks, the president's will would prevail.

In the midst of the Iraq debate, and largely because of it, the president's soaring popularity also delivered, in November 2002, a resounding victory for his party in the midterm elections. Typically, and for many reasons, a president's party loses Congressional seats in midterm elections, but not in 2002. The Republicans took over control of the Senate from the Democrats and increased their control in the House.

The magnitude of their victory was historic. It had been almost seventy years—the 1934 midterm elections during Franklin Roosevelt's first term—since a president's party had gained strength in both the House and the Senate in a midterm election. Bush's sky-high approval numbers reached into state elections as well. After the 2002 elections, Republican governors outnumbered Democratic governors for the first time in fifty years.

The Republicans' extraordinary national victory was plainly the by-product of the towering popularity of President Bush, buttressed by his bellicose posture toward Iraq, which became the centerpiece of the 2002 campaign. The nation had coalesced behind its president, and even though he was not on the ballot, the deep faith placed in his leadership among Republicans, Independents, and even many Democrats led to a historic victory for his party.

The president's popularity cannot be attributed exclusively to the happenstance of the 9/11 attacks. Particularly in the weeks and even months following those attacks, much of the president's conduct generated confidence both in his abilities and in his judgment. As it appeared at the time, the invasion of Afghanistan and the subsequent overthrow of the Taliban was a creatively executed and rapid success. Moreover, although his initial post-9/11 appearances were shaky, the president's speeches quickly became resolute, eloquent, and even inspiring. He expressed a focused and restrained anger but steadfastly avoided vengeful rhetoric. He pledged to pursue the planners and perpetrators of the attack relentlessly, but appeared to eschew rash or reckless overreaction.

And the president repeatedly emphasized that the enemy was defined neither as adherents to Islam nor as Middle Eastern countries and their citizens, but instead was a band of fanatics who exploited Islam as a pretext for terrorism and violence. In his September 20, 2001, speech to the Joint Session of Congress, he declared:

Americans are asking: Who attacked our country? The evidence we have gathered all points to a collection of loosely affiliated terrorist organizations known as al Qaeda. They are the same murderers indicted for bombing American embassies in Tanzania and Kenya, and responsible for bombing the USS *Cole*. . . .

The terrorists practice a fringe form of Islamic extremism that has been rejected by Muslim scholars and the vast majority of Muslim clerics—a fringe movement that perverts the peaceful teachings of Islam.

And in the midst of emerging, isolated reports that American Muslims (or those perceived to be such) were the victims of attacks, and even of murder, the president pointedly emphasized:

I ask you to uphold the values of America, and remember why so many have come here. *We are in a fight for our principles, and our first responsibility is to live by them* [emphasis added]. No one should be singled out for unfair treatment or unkind words because of their ethnic background or religious faith. (*Applause.*)

Three days earlier, President Bush had purposefully made a public appearance at the Islamic Center in Washington and afterward delivered this pointed statement:

Those who feel like they can intimidate our fellow citizens to take out their anger don't represent the best of America. They represent the worst of humankind, and they should be ashamed of that kind of behavior. This is a great country. It's a great country because we share the same values of respect and dignity and human worth. And it is my honor to be meeting with leaders who feel the same way I do. They are outraged. They are sad. They love America just as much as I do. . . .

Women who cover their heads in this country must feel comfortable going outside their homes. Moms who wear cover must not be intimidated in America. That's not the America I know. That's not the America I value.

Attacks or intimidation efforts against Muslim Americans or Arab Americans, warned the president, would be aggressively prosecuted.

In addition to a firm insistence on tolerance for all citizens, including Muslims, the president expressed goodwill toward other countries—and toward Democratic leaders—in his opening remarks before the Joint Session, remarks that are striking in light of how little such sentiments would be present for the remainder of the Bush presidency:

> Speaker Hastert, Minority Leader Gephardt, Majority Leader Daschle and Senator Lott, I thank you for your friendship, for your leadership and for your service to our country. *(Applause.)*
>
> And on behalf of the American people, I thank the world for its out-pouring of support. America will never forget the sounds of our National Anthem playing at Buckingham Palace, on the streets of Paris, and at Berlin's Brandenburg Gate.

Unquestionably, the 9/11 attacks would have united the country behind any president; external attacks on a nation virtually always prompt the citizenry's solidarity behind their leaders. But sustained support for President Bush was not merely the by-product of emotion-driven reactions to the attack. The president himself was responsible for a wide and deep admiration and trust on the part of many Americans who, though initially skeptical of him, were eager that their country be led by an empowered and able president.

Predictably, the president's approval ratings eroded from the unnatural 90 percent level, but, as noted, they remained high over the course of the next two years. And the March 2003 invasion of Iraq boosted the approval ratings once again to near 70 percent.

The president's approval ratings did not decline substantially until it became apparent that, contrary to the predominant justification given for the invasion of Iraq, that country did not possess any weapons of mass destruction and was not even actively pursuing development of such weapons at the time the United States invaded. Though the lack of WMDs in Iraq was apparent for some time to those closely following political events, it was the issuance of the "Duelfer Report" in October 2004 which solidified that fact as undisputed conventional wisdom among the country's media and pundit classes. That report, issued by the CIA under the supervision of its principal Iraqi weapons expert, Charles Duelfer, was intended by the Bush administration to constitute the official and definitive findings with respect to Saddam's weapons programs. And those findings could not have been more definitive—or more incriminating.

Most Americans did not, of course, read that report, but its impact on America's political discourse and public opinion about Iraq is nonetheless difficult to overstate. It single-handedly put an end to any ambiguity among America's punditry, political elite, and other opinion-makers as to the complete nonexistence of the WMDs. In the wake of the "Duelfer Report," the nonexistence of WMDs in Iraq became such a widely accepted fact that even Bush-friendly media outlets such as Fox News reported it in clear and unambiguous terms. As one Fox report from October 2004 put it:

> The chief U.S. arms inspector in Iraq has found no evidence of weapons of mass destruction production by Saddam Hussein's regime after 1991. . . .
>
> "It appears that he did not vigorously pursue those programs after the inspectors left," a U.S. official said on condition of anonymity, ahead of the report's Wednesday afternoon release by the CIA.

Such an incontrovertible finding was directly contrary to the most critical prewar claims that the president and his top officials had repeatedly represented not as being merely likely, but as *hard facts* beyond the realm of doubt. As the Fox report went on to note somewhat pointedly:

> Vice President Dick Cheney said in an Aug. 26, 2002 speech, 6½ months before the invasion, that "simply stated, there is no doubt that Saddam Hussein now has weapons of mass destruction. There is no doubt he is amassing them to use against our friends, against our allies and against us."

The "Duelfer Report" was issued one and a half years after the invasion of Iraq. By then, in light of the failure to find any WMDs (despite the administration's continuous assurances that they "knew" where they were located), it was readily apparent that there were none.

Nonetheless, up until the definitive conclusions were issued by an authoritative report, the president and his supporters were able to cloud the issue of WMDs with obfuscating assertions that no such weapons had been found "yet"—as though they existed but were hidden—or with murkier assertions that the United States *had* located something called "weapons of mass destruction related program activities." No Bush official, and certainly not the president himself, acknowledged (until after the 2004 election) that Saddam simply had no WMDs. The "Duelfer Report" and its uncompromising, absolute language put an end to those evasions and compelled the widespread recognition of the truth.

An October 2004 article in the *Washington Post* provides a flavor of the type of statements about the administration's prewar claims that became commonplace once the "Duelfer Report" was issued:

> Duelfer's report, delivered yesterday to two congressional committees, represents the government's most definitive accounting of Hussein's weapons programs, the assumed strength of which the Bush administration presented as a central reason for the war. While previous reports have drawn similar conclusions, Duelfer's assessment went beyond them in depth, detail and level of certainty.
>
> "We were almost all wrong" on Iraq, Duelfer told a Senate panel yesterday.

CNN led its coverage of the report's findings by underscoring not only the complete absence of WMDs in Iraq for more than ten years, but the absence of any efforts whatsoever on Saddam's part to develop such weapons:

> Saddam Hussein did not possess stockpiles of illicit weapons at the time of the U.S. invasion in March 2003 and had not begun any program to produce them, a CIA report concludes.
>
> In fact, the long-awaited report, authored by Charles Duelfer, who advises the director of central intelligence on Iraqi weapons, says Iraq's WMD program was essentially destroyed in 1991 and Saddam ended Iraq's nuclear program after the 1991 Gulf War.

In terms of assessing the Bush legacy, the definitive finding that Saddam had no WMDs whatsoever—issued by the president's handpicked weapons experts—is certainly one of the most symbolically significant events, and one of the most consequential.

While Americans differed (and continue to differ) on exactly what caused the vast discrepancy between the president's prewar claims and the reality in Iraq—an honest mistake, a reckless disregard for whether the claims were true, pressure on the intelligence community to issue findings that justified an invasion, or outright, deliberate deceit—there was little dispute, once the report was issued, that the primary justification used to persuade Americans to support the president's attack on Iraq was simply false. It dramatically altered the opinions of many Americans with regard to the president, and it helped catalyze what can only be described as a near-total collapse of the Bush presidency.

The U.S. had alienated most of the world by commencing an optional war "justified" by the urgent need to eliminate weapons that simply did not exist. At best, the revelation meant that the U.S. had committed a horrifying and embarrassing blunder in front of the entire world. And as the situation in Iraq became more chaotic and it was clear that the president had lost control of events in that country (if he ever had such control in the first place), the "blunder" became not merely embarrassing but dangerous, destructive, and increasingly difficult to defend.

The inescapable fact that WMDs did not exist had a more significant impact on the perceptions of Bush supporters than it did on Bush opponents, since the latter were predominantly already against the war and already harbored serious doubts about the president's judgment and honesty. There were large numbers of Independents, moderates, and even liberal Democrats who were not natural political allies of the president but who put aside those political differences and supported the invasion of Iraq. Many did so despite holding reservations about the wisdom of invading a sovereign country that had not attacked the United States, but ultimately deferred to the president's judgment and integrity by accepting his insistent claims that the invasion was critical to U.S. national security.

The realization by war supporters that the president's primary prewar justification was false, and that their good-faith support for him had been exploited to enable an agenda having nothing to do with terrorism, led to a sense of deep betrayal and irreversible mistrust. From that point forward, many reasonable people were unwilling to place faith in the accuracy of the president's statements.

Making matters worse for the president, the definitive finding that there were no WMDs came at the time when the occupation of Iraq—which Americans had been led to expect would be quick and easy—was plagued by chaos, violence, and increasingly high American casualties. That there was no end in sight was becoming rapidly apparent. And rather than making progress, Iraq began to resemble the lawless and violence-plagued state that—at the time of the Afghanistan invasion— Americans were told was the climate most likely to breed terrorism.

The revelation of no WMDs, coming as Iraq was falling apart, thus had the devastating effect of undermining Americans' faith in the integrity of the president *as well as* his administration's competence. Those two attributes—personal honesty and competence in foreign affairs— had been the pillars of the president's political strength, and both were subjected to severe assault by the "Duelfer Report" and the accompanying deterioration of Iraq. Polls thus demonstrated not only that previously pro-Bush Americans were expressing disapproval of his performance as president, but that their assessment of the president as a person—his honesty, reliability, and judgment—was dramatically worsening.

According to the Pew Research Center, in September 2003, 62 percent of Americans believed President Bush was *trustworthy.* By July 2005, that number had dropped to 49 percent, and by March 2006, the number had plummeted to 40 percent.

Similarly, when asked to describe President Bush using only one word, the leading response in February 2005 was *honest,* given by 38 percent of respondents. The word *incompetent* finished a distant fifth, garnering only 14 percent. But only a year later, in March 2006, those numbers reversed. *Incompetent* became the leading response with 29 percent, while *honest* tumbled to sixth place, with only 14 percent—tied with the word *liar* (14 percent) and behind the epithet *idiot* (17 percent). As Pew put it in a March 2006 report accompanying its polling data:

> President Bush's declining image also is reflected in the single-word descriptions people use to describe their impression of the president. Three years ago, positive one-word descriptions of Bush far outnumbered negative ones. Over the past two years, the positive-negative balance has been roughly equal. But the one-word characterizations have turned decidedly negative since last July.
>
> Currently, 48% use a negative word to describe Bush compared with just 28% who use a positive term, and 10% who use neutral language.

The 2007 Pew poll was even worse for the president. *Incompetent* continued to be the leading adjective, this time from 34 percent of the respondents. Second was *arrogant,* the adjective selected by 25 percent; the word *idiot* continued to attract a sizable portion as well (19 percent).

The Duelfer Report was issued in October 2004—less than one month prior to the 2004 election. As a result, the unraveling of the Bush presidency was still in its initial stage when America decided to re-elect him. Bush's approval rating, after remaining near or above 60 percent for most of 2002 and 2003, descended to the 50 percent level in 2004—generally considered the danger zone for the re-election prospects of incumbent presidents—and it hovered there throughout the year, up to and including the election.

Opinion polls in the weeks before the election reflected a dead heat between Bush and John Kerry. Ultimately, Bush won the 2004 race by a popular-vote margin of 2.7 percentage points, the smallest margin of victory for any incumbent president since 1828. As the *Los Angeles Times'* Ron Brownstein noted after the election: "Apart from Truman in 1948 (whose winning margin was 4–5 percentage points), every other president elected to a second term since 1832 has at least doubled the margin that Bush had over Kerry." And just as was true in 2000, Bush's 2004 victory was dependent upon a narrow victory in a single state, this time in Ohio.

Most remarkable about the narrowness of Bush's 2004 victory is the vast array of overwhelming electoral advantages he enjoyed as an incumbent War President. Those advantages ought to have made re-election nearly assured.

Incumbent American presidents rarely lose under any circumstances. But Americans have *never* voted a president out of office during wartime, having comfortably re-elected all four previous wartime presidents who ran again (Madison, Lincoln, Franklin Roosevelt, and Nixon).

Beyond those towering inherent advantages, Bush barely squeaked by despite running against John Kerry, one of the most politically ungifted major party nominees in several decades; despite Kerry's running an inept and passive presidential campaign, leading former DNC chair Terry McAuliffe to call the campaign's failure to attack Bush's record "one of the biggest acts of political malpractice in the history of American politics"; and despite a significant financial advantage. Even with all of those formidable advantages, facing a weak opponent and an unskillful campaign, the War President, after four years of governing, won only two states in 2004 that he did not take in 2000 (Iowa and New Mexico) and even lost New Hampshire for a net gain of only one state.

Since his re-election, the president's popularity has continued to decline steadily—at times even precipitously—to the point where George Bush has reached historic levels of sustained unpopularity. To put the collapse of the president's popularity into context, at the time Richard Nixon was forced to resign the presidency after being battered for two years by the Watergate scandal, Nixon's approval rating had plummeted to 25 percent—a mere seven points lower than the 32 percent approval rating registered by President Bush multiple times throughout 2006. On January 21, 2007, when CBS News issued a poll placing the president's approval rating at 28 percent, the right-wing website Drudge Report posted a headline which read: "Bush poll ratings fall to Nixon levels."

On the eve of the president's 2007 State of the Union address, Bloomberg News reported that "President George W. Bush's approval ratings are now the lowest for any president the day before a State of the Union speech since Richard Nixon in 1974." And unlike previous presidents, most of whom reached all-time approval-rating lows in the mid-30s, George Bush's unpopularity has been sustained, spending virtually all of 2006 and the early months of 2007 mired in the mid-to-low 30s. The only convincing comparison one can make is the collapse of the Lyndon Johnson presidency, which—like Bush's collapse—was tied not to some fleeting event or scandal, but to a deeply unpopular war that dragged on without end.

Even as early as the end of 2005, Gary Langer of ABC News noted the historic nature of George Bush's unpopularity and drew the comparison this way:

> An increasingly unpopular war, an ethics cloud, and broad economic discontent have pushed public opinion of the Bush administration from bad to worse, infecting not only the president's ratings on political issues but his personal credentials for honesty and leadership as well. . . .

A striking feature of the president's predicament is the intensity of sentiment against him. Just 20 percent of Americans "strongly" approve of his work in office, the fewest of his career; more than twice as many, 47 percent, strongly disapprove, the most yet seen. . . .

Bush's troubles stand out, in large part because they're rooted not just in economic concerns but in an increasingly unpopular war. That invites comparisons to Lyndon B. Johnson, whose approval rating suffered each year as the country became more enmeshed in Vietnam—dropping in Gallup data from 75 percent on average in 1964, to 43 percent in 1967 and 1968. Bush, for his part, has gone from an average of 73 percent approval in 2000 and 2001 to 46 percent, on average, so far this year. The trend lines are strikingly similar.

This dramatic, wholesale erosion of support for the president continued after Langer drew the LBJ comparison and it has now been sustained over a much longer period of time. It spans the ideological and demographic spectrum and appears largely irreversible. Analyzing a February 2006 poll showing the president with new lows in approval and popularity ratings, political scientist Richard Stoll of Rice University observed that it "suggests that he's pretty much down to his core supporters out there . . . and *everyone else has left*" (emphasis added).

Though catalyzed by the catastrophe in Iraq, this collapse had plenty of other authors. From the outset, the president's second term was plagued by a series of embarrassing domestic failures that, as an accompaniment to the unraveling of Iraq, exacerbated perceptions of Bush's startling ineptitude. The president's campaign to overhaul Social Security—his flamboyantly touted second-term "legacy" program—flopped from the start, his proposals pushed away even by his own party, which made him appear weak and ineffective. The failed Supreme Court nomination of his loyal aide Harriet Miers was fueled almost entirely by his own supporters and further eroded the powerful, almost omnipotent aura that had surrounded him during the heyday of his first term. The palpable sloth and indifference that characterized his reaction to the Katrina disaster chipped away further at his image of strength and Americans' confidence in his ability to "protect" them. The fiasco over his attempt to turn over America's port operations to a company owned by the United Arab Emirates even raised questions about whether he was sufficiently committed to protecting the country against the threat of Islamic terrorism, the only asset which had, until that point, been immune from attack. As the president's second term slogged along, his few remaining strengths were gradually diluted until they disappeared completely.

But it was the disaster in Iraq that provided the essential framework in which all of these other failures unfolded. There is certainly a good argument to make that the nonexistence of WMDs was so harmful to the president *only* because the war that those weapons "justified" had been managed so ineptly, to the point where America actually appeared to be losing. Many Americans, perhaps most, hate a losing war more than they hate an unjust war. To be burdened with an image of weakness and defeat is arguably more damaging for an American president than to be revealed as dishonest. A substantial bulk of the Iraq-fueled hostility toward the president had as much to do with the fact that he failed to win the war—that he seemed to be *losing*—as it did with the fact that he justified the war in the first place with pretexts that were revealed to be false. But in all events, the confirmed nonexistence of WMDs did not mean merely that the war was sold on false pretenses. The revelation itself was a failure, a defeat. It brought embarrassment to the United States and vindication to war opponents. And even many Americans who were not bothered by the invasion were deeply disturbed by the humiliation when America appeared in the eyes of the world as incapable of doing anything right in its attempt to subdue Iraq.

By early 2006, the vast majority of Americans irreversibly opposed the war in Iraq—the centerpiece of the Bush presidency—and believed that it had been a mistake to invade. Worse, Americans largely believed that they were misled into supporting the invasion of Iraq not by virtue of erroneous intelligence but due to *deliberate deceit*. The *Washington Post* reported at the end of 2005: "A clear majority—55 percent—now says the administration deliberately misled the country in making its case for war with Iraq—a conflict that an even larger majority say is not worth the cost."

This staggering unpopularity is all the more striking considering its contrast with the political omnipotence the president enjoyed for the first two and a half years after the 9/11 attacks. On one level, this near-complete reversal is difficult to understand because the president has not changed his approach or his worldview in the slightest. But on another, the collapse of his support is due precisely to the fact that the president's governing approach and mind-set never change, even when his policies are glaring failures and the issues he is forced to address are entirely unsuitable to his worldview.

It is difficult to overstate the extent to which the Bush presidency imploded, but the November 2006 midterm elections provide a potent illustration. The Republican Party's smashing electoral defeat in the 2006 midterms was as rare and as mammoth as was that party's midterm victory in 2002. For only the third time in sixty years, there was a change in control of the Congress, as Democrats took over both the House and the Senate.

The magnitude of the Republican losses was staggering. The Democrats defeated six Republican senators to take control of the Senate, and picked up a total of thirty-one House seats. Six governorships switched from Republican control to Democratic, returning majority control of governorships back to the Democrats, by a margin of 28 to 22.

More notably still, not one incumbent House Democrat lost, and therefore not one single Republican challenger won—the first time since 1938 that one of the two major parties failed to defeat a single House incumbent. All incumbent Senate Democrats also won. Thus, the 2006 midterm election was only the second election in U.S. history in which one of the major parties failed to defeat even a single incumbent from the other party.

Dissatisfaction with the president's Republican Party was so pervasive that it extended down to multiple state races. All incumbent Democratic governors won re-election as well. Democrats seized control of four different state legislatures previously under Republican control, while Republicans failed to take over any Democratic-run state legislatures. The 2006 rejection by American voters of George Bush's Republican Party was total and evident across-the-board in every region outside of the Deep South.

With that humiliating development, the collapse of the Bush presidency was virtually complete. By the end of 2006, vast majorities of Americans believed that the president was untrustworthy, incompetent, and even unlikable. They believed he misled them into supporting the invasion of Iraq not by virtue of erroneous intelligence but through deliberate deceit. Americans' dislike for George Bush was so widespread and intense that it infected the entire Republican Party.

THE ESTABLISHMENT REBELS

After the American electorate signaled its profound dissatisfaction with the Bush presidency, and as events in Iraq continued their downward spiral, even the Washington Establishment, including its Republican standard-bearers, abandoned the president. It is as though the country collectively acknowledged the severity of America's crisis the administration had inflicted and resolved to take action, leaving the president standing alone—weak, isolated, and unpopular—as his war lay in ruins. By the time the president unveiled his so-called Iraq "surge" strategy at the beginning of 2007, the war in Iraq was spoken of not as a mere mistake or serious problem, but as a strategic disaster of historic proportions.

Republican senator Chuck Hagel, at a Senate Committee on Foreign Relations hearing where Secretary of State Condoleezza Rice was testifying, called the escalation "morally wrong" and declared: "I have to say, Madam Secretary, that I think this speech given last night by this president represents the most dangerous foreign policy blunder in this country since Vietnam." The day after President Bush announced his "surge" strategy, Al Gore declared it "the worst strategic mistake in the entire history of the United States."

Such rhetoric suddenly began issuing from even moderate, establishment-defending journalists and pundits whose principal function typically is to recite Beltway conventional wisdom and the political orthodoxies prevailing among the Beltway elite. The *Washington Post* columnist David Ignatius, a vigorous champion of moderation in all things—policy, politics, and rhetoric—wrote that the president's January 2007 "surge" speech revealed "a presidency in eclipse: He has lost the House and Senate; he has lost the public on the war; and he has attached his presidency to a riderless horse." Similarly, CBS News' Dick Meyer observed:

> Rarely in our history has a president made a speech like this—an announcement that a large number of American soldiers will be sent to a

foreign war—with less public, political, and international support. The president really is alone.

In war and politics, an essential measure of power is allies. Bush has few, and they are not powerful.

By 2007, unrestrained attacks on the president and his policies had become commonplace and were but a symptom of the wholesale insurrection by the Washington Establishment against the presidency that it had propped up for so long. The most surprising indignity suffered by the Bush presidency—and perhaps the most harmful as well—was the unabashed critical conclusion issued by the blue-chip, bipartisan panel, the so-called Iraq Study Group, or Baker-Hamilton Commission, which was composed of some of Washington's most institutionally respected figures. Commissions of this sort are typically assembled in response to problems with the expectation that they will recommend, at most, incremental changes on the margins.

But the sheer scope of Bush's Iraq failure, and the grave danger posed to the United States by its continuation (let alone escalation), did not permit the commission the luxury of such tempered and polite findings. Instead, the report was emphatic, at times even scathing, in its assessment that the war had gone terribly awry.

The day the report was issued, the commission's co-chair, Lee Hamilton, summarized its conclusion: "The situation in Iraq today is grave and deteriorating"; the report itself warned: "If the situation continues to deteriorate, the consequences could be severe." The report never referenced the possibility of "victory," instead aiming for efforts to stabilize the country in order for all American troops not necessary for force protection to be out of Iraq by early 2008.

The report even accused the administration of "significant underreporting of the violence in Iraq." It then proceeded to echo a charge made over the course of several years by war opponents—namely, that the administration was concealing negative information about Iraq from the American public in order to maintain support for the war. The report pointedly noted: "Good policy is difficult to make when information is systematically collected in a way that minimizes its discrepancy with policy goals."

The bipartisan commission, composed of five Republicans and five Democrats, was the very embodiment of The Respected Washington Establishment. It was chaired by longtime Bush family supporter James Baker, who served as secretary of state for Bush's father and who led the charge on behalf of Bush's successful battle over the 2000 Florida election results, a success resulting in Bush's becoming president. Another of the commission's Republican members, Sandra Day O'Connor, was one of the five justices whose vote halted Al Gore's requested recount, ensuring George Bush's inauguration.

The report rejected not merely the president's handling of the war but also, more critically, the overall approach of the Bush administration toward the Middle East. The report's key recommendations constituted wholesale rejections of the basic premises of the Bush approach to the Middle East—specifically, it concluded that the United States should open negotiations with the regimes in Iran and Syria to achieve stability in Iraq, and should also exert far more efforts toward facilitating an Israeli-Palestinian peace agreement.

These recommendations, unanimously embraced by the commission, were clear repudiations of the pillars of the Bush foreign policy. The president's approach to the Middle East was informed by his view that "Evil" regimes (his characterization of those that rule Iran and Syria) cannot be reasoned or negotiated with. The president has been equally insistent that the U.S. should remain firmly on Israel's side rather than acting as an "honest broker" between it and its "Evil terrorist" enemies.

That such a panel—composed of wise, respected Washington elites, including some Bush supporters—would issue such a resounding rejection of the president's handling of the war and his overall foreign policy constituted nothing short of the political establishment's full-scale rebellion over the course the president had chosen for the United States. Writing in *Salon*, Gary Kamiya described the report as "a call for the United States to radically change its policies in the Middle East," and explained:

Under normal circumstances, the chances would be nil that a bipartisan panel made up of such wild radicals as Sandra Day O'Connor, Vernon Jordan and Alan Simpson would bluntly assert that "the United States will not be able to achieve its goals in the Middle East unless the United States deals directly with the Arab-Israeli conflict," or insist that we begin talking with states we deem supporters of terrorism. Holding Israel's feet to the fire, which is what "dealing directly" with the conflict means, is politically radioactive in Washington—or it was.

But Bush's Iraq debacle has exacerbated the contradictions and weaknesses of our Mideast policy and raised the stakes for the United States so high that it has become impossible for neutral observers to simply mouth the party line. Just as the thought of the gallows concentrates the mind, so a war that has cost almost 3,000 American lives and $2 billion a week, weakened America's standing in the world, and strengthened our terrorist enemies, has forced the Washington power elite to acknowledge reality.

Bush's almost immediate rejection of the report's key findings, and his announced intention to escalate the war instead, was a potent sign of how isolated he had become.

The Iraq War had become so manifest a failure by the end of 2006 that some prominent war supporters and prowar pundits were not merely changing their minds about the war, but were affirmatively denying that they ever supported it in the first place. In January 2007, Joe Klein, the longtime columnist for *Time* magazine, claimed on a *Time* website: "I've been opposed to the Iraq war ever since . . . 2002." But on February 23, 2003—exactly one month before the invasion of Iraq—Klein had been a guest on *Meet the Press* and had this exchange with Tim Russert:

KLEIN: This is a really tough decision. War may well be the right decision at this point. In fact, I think it—it's—it—it probably is.
RUSSERT: Now that's twice you've said that: "It's the right war." You believe it's the wrong time. Why do you think it's the right war?
KLEIN: Because sooner or later, this guy has to be taken out. Saddam has—Saddam Hussein has to be taken out.

For a public figure like Klein to claim that he was opposed to the Iraq War—even though he went on national television one month before it started to pronounce that war "probably" is "the right decision at this point"—demonstrates just how damaging Klein perceives being associated with the president's decision to invade.

Like Klein, Michael Ledeen—a contributing editor of *National Review* and a Freedom Scholar at the influential neoconservative think tank American Enterprise Institute—wrote on the *National Review* blog in November 2006: "I had and have no involvement with our Iraq policy. I opposed the military invasion of Iraq before it took place."

Ledeen, however, wrote in August 2002 of "the desperately-needed and long overdue war against Saddam Hussein"; and when he was interviewed for *Front Page Magazine* the same month and asked, "Okay, well if we are all so certain about the dire need to invade Iraq, then when do we do so?" Ledeen replied: "Yesterday." There is obvious, substantial risk in falsely claiming that one opposed the Iraq War notwithstanding a public record of support. But that war has come to be viewed as such a profound failure that that risk, at least in the eyes of some, is outweighed by the prospect of being associated with Bush's invasion.

Perhaps most notably, even the aggressively loyal band of Bush supporters who have long stood behind the president on virtually every issue—who cheered on and enabled almost every decision—has been abandoning him as the perception grows that he is a weak and failed president.

For the first several years of the Bush presidency—up to and including his re-election—Peggy Noonan, the former speechwriter to the president's father who wrote Bush 41's "thousand points of light" speech, employed her trademark effusiveness in her *Wall Street Journal* column and frequent television appearances in praise of the president's character and integrity.

Yet by 2006, she began attacking him regularly—his performance in office as well as his character. Noonan focused specifically on what had previously been, in the eyes of his supporters, a great strength—namely his refusal to consider the possibility that he had erred and his belief that failure requires nothing more than increased determination to succeed. Noonan wrote in an October 2006 column:

> I think that Americans have pretty much stopped listening to him. One reason is that you don't have to listen to get a sense of what's going on.

He does not appear to rethink things based on new data. You don't have to tune in to see how he's shifting emphasis to address a trend, or tacking to accommodate new winds. For him there is no new data, only determination.

But whereas certain fans began abandoning Bush on the ground that he is too stubborn and resistant to change even in the face of failure, others began turning against him on the exact opposite ground—namely, that he had become too weak and irresolute. Former Bush speechwriter David Frum—whose 2003 book had anointed Bush *The Right Man* and "tells the story of Bush's transformation: how a president whose administration began in uncertainty became one of the most decisive, successful, and in the US at least, popular leaders of our time"—painted a picture of Bush in a November 2006 *Wall Street Journal* op-ed as a weak, confused, defeated figure:

> The Bush administration woke up yesterday morning to a deeply ugly political situation. Those polls that show the president below 40 percent approval? They would look even worse if they surveyed only Republican members of Congress. As for the president's opponents: They are slavering for a nice two-year-long munch on the administration's haunches.
> Worst of all, the administration seems to have exhausted its energy. Frustrated by Iraq, wounded by Katrina, thwarted in its two most recent major domestic initiatives (Social Security and immigration), the administration looks baffled, uncertain and often strangely passive.

John Podhoretz has long used his pundit space in the *New York Post* and *National Review* to hail the greatness of George Bush. Further, his *Bush Country* (2004) is devoted, literally, to establishing Bush's greatness. Therein, he described the invasion of Iraq as "the gift George W. Bush has given to the world" and even praised him as the "best presidential speaker since Franklin Delano Roosevelt." A more adoring fan of President Bush would be hard to find. Yet in his *New York Post* column, Podhoretz called a December 2006 press conference regarding Iraq "unquestionably the most dispirited performance of his presidency." Podhoretz went on to argue that the performance was indicative of a weakened, crippled president:

The question was this: How would Bush, who himself had only suffered electoral success since seeking higher office in 1994, handle defeat? The answer: Not well. . . .

As usual, the president took pains to warn the enemy in Iraq that "they can't intimidate America." But, by offering no real sense that he knows what "the way forward in Iraq" is, he seemed unsteady—and unsteadiness is exactly the quality that should and will gladden the hearts of the enemy in Iraq.

If you combine the effect of yesterday's press conference with his remarkably depressing interview with *The Washington Post* the day before—when he said that victory was "achievable" in Iraq, a defeatist word that must have had Winston Churchill rolling in his grave—you can't help but feel that Bush has had the stuffing knocked out of him by the twin blows of the November election results and the bloody chaos in Baghdad.

Yet this is not a moment when we or the troops in Iraq can afford to have a winded and stunned president.

Fundamental shifts in one's perception of President Bush are now commonplace from those who had previously revered him. *Washington Post* reporter Bob Woodward has written a three-book series about the administration, with a focus on the president's personality traits and decision-making methods. *Bush at War*, the 2002 first of the three, is almost entirely brimming with praise for Bush the Great and Strong Leader.

But in September 2006, Michiko Kakutani, book critic of the *New York Times*, noted that in *State of Denial*, the third and last in the series, the president described by Woodward appears to be a completely different person than the one he glorified in his 2002 treatment:

President Bush [in *State of Denial*] emerges as a passive, impatient, sophomoric and intellectually incurious leader, presiding over a grossly dysfunctional war cabinet and given to an almost religious certainty that makes him disinclined to rethink or re-evaluate decisions he has made about the war.

It's a portrait that stands in stark contrast to the laudatory one Mr. Woodward drew in "Bush at War," his 2002 book, which depicted the president—in terms that the White House press office itself has purveyed—as a judicious, resolute leader, blessed with the "vision thing" his father was accused of lacking and firmly in control of the ship of state.

Thus, while the Bush in Woodward's 2002 depiction is an admirable man of resolve, by 2006 the president is a profoundly flawed "prisoner of his own certitude."

As 2006 drew to a close, Tony Blankley, a *Washington Times* editor and former press spokesman to Newt Gingrich, described the president's predicament as one of great loneliness, abandoned even by most of his prior supporters, and under attack from all precincts:

> The American presidency has been called "A Glorious Burden" by the Smithsonian Museum, and the loneliest job in the world by historians. As we approach Christmas 2006 Anno Domini, President Bush is surely fully seized of the loneliness and burden of his office.
>
> For rarely has a president stood more alone at a moment of high crisis than does our president now as he makes his crucial policy decisions on the Iraq War. His political opponents stand triumphant, yet barren of useful guidance. Many—if not most—of his fellow party men and women in Washington are rapidly joining his opponents in a desperate effort to save their political skins in 2008. Commentators who urged the president on in 2002–03, having fallen out of love with their ideas, are quick to quibble with and defame the president.

Blankley is one of the remaining few who admire Bush, yet even his depiction of the formerly cocksure and powerful president as an abandoned and lonely figure is almost pity inducing.

And on Fox News, long an outpost of pro-Bush loyalty, the pro-war, generally pro-Bush Mort Kondrake appeared the day after Bush's 2007 State of the Union address and summarized the Bush legacy as follows:

> In this world in which we live, the chances are that unless something miraculous happens, that George Bush is going to leave us with a world in which everything's a mess and we've got to restore our likeability in the world without losing our leadership capacity.

And in the wake of the growing scandal in March 2007 involving the administration's firing of eight U.S. attorneys, conservative pundit Bob Novak—noting that virtually nobody, including House Republicans, was defending the president—made this rather startling observation in his syndicated column:

> With nearly two years remaining in his presidency, George W. Bush is alone. In half a century, I have not seen a president so isolated from his own party in Congress—not Jimmy Carter, *not even Richard Nixon as he faced impeachment* [emphasis added].

THROWING BUSH OVERBOARD

Bush's unpopularity has become so intense and toxic that self-identified political conservatives have taken to distancing themselves from Bush by insisting he was never really a "conservative" at all. In the aftermath of the 2006 midterm elections, the *New York Times* reported:

> Since the election, a chorus from the right has been noisily distinguishing between conservative and Republican, blaming deviation from conservative principles for the election losses. From George Will to Rush Limbaugh, conservatives cut loose with criticisms of the Republicans for spending too much at home and getting bogged down in Iraq.

The day following the election, Rush Limbaugh assured his conservative audience: "Liberalism didn't win anything yesterday; Republicanism lost. Conservatism was nowhere to be found except on the Democratic side." Writing in *National Review*, Jonah Goldberg in 2006 actually went so far as to claim that Bush is a "liberal" Republican: "But there is one area where we can make somewhat useful comparisons between Nixon and Bush: *their status as liberal Republicans* (emphasis added)." Thus, reasoned Goldberg, Bush is exactly the opposite of what "conservatives" support: "The modern conservative movement, from Goldwater to Reagan, was formed as a backlash against Nixonism."

Yet when Bush was highly popular, Goldberg decreed precisely the opposite—namely, he anointed George W. Bush as the heir to Reagan conservatism and the Bush-led Republican Party as the vessel of pure Reaganism:

But it is now clear that Bush's own son takes far more after his father's old boss than he does his own father, at least politically speaking. From tax cuts (and deficits, alas), to his personal conviction on abortion, to aligning America with the historical tide of liberty in the world, *George W. Bush has proved that he's a Reaganite, not a "Bushie." He may not be a natural heir to Reagan, but that's the point. The party is all Reaganite now* [emphasis added]. What better sign that this is now truly and totally the Gipper's Party than the obvious conversion of George Bush's own son?

The dramatic turnabout in conservative characterizations of Bush is nowhere better demonstrated than by comparing Goldberg's accusation in 2006 that Bush's governing approach is like his father's rather than Ronald Reagan's ("Bush was always loyal to his father, who came out of the Nixon wing of the party") to Goldberg's 2002 polar opposite claim that Bush "takes far more after his father's old boss [Ronald Reagan] than he does his own father" and that "George W. Bush has proved that he's a Reaganite, not a 'Bushie.'"

As Bush's popularity has plummeted, so, too, has the esteem in which his own followers hold him. Self-identified conservatives during Bush's first term were writing truly worshipful books about George Bush, devoted to paying homage to his greatness as a leader and as a wise, resolute yet humble man; in 2006 they were denouncing him as a stubborn and weak failure who, in addition to those "sins," was never a conservative at all, and perhaps was even a closeted "liberal." The conservatives' frantic scampering to distance themselves and to disassociate their political movement from Bush stands as a powerful testament to the president's steep fall and isolation.

In that regard, there is a serious, and quite revealing, fraud emerging in the political landscape—namely, that the so-called conservative movement is *not responsible* for the destruction wrought on the country by the Bush presidency and the loyal Republican Congress that followed him. Even more audacious, the claim is emerging that the conservative movement is actually the prime *victim* here, because its lofty "principles" have been betrayed and repudiated by the Republican president and Congress that have ruled our country for the last six years.

This cry of victimization was the principal theme at the National

Review Institute Conservative Summit held in January 2007, at which one conservative luminary after the next paraded on stage to lament that the unpopular president and rejected GOP-controlled Congress "abandoned" conservatism and failed for that reason. As but one illustrative example, the following is a passage from *National Review* editor Rich Lowry's opening remarks, introducing Newt Gingrich (whom Lowry afterward described as "inspiring, brilliant, creative, visionary"):

> It is, in all seriousness, it is a distressing and depressing time to be a conservative. I'm reminded of the old saying by Mao—things are always darkest before they go completely black.
>
> In recent years, we have watched a Republican Congress disgrace itself with its association with scandal, with its willful lack of fiscal discipline, and with its utter disinterest in the reforms that America needs. And at the same time, we watched a Republican President abet or passively accept the excesses of his Congressional party and, more importantly, fail to take the steps—until perhaps now—fail to take the steps to win a major foreign war. . . .
>
> So we need to figure out a way how to make conservative policy and principles appealing and relevant again to the American public, and we need to do it together.

Note the passive tone Lowry uses to signify a lack of agency, even victimhood—"we have watched a Republican Congress disgrace itself " and "we watched a Republican President abet or passively accept the excesses of his Congressional party." Lowry depicts himself and his poor fellow movement conservatives as victims: They have stood by helplessly and with such sadness as the country was damaged by a president and Congress that abandoned and violated their conservative principles and left conservatives isolated and with nowhere to turn.

But the deceit here is manifest. Lowry and his "conservative" comrades were anything but passive observers over the last six years. They did far more than "watch" as the president and the Congress "disgraced" themselves and damaged this country. It was self-identified "conservatives" who were the principal cheerleaders, the most ardent and loyal propagandists, propping up George Bush and his blindly loyal Republican Congress.

It was they who continuously told America that George Bush was the reincarnation of the Great American Conservative Hero Ronald Reagan and the Great Warrior Defender of Freedom Winston Churchill all wrapped up in one glorious, powerful package. It was this same conservative movement—now pretending to lament the abandonment of conservatism by Bush and the Congress—that was the single greatest source of Bush's political support, that twice elected him and propped up his presidency and the movement that followed it.

So why, after six years of glorifying George Bush and devoting their full-fledged loyalty to him and the Hastert-and-DeLay-controlled Congress are conservatives like Lowry, Limbaugh, and Gingrich suddenly insisting that Bush is an anti-conservative and the GOP-led Congress the opposite of conservative virtue? The dynamic is as obvious as it is corrupt. They are desperately trying to disclaim responsibility for the disasters that they wrought in the name of "conservatism" by repudiating the political figures whom they named as the standard-bearers of their movement but whom America has now so decisively rejected.

George Bush has not changed in the slightest. He is exactly the same as he was when he was converted into the hero and icon of the conservative movement. The only thing that has changed is that Bush is no longer the wildly popular president that conservatives sought to embrace, but instead is a deeply disliked figure, increasingly detested by Americans, from whom conservatives now wish to shield themselves. And in this regard, these self-proclaimed great devotees of conservative political principles have revealed themselves to have *none*.

When he was popular, George Bush was the embodiment of conservatism. Now that he is rejected on a historic scale, he is the betrayer of conservatism. That is because "conservatism"—while definable on a theoretical plane—has come to have no practical meaning in this country other than a quest for ever-expanding government power for its own sake. When George Bush enabled those ends, he was the Great Conservative. Now that he impedes them due to his unprecedented unpopularity, he is the Judas of the conservative movement.

What is going on here, quite transparently, is a rehabilitation project. Bush's presidency cannot be salvaged, but the reputation of conservatives and conservatism can be—though only by separating the former from the latter. Given Bush's policies—massive increases in federal spending (including discretionary domestic spending), wildly expanding deficits, drastically increased domestic surveillance powers, and foreign wars fought ostensibly to export American values—there is and always has been a strong case to make that the Bush administration adhered to very few of the defining tenets of political conservatism, at least as it exists in theory. For that reason, had a substantial cohort of conservatives insisted upon distinguishing between Bush and conservatism when the Bush presidency was an epic success, the argument that the president is not a "true conservative" would have been reasonable. During Bush's high-flying years, however, conservatives overwhelmingly claimed him as one of their own. Further, even as Bush's popularity ratings tumbled, his remaining loyal supporters were preponderantly self-identified conservatives.

According to Pew, in March 2006, the president's approval ratings had plummeted to an all-time low of just 33 percent. But a robust 78 percent of self-identified "conservatives" continued to approve of his job performance.

Thus, it is disingenuous, to put it generously, for right-wing activists to disclaim Bush so belatedly as a member of the fold, for it is the "conservative" movement that is centrally responsible for Bush's presidency. Until his popularity plunged steeply and irrevocably, they claimed him as one of their own and engineered both of his electoral victories.

Means exist for political movements to eject the leaders they choose in the event that those leaders stray from the "right beliefs." In 1976, Gerald Ford was the Republican president, but conservatives believed he was insufficiently conservative: so they supported the primary challenge of Ronald Reagan.

In 1980, Jimmy Carter was the Democratic president, but liberals believed he was insufficiently liberal, so they supported the primary challenge of Ted Kennedy. As *The Washington Monthly* recounted: "By 1980, many liberals were in open revolt against Carter, abandoning him to support Ted Kennedy's ultimately-doomed primary challenge even as the public was sending unmistakable signals that it was sick of Kennedy-style big government."

In 1992, the first George Bush was the Republican president, but many conservatives believed he was insufficiently conservative, so they supported the primary challenge of Pat Buchanan. As *New York Times* columnist William Safire described it at the time: "Buchanan is using the Republican primary campaign in 1992 as the springboard for his long-range plan to wrest control of the party from hawkish neoconservatives and pragmatic moderates. Right from the start, he was a Goldwater 'true believer,' never happy with the necessary compromises of Nixon and Reagan."

George W. Bush, however, with very rare exception, was enthusiastically embraced by conservatives—in his 2000 primary fight against John McCain, in the 2000 general election, and again in the 2004 general election. Conservatives made George Bush (and the individuals who controlled Congress) the standard-bearer of their political movement for the last six years, and there was little attempt to separate conservatism from the president or from the GOP leadership embodied by Denny Hastert and Tom DeLay. The handful of right-wing figures who insisted that the Bush presidency deviated fundamentally from political conservatism—a Pat Buchanan here or an Andrew Sullivan there—were castigated and declared not to be "real conservatives" solely by virtue of their refusal to support George Bush's policies.

Who, then, are the ostensible "real conservatives" who were repudiating George Bush and the GOP Congressional leaders when Bush's approval ratings were respectable? Is it Mitt Romney, who in 2004 hailed "the courageous and compassionate leadership of President George W. Bush and Vice President Dick Cheney"? Is it Rick Santorum, who solemnly told Americans: "every generation has but a moment to carry the torch that defines who we are and what we will be," and then identified who he thinks will do that for conservatives: "George Bush has shown his compassion by advancing his faith-based initiatives, strengthening marriage, and fighting to let the American people define marriage, not left-wing judges"?

Perhaps it is Rush Limbaugh, who, at the time of Reagan's 2004 death, said: "Reagan was right just as George W. Bush is today, and I really believe that if Reagan had been able he would have put his hand on Bush's shoulder and say to him, 'Stay the course, George.' I really believe that." Or James Dobson, who boasted of the critical role played by conservatives in re-electing George Bush: "According to Dobson, evangelical Protestants played a major role in re-electing President George W.

Bush, giving him a 'great mandate.'" And in May 2003, longtime conservative pundit Bob Novak called Bush "a president who may be more basically conservative than Ronald Reagan."

The leading right-wing political magazine, *National Review*—with the aforementioned Rich Lowry at the helm—in 2004 told its readership about George Bush and "conservatism": "In his bid for reelection, George W. Bush deserves the support of conservatives." Although the editors acknowledged that "mistakes" were made, they said that "Bush has shown evidence of being able to learn from his mistakes. We have made political strides in Iraq." While noting the "legitimate conservative criticisms that can be made of his record," they also wrote that "Bush deserves conservative support, as well, on domestic issues." Thus, "For conservatives . . . backing Bush's reelection should be an easy decision."

During the years of 2002 through 2004, George Bush was venerated like few other presidents, spoken of in terms so reverent that at times it seemed almost improper to criticize him. And it was American conservatives leading these virtual canonization rituals. Such a sudden "recognition" that Bush is not a true conservative, then, is transparently prompted by the collapse of the Bush presidency, by the collective realization that he has been an epic failure, and the consequent desire to shield conservatism from the toxic fallout.

Independent of the abstract debate as to whether George Bush has governed as a "conservative" in some theoretical, academic sense of that term, the near-complete reversal in how right-wing leaders speak of George Bush is simply remarkable. The fundamental reversal reveals the extent to which the Bush presidency has become so politically poisonous that even his own supporters now fear being held responsible for its legacy.

Destroying the Republican Brand

The abandonment of the president is so cataclysmic that it is actually reshaping the American political landscape. A March 2007 Pew poll revealed some truly startling findings. George Bush's unpopularity was literally driving Americans away in droves from the Republican

Party. Bush was single-handedly coming close to destroying the Republican brand. Whereas in 2002 the percentage of Americans who identified or leaned toward one of the parties was split almost evenly (43–43 percent), Democrats had opened up a huge gap after six years of the Bush presidency. According to Pew, 50 percent of Americans now identify as or lean toward the Democratic Party, while Republicans attract only 35 percent. As the *Los Angeles Times* put it in reporting on the Pew findings:

> Public allegiance to the Republican Party has plunged during George W. Bush's presidency, as attitudes have edged away from some of the conservative values that fueled GOP political victories, a major survey has found.
>
> The survey, by the nonpartisan Pew Research Center for the People & the Press, found a "dramatic shift" in political party identification since 2002, when Republicans and Democrats were at rough parity. Now, 50% of those surveyed identified with or leaned toward Democrats, whereas 35% aligned with Republicans. . . .
>
> "Iraq has played a large part; the pushback on the Republican Party has to do with Bush, but there are other things going on here that Republicans will have to contend with," said Andrew Kohut, director of the Pew Center. "There is a difference in the landscape."

Political journalist Rod Dreher is as conservative as an individual can be—a longtime contributor to *National Review,* a self-described "practicing Christian and political conservative," and a columnist for the *Dallas Morning News.* Yet his rejection of George Bush *and* Bush's vision of America is now complete, and the reasoning that led him to that point is shared by many other Americans who previously supported the president.

In January 2007, Dreher recorded an extraordinary oral essay for National Public Radio in which he recounts how the conduct of President Bush (for whom he voted twice) in the Iraq War (which he supported) is causing him to question, really to abandon, the core political beliefs he has held since childhood. Dreher, forty, explains that his "first real political memory" was the 1979 failed rescue effort of the U.S. hostages in Iran. He states that he "hated" Jimmy Carter for "shaming

America before our enemies with weakness and incompetence." When Reagan was elected, Dreher believed "America was saved." Reagan was "strong and confident." Democrats were "weak and depressed."

In particular, Dreher recounts how much, during the 1980s, he "disliked hippies—the blame-America-first liberals who were so hung up on Vietnam, who surrendered to Communists back then just like they want to do now." In short, to Dreher, Republicans were "winners." Democrats were "defeatists." On September 11, Dreher's first thought was: "Thank God we have a Republican in the White House." The rest of his essay recounts his political transformation as a result of the Bush presidency:

> As President Bush marched the country to war with Iraq, even some voices on the Right warned that this was a fool's errand. I dismissed them angrily. I thought them unpatriotic.
>
> But almost four years later, I see that I was the fool.
>
> In Iraq, this Republican President for whom I voted twice has shamed our country with weakness and incompetence, and the consequences of his failure will be far, far worse than anything Carter did.
>
> The fraud, the mendacity, the utter haplessness of our government's conduct of the Iraq War have been shattering to me.
>
> It wasn't supposed to turn out like this. Not under a Republican President.
>
> I turn forty next month—middle aged at last—a time of discovering limits, finitude. I expected that. But what I did not expect was to see the limits of finitude of American power revealed so painfully.
>
> I did not expect Vietnam.
>
> As I sat in my office last night watching President Bush deliver his big speech, I seethed over the waste, the folly, the stupidity of this war.
>
> I had a heretical thought for a conservative—that I have got to teach my kids that they must never, ever take presidents and generals at their word—that their government will send them to kill and die for noble-sounding rot—that they have to question authority.
>
> On the walk to the parking garage, it hit me. Hadn't the hippies tried to tell my generation that? Why had we scorned them so blithely?
>
> Will my children, too small now to understand Iraq, take me seriously when I tell them one day what powerful men, whom their father once believed in, did to this country? Heavy thoughts for someone who is still a conservative despite it all. It was a long drive home.

Dreher's essay is extreme and intense but also increasingly commonplace and illustrative. The unparalleled magnitude of the disaster that President Bush has wrought on this country will carry a profound impact on American strength and credibility for a long, long time to come and also on the views of Americans—including many conservatives—toward their political leaders and, almost certainly, toward the Republican Party.

Yet another illustrative example is *Newsweek*'s Fareed Zakaria, who was not only a supporter of the war in Iraq but also one of two journalists invited to a secret meeting with senior Bush Defense Department officials in November 2001 at which the participants strategized on ways to persuade the president of the need to invade Iraq. But by 2006, Zakaria had turned against the administration almost completely, and by the middle of the year was issuing sweeping condemnations of both Bush and the legacy of his presidency:

> Leave process aside: the results are plain. On almost every issue involving postwar Iraq—troop strength, international support, the credibility of exiles, de-Baathification, handling Ayatollah Ali Sistani—Washington's assumptions and policies have been wrong. By now most have been reversed, often too late to have much effect. This strange combination of arrogance and incompetence has not only destroyed the hopes for a new Iraq. It has had the much broader effect of turning the United States into an international outlaw in the eyes of much of the world.
>
> Whether he wins or loses in November, George W. Bush's legacy is now clear: the creation of a poisonous atmosphere of anti-Americanism around the globe. I'm sure he takes full responsibility.

The enormity of the damage Bush has done to America is reflected by the palpable change in the content as well as the tone of our political dialogue. By the end of 2006, op-ed themes such as historian Douglas Brinkley's in the *Washington Post* became commonplace. Brinkley is a highly regarded presidential historian, having written books about Franklin Roosevelt, Jimmy Carter, and John Kennedy.

In his first paragraph, Brinkley recounts a meeting he had with Reagan biographer Lou Cannon: "Like many historians these days, we discussed whether George W. Bush is, conceivably, the worst U.S. president ever."

While Cannon "bristled" at the idea, he did so, according to Brinkley, *not* because anything in Bush's presidency thus far precludes such an assessment, but only because, with two years left, declaring Bush "the worst" was premature. After all, unforeseen events could unfold in such a way as to improve Bush's standing.

But Brinkley had no such qualms, barely qualifying his ready conclusion about Bush's place in history:

> But we live in speedy times and, the truth is, after six years in power and barring a couple of miracles, it's safe to bet that Bush will be forever handcuffed to the bottom rungs of the presidential ladder.

In February 2007, Al Neuharth, founder of *USA Today*, the newspaper with the highest circulation in the country, announced that he had reconsidered his view of Bush's place in history. Headlined "Mea Culpa to Bush on Presidents Day," Neuharth wrote:

> Our great country has had 43 presidents. Many very good. A few pretty bad. On Presidents Day next Monday, it's appropriate to commemorate them all. . . .
>
> A year ago I criticized Hillary Clinton for saying "this (Bush) administration will go down in history as one of the worst."
>
> "She's wrong," I wrote. Then I rated these five presidents, in this order, as the worst: Andrew Jackson, James Buchanan, Ulysses Grant, Hoover and Richard Nixon. "It's very unlikely Bush can crack that list," I added.
>
> I was wrong. This is my mea culpa. Not only has Bush cracked that list, but he is planted firmly at the top. . . .
>
> Bush admitting his many mistakes on Iraq and ending that fiasco might make many of us forgive, even though we can never forget the terrible toll in lives and dollars.

The collapse of the Bush presidency brings to mind the plight of the Greek tragic figure Icarus, whose father built wings made of feathers and wax to enable them to escape from their exile on Crete. Intoxicated by hubris and uncontrollable sensations of his own potency, Icarus exceeded his limits and flew too close to the sun, which melted his wings and caused him to plunge helplessly into the sea.

One can draw a straight line between the unprecedented heights reached by George Bush in his post-9/11 glory days and the hubris- and arrogance-driven collapse—now sustained and total—of his presidency.

By any measure, things have not gone well for the United States over the first six years of the Bush presidency. Is there anyone who really claims otherwise? In any area, what metrics could possibly be adopted, what achievements invoked, in order to argue that the interests and welfare of America have been enhanced during this administration?

As Brinkley points out, while Bush and Lyndon Johnson both presided over a deeply unpopular war, Johnson's place in history is vastly improved by substantial "major domestic accomplishments to boast about when leaving the White House, such as the Civil Rights Act and Medicare/Medicaid." By stark contrast, Brinkley pointed out, "Bush has virtually none."

It appears highly likely, even inevitable, that until Bush leaves office on January 20, 2009, the United States is going to be saddled with a failed president, one who is lost, aimless, weak, and isolated in the extreme. Yet he continues as inflexibly as ever to be driven by a worldview that has come to be almost universally rejected as useless, even dangerous, for dealing with the challenges facing the nation.

A failed, lame-duck president, with nothing to lose, can either accept his impotence and passively muddle through the remainder of his term or do the opposite—move furiously forward on an extremist course, free of the constraints of facing the electorate again and convinced that he is on the side of Good and Right. Such a conviction can lead to the belief that his unpopularity is not an impediment, but a challenge, even a *calling*, to demonstrate his resolve and commitment by persisting *even more tenaciously* in the face of almost universal opposition.

The embrace of that latter course renders public opposition and all other forms of outside pressure irrelevant, even counterproductive. It is human nature that when one is rejected and condemned by contemporary opinion, a temptation arises to reject that contemporary opinion as misguided and worthless. One instead seeks refuge in other less hostile metrics of success—universal moral standards, or the judgment of a Supreme Being, or the future vindication of history.

It has long been evident that the president's worldview compels such refuge. Convinced that his core beliefs are preordained as Right, he will reject any measurement that rejects his beliefs and embrace any that affirms them. What matters to him now is not the judgment of contemporary politicians, journalists, or even the majority of American voters. The rightness of his actions are determined not by public opinion polls or editorials or even empirical evidence but instead by adherence to what he perceives to be objectively moral notions of Right and Wrong, Good and Evil. As the president himself has made expressly clear, his calling is to wage war against Evil on behalf of Good—as he conceives of those concepts—and he will not be deterred in that mission, not even slightly, by pragmatic impediments, whether they be political pressures, resource constraints, ongoing failures, or the objections of American citizens.

CHAPTER TWO

The Manichean Warrior

You know, you've heard me talk about this probably, but I really, truly view this as a conflict between good and evil. And there really isn't much middle ground—like none. The people we fight are evil people. . . .

Either you're with us or you're against us. Either you're on the side of freedom and justice or you aren't.

—**GEORGE W. BUSH**, Winston-Salem, North Carolina, January 30, 2002

One of the aspects of the Bush presidency that has often confounded supporters and opponents alike is that George Bush's political beliefs do not fit comfortably, or even at all, within any of the familiar, commonly assigned ideological categories. Certainly Bush is typically referred to as a conservative, and as was demonstrated in the preceding chapter, the conservative political movement claimed him as its own and was largely responsible for both his 2000 and 2004 election victories.

Political conservatism in the United States, however, has two meanings. In one sense, it is an abstract theory of government that—in its pure, academic form—advocates various political principles. In this academic formulation, *conservatism* is defined by a belief in (a) restrained federal government power, (b) minimal federal taxes and responsible and limited spending, (c) a generalized distrust of the federal government and its attempts to intervene into the private lives of citizens, (d) reliance on the private sector rather than the federal government to achieve "Good" ends, (e) a preference for state and local autonomy over federalized and centralized control, (f) trusting in individuals rather than government officials to make decisions, and (g) an overarching belief in the supremacy of the rule of law.

But the term *conservatism* also refers to a group of political figures and their supporters who call themselves conservatives. In this version, *conservatism* is defined by the actions taken and the policies implemented *in reality* by conservatives when they are in power rather than by what think tanks and theorists set forth as conservative principles.

This dichotomy is not unique to conservatism. All political theories can be understood as a set of principles, or, independently, as the collection of policies and methods of governance that its adherents, *in practice*, undertake when in power. Communism, for instance, exists as a sterile, academic theory in the works of Karl Marx and the speeches of Mao Tse-tung and Fidel Castro. At that theoretical level, communism constitutes harmonious egalitarianism in which all are liberated from capitalistic enslavement and material wants, and thus are freed to pursue more elevated levels of creativity and personal fulfillment.

But when its adherents—"Communists"—have obtained power, they have not behaved in conformity with these pretty utopian principles. They have almost uniformly imposed tyranny and wrought profound misery. The term *communism,* then, is not understood exclusively—or even primarily—by reference to the abstract principles defining it in books and in speeches. Rather, it is best and most commonly understood to describe the actions of Communists when in power.

Like communism, the theory of American political "conservatism" in the pure, abstract Hayek-Goldwater sense has rarely, if ever, converged with the actions and policies of self-described conservatives when in power. And, like communism, perhaps the very nature of theoretical conservatism means that it never can.

Arguably, the imperatives of human nature and the instincts of government leaders—to attempt to enhance rather than restrict their own power—constitute an insurmountable barrier to the implementation of "pure" conservatism, an idealistic vision where elected government officials proceed to limit or even dismantle the mechanisms of their own power. Additionally, elected officials in the American political system must often support government programs benefiting a political movement's constituents as a condition of retaining their power, thereby rendering the reduction, let alone the abolition, of excessive government spending virtually impossible.

Whether political conservatism in the United States has ever really existed can be and continues to be endlessly debated. The allegedly purest form of it, as embodied by Ronald Reagan, oversaw an expansion of the power of the federal government in countless ways. That expansion of power was accompanied by wild deficit spending. The Reagan administration ushered in a significant increase in domestic discretionary spending (though far less than that which has occurred under the Bush administration). And multiple Reagan officials were indicted, and some convicted, as a result of a scandal that grew out of the administration's violations of legal prohibitions on providing aid to the Nicaraguan contras. To be sure, Reagan paid rhetorical homage to conservative theories, but his actual governance deviated in multiple ways from those principles.

Regardless of one's view of *that* debate, it is beyond reasonable dispute that President Bush's actions and policies deviate fundamentally, and in almost every area, from the theoretical precepts of political conservatism. Whatever one might call the set of guiding principles animating President Bush, political conservatism—at least as it exists in its storied, theoretical form—is not it.

Since President Bush was inaugurated, discretionary domestic spending has skyrocketed, both in absolute terms and when compared to the budget-balancing Clinton administration. In 2003, the right-leaning Cato Institute published a detailed assessment of federal government spending over the preceding thirty years—entitled " 'Conservative' Bush Spends More Than 'Liberal' Presidents Clinton, Carter." It concluded:

> But the real truth is that national defense is far from being responsible for all of the spending increases. According to the new numbers, defense spending will have risen by about 34 percent since Bush came into office. But, at the same time, non-defense discretionary spending will have skyrocketed by almost 28 percent. Government agencies that Republicans were calling to be abolished less than 10 years ago, such as education and

labor, have enjoyed jaw-dropping spending increases under Bush of 70 percent and 65 percent respectively. . . .

After all, in inflation-adjusted terms, Clinton had overseen a total spending increase of only 3.5 percent at the same point in his administration. More importantly, after his first three years in office, non-defense discretionary spending actually went down by 0.7 percent. This is contrasted by Bush's three-year total spending increase of 15.6 percent and a 20.8 percent explosion in non-defense discretionary spending.

Those profligate spending patterns only worsened as the Bush presidency proceeded. In 2005, the right-wing American Enterprise Institute (AEI) published a study by its own Veronique de Rugy and *Reason* magazine's Nick Gillespie. The report was entitled "Bush the Budget Basher" and concluded: "After five years of Republican reign, it's time for small-government conservatives to acknowledge that the GOP has forfeited its credibility when it comes to spending restraint."

President Bush has not only violated every claimed tenet of conservatism when it comes to restraints on federal spending, but he ranks among the most fiscally reckless presidents in modern times—so insists the pro-Bush AEI:

> "After 11 years of Republican majority we've pared [the budget] down pretty good," Rep. Tom DeLay (R-Texas) crowed a few weeks back during ongoing budget deliberations. But nothing could be farther from the truth, at least since the GOP gained the White House in 2001.
>
> During his five years at the helm of the nation's budget, the president has expanded a wide array of "compassionate" welfare-state, defense, and nondefense programs. When it comes to spending, Bush is no Reagan. Alas, he is also no Clinton and not even Nixon. The recent president he most resembles is in fact fellow Texan and legendary spendthrift Lyndon Baines Johnson—except that Bush is in many ways even more profligate with the public till.

These massive spending increases are entirely independent of any 9/11-related or defense-based expenditures: "When homeland security spending is separated out, the increase in discretionary spending is still huge: 36 percent on Bush's watch," according to the AEI. During the Bush presidency, total real discretionary outlays increased by 35.8 percent. By comparison, the same figure increased by only 11.2 percent during the deficit-plagued Reagan administration, and during the budget-balancing Clinton administration, it *decreased by 8.2 percent.* All of this led the AEI report to conclude: "It seems incontestable that we should conclude that the country's purse is worse off when Republicans are in power."

The Bush administration has also repeatedly asserted the prerogatives of federal power in areas traditionally reserved to the states. It has, for instance, sought to eliminate the right of the states to enact laws governing marriage, assisted suicide, and the use of medical marijuana. In each of those areas, various states have enacted laws—in some instances by referenda—that President Bush disliked. As a result, the Bush administration fought to override the judgment of the states by federalizing those issues and imposing the policy preferences of the president as a uniform, compulsory standard, which no state was to be free to reject. Hence: No gay marriage. No physician-assisted suicide. No permitting terminally ill individuals to obtain prescriptions for marijuana to treat their afflictions or alleviate their symptoms.

The Bush administration's disdain for the ostensibly conservative belief in limited federal power and the sanctity of states' rights became most apparent in the case of Terri Schiavo. A lifelong Republican and Southern Baptist state court judge had been presiding over the Schiavo matter for several years, faithfully applying clear Florida state law to resolve the battle between Schiavo's husband and her parents as to what end-of-life decisions would be made about Schiavo. Florida appellate courts upheld virtually all of that judge's substantive rulings.

But the outcome of those state judicial proceedings deviated from the president's moral preferences and those of his "conservative" Congressional allies. As a result, in an atmosphere of intense drama, Congress enacted and the president signed "emergency" legislation vesting authority in the federal courts to override the judgment of the Florida courts. Wielding the tools of federal power, they sought to take it upon themselves to resolve the end-of-life issues faced by Terri Schiavo's family, issues that were controlled by clear Florida law.

The list of the Bush administration's systematic deviations from fundamentally "conservative principles" (as they exist in theory) is too lengthy to chronicle here. Suffice it to say, while the Bush presidency is consistent with the actual decisions and policies of previous "conservative" politicians, a belief in conservative theories of government is plainly not what has guided the president or his administration.

MORALISM TRUMPS CONSERVATISM

That political conservatism (in its theoretical sense) has not been the North Star of the Bush presidency defies reasonable dispute. That reality leads to the question, What does drive the president? When aggregated, the Bush administration's actions, policies, and political arguments can appear jumbled and incoherent, bereft of a philosophical center. But the opposite is true. At the heart of the Bush presidency exists a coherent worldview, one the president has applied with exceptional consistency and unyielding conviction.

Many Bush critics, and even some of his supporters, have long depicted the president as a weak and malleable individual—more of an aimless figurehead than a resolute leader—whose actions are the by-product not of personal agency but manipulation and control by advisers shrewder and more willful than he. But that portrayal is pure mythology, for which there is virtually no support.

It is certainly true that throughout his presidency, Bush has relied heavily on advisers who focus on details, has delegated even significant tasks to aides, and has trusted those around him to inform him of critical matters and to educate him on issues about which he knew little. In those regards, his reliance on his advisers and top aides is substantial. But when the president, in a mid-2006 press conference, anointed himself as "the Decider," it struck many as arrogant, but few as inaccurate: George Bush's strong personality traits and deeply held personal beliefs have, more than anything else, defined and propelled the Bush presidency.

In his book *The Right Man: The Surprise Presidency of George W. Bush*, Bush speechwriter David Frum recounted several incidents early on in the Bush presidency, even prior to the 9/11 attacks, in which an engaged, aggressive, and even sometimes shrewd George Bush left no doubt that he was in charge, that he was the Decider well before he coined that term. After describing a meeting in which the president was particularly decisive and calculating, Frum concluded:

> In that hour, Bush had settled one thing in my mind: I could never again take seriously the theory that somebody else was running this administration—not Cheney, not Rove, not Card. Bush was leading us all right—but where was he leading us all to?

As is true with any decision-maker, those close to the president are able to exert influence over his decisions by molding their advice to comport with the president's worldview, thereby enhancing the likelihood that the president will find their recommended course of action persuasive. The president's advisers certainly are aware of the president's impulses and belief system and conform their cases accordingly. Nonetheless, each defining aspect of the administration—the policies it has undertaken, its interaction with the outside world, and the manner in which decisions are made—has been shaped and determined by the worldview and personal leadership attributes of the president himself. As a result, all of the seemingly disparate component parts and disconnected events of the Bush administration have a common origin.

They all are, to varying degrees, outgrowths of the president's core view that the world can be understood as an overarching conflict between the forces of Good and Evil, and that America is "called upon" to defend the former from the latter. That view finds a corresponding expression for the president on the personal level, where the moral and religious duty of the individual is to divine God's will (the Good) and to act in accordance with it.

By definition, this premise demands the identification of Evil, which is the enemy—an enemy that is pure in its Evil and that, by its very nature, cannot be engaged, offered compromises, negotiated with, understood, managed, contained, or ignored. It can only be attacked, hated, and destroyed.

When expressed and implemented as a governing philosophy, this belief in the centrality of Good vs. Evil results *not* in an effort to limit government power, but rather to expand it drastically, both domestically and abroad, in order to accumulate power in service of the battle against (perceived) Evil and to impose (perceptions of) Good. Such a philosophy is centrally predicated on the certainty that government leaders can divine God's will—not with regard to specific issues and policies but in a generalized moral sense—and can therefore confidently enlist and expand the awesome power of the American government in service to universal moral dictates. As a political philosophy, it is therefore far from "conservative." Rather, it is messianic, evangelical, and Manichean.

The term *Manichean* refers in its most literal sense to a religion founded in the third century by the Persian prophet Manes. The movement attracted large numbers of followers who were drawn to its simplicity and moral clarity. The religious movement spread throughout large parts of the Roman Empire and into China. Its central precept was that the entire world could be cleanly divided into two opposing spheres—God and Satan in the world of the eternal, and a corresponding dualistic battle of Good and Evil playing out on Earth. A stark dichotomy lies at the heart of the worldview, with God as father of goodness, and the Prince of Darkness as the ultimate author of all Evil.

World events were all driven by, were all the by-product of, an ongoing, endless conflict between the forces of Good and the forces of Evil. One's overarching moral duty was to maintain adherence to God's will by siding with Good and battling against the forces of Evil.

One of Christianity's most influential moral philosophers, St. Augustine, was a devotee of Manicheanism in his youth. But ultimately, its doctrinal deviations from Christianity led to its being condemned as heretical by various Christian emperors. Nonetheless, the similarities between Manichean and Christian moralism are self-evident, and the influence of the former on the latter is beyond doubt.

But the historical fate of the Manichees is of far less interest than is contemporary reliance on their religion's central moral tenets. In the overwhelming majority of President Bush's significant speeches and interviews throughout his political career—but particularly since the 9/11 attacks—he evinces a dualistic worldview lodged at the core of his belief system.

Both the president's deeds and, frequently, his own self-descriptions leave no doubt he holds that world events are driven by the forces of Good vs. Evil. And it is equally clear that the duty to side with Good and battle against Evil motivates the president—not merely in his private life but also as a leader, as the American president. The tools for fulfilling that duty are the powers and resources of the U.S. government.

Many people, probably most, believe in the existence of Good and Evil—that is to say, they perceive certain isolated acts, perhaps even certain individuals, as composed not of a mixture of good and evil, but rather as pure Good or pure Evil. Indeed, wide agreement exists that certain actions can be understood only as pure Evil: Nazis devoting themselves to the extermination of targeted groups; whites treating blacks as property to be bought and sold; cold-blooded murders committed for no reason, or petty reasons, without mercy or remorse; theocracies putting to death heathens, infidels, homosexuals, rape victims, and others who deviate from mandated orthodoxies; and terrorists flying fuel-laden jets filled with innocent people into office buildings also filled with innocent people in order to slaughter as many as possible. One could compile a long list of acts that most would agree are Evil.

Conversely, there are acts that seem accurately characterized as pure Good: one who risks his own life to save another or one who devotes his life to the well-being of those in need. It is true that plausible arguments can be advanced that such behavior is driven by mixed motives—the life-saver becomes a hero and receives adulation, Mother Teresa becomes famous and widely admired for her aid to the sick and destitute, etc. But it is difficult to dispute that, on an intuitive if not rational level, these acts seem to be propelled by a force for Good (whatever its origins), just as murderous or genocidal acts (even when there is a perceived justification for them) seem driven by Evil.

But deeds that are pure Good or pure Evil—and, even more so, individuals who are pure Good or pure Evil—are rarities, the exception and not the norm. In truth, the vast, vast majority of individuals are capable of both Good and Evil, and even those who may commit an Evil act are capable of acts of great Good (and those who commit acts of Good are capable of Evil). Human beings and their psyches are complex and shaped by numerous, often conflicting influences.

Moreover, most behaviors are not susceptible to moral judgment at all. They are morally neutral, purely pragmatic endeavors geared toward effecting a desired outcome rather than in the service of moral dictates. When one applies for a job or carries out one's job duties or reads a book or eats a meal or chats with a friend or invents a new product or repairs a malfunctioning machine, pragmatic rather than moral considerations predominate. Routine decisions and actions such as these are not motivated by moral considerations, even if they have a moral component to them.

But the Manichean mind-set does not admit to the merely isolated or occasional appearance of Good and Evil. Rather, in this view, the battle between Good and Evil is the ongoing dynamic at the epicenter of world events, and more so, acting in defense of the Good constitutes the overarching duty. It is that mind-set that has driven President Bush and his presidency. He lays the template of the glorious and all-consuming battle between Good and Evil over all significant matters, personal and public/political.

Further, for the Manichean believer, the battle between Good and Evil is paramount. It subordinates all other considerations and never gives way to any conflicting or inconsistent goals. Measures intended to promote Good or undermine Evil are, by definition, necessary and just. They cannot be abandoned for pragmatic or prudential reasons, or because of growing opposition, or in response to evidence of failure. Insufficient progress when attacking Evil never justifies re-examination of the wisdom of the action, but instead compels a redoubling of one's determination to succeed. In sum, complexities, pragmatic considerations, the restraints of reality are trumped by the imperative of the moral crusade.

This Manichean paradigm unites and explains the president's personal approach to all matters—his foreign policy decisions; his relations with other countries; his domestic programs; the terms he adopts when discussing, debating, and analyzing political matters; his attitude toward domestic political opponents (including his own former officials and allies who have become critical); and his treatment of the national media. For the president, there always exists a clear and identifiable enemy who is to be defeated by any means, means justified not only by the pureness of the enemy's Evil but also by the core Goodness that he believes motivates him and his movement.

Religious faith is but one path to a Manichean mind-set, but it is far from the only one. Many people come to view the world as an all-consuming Manichean battle due to a variety of factors having nothing to do with religion—including extreme nationalism (manifested as a belief that one's own country is intrinsically Good and anyone who opposes it is pure Evil); ideological, racial, or ethnic supremacy; or even unrestrained fear (causing one to adopt a view of themselves as a "Good" victim with the sole priority being "protection" from the threat posed by forces of Evil). And while much of the support for President Bush's Manichean crusades may be explained by some combination of those factors, it is George Bush's religious faith—as he himself acknowledges—in which his personal Manichean worldview is rooted.

A critically important caveat is in order here. In the hands of political leaders, Manichean moralism can operate on at least two different levels. For some, it serves as a sincerely held belief system, genuinely animating their actions and decisions. Government leaders authentically driven by Manicheanism believe that there is objective Evil in the world and deploy state resources to attack and defeat it. Even the most tyrannical and extremist religious leaders, for instance, or the most brutal tyrants presiding over empires, or the most repressive Communist dictators (such as Mao Tse-tung or even Fidel Castro) often come to believe that they are acting in pursuit of moral Good, and that their tyranny is justified—even compelled—by the threat of Evil which surrounds them. Whether the forces they attack are *in fact* Evil and/or whether they are acting in pursuit of the *genuine* Good is an independent question entirely. The salient point is that Manichean leaders, by definition, *believe* that they are acting in pursuit or defense of the Good and against Evil.

Independently, political leaders can cynically adopt the template and language of Manichean moralism as a tool for persuading citizens of the necessity and justifiability of certain actions. Controversial actions that, in fact, have little or nothing to do with a concern for Good and Evil, and which political leaders *know* have little or nothing to do with either, can nonetheless be rhetorically justified via a dualistic appeal—that the action in question is necessary to fight for Good and defend against Evil. Thus, issues can be framed in Manichean terms by insincere leaders to manipulate public opinion, to cast morally neutral or even immoral policies as necessary for defense of the Good, and to thereby generate support for actions they wish to undertake.

Bush supporter and *Commentary* magazine founder Irving Kristol—generally credited as the "Father of Neoconservatism" and the father of

Bill Kristol, *The Weekly Standard*'s influential prowar editor—has expressly argued that society works best when a vanguard of elite leaders decide what is best and then disguise those conclusions in a Manichean package in order to induce what neoconservatism essentially regards as the idiot masses to accept and ingest those decisions. Kristol explained this approach in an interview, quoted by *Reason* magazine's Brian Doherty in July 1997:

> There are different kinds of truths for different kinds of people. There are truths appropriate for children; truths that are appropriate for students; truths that are appropriate for educated adults; and truths that are appropriate for highly educated adults, and the notion that there should be one set of truths available to everyone is a modern democratic fallacy. It doesn't work.

Writing in *Free Inquiry* magazine, Shadia Drury, a professor of philosophy and political science at the University of Regina (Saskatchewan, Canada), documented that Manicheanism as a manipulative tool has deep roots in neoconservative theory:

> There is a certain irony in the fact that the chief guru of the neoconservatives is a thinker who regarded religion merely as a political tool intended for the masses but not for the superior few. Leo Strauss, the German Jewish émigré who taught at the University of Chicago almost until his death in 1973, did not dissent from Marx's view that religion is the opium of the people; but he believed that the people need their opium. He therefore taught that those in power must invent noble lies and pious frauds to keep the people in the stupor for which they are supremely fit.

Drury notes that—beyond Irving Kristol—self-proclaimed followers of Strauss's theory include some of the most influential figures in the shaping and selling of Bush's foreign policy, such as Paul Wolfowitz, Bill Kristol, and various other Pentagon officials under former Secretary Rumsfeld. In his autobiographical essay, Irving Kristol specifically lauded the Straussian belief that the masses in a democracy need to be pacified with moral imperatives, and that "truth" was only for the elite leadership:

> What made [Strauss] so controversial within the academic community was his disbelief in the Enlightenment dogma that "the truth will make

men free." . . . Strauss was an intellectual aristocrat who thought that "the truth could make *some* minds free" [emphasis added], but he was convinced that there was an inherent conflict between philosophic truth and political order, and that the popularization and vulgarization of these truths might import unease, turmoil and the release of popular passions hitherto held in check by tradition and religion with utterly unpredictable, but mostly negative, consequences.

Thus, in the eyes of neoconservatives, concepts of Manichean morality are but tools used to blind, rather than enlighten, the masses, to keep them loyally in line behind their leaders' "superior" wisdom and insight. Leaders make decisions about complex matters and then package those decisions in simplistic moralistic terms in order to manipulate public support. Such packaging is how the neoconservatives' long-standing, pre-9/11 desire to invade Iraq for all sorts of geopolitical reasons was transformed into what Bush chief of staff Andy Card called a "marketing product," justifying that invasion based on the claims that 9/11 Changed Everything; that Saddam was connected to those attacks and he would give his Bad Weapons to the Terrorists; and that Freedom was On the March.

One can debate endlessly (without much hope of a definitive resolution) the question of whether George Bush has followed this neoconservative stratagem of cynically wielding Manichean concepts in order to persuade Americans to support his international aggression or whether, instead, such techniques were first cynically wielded to persuade Bush himself of the wisdom and moral necessity of these policies. Either way, that George Bush has invoked Manichean moralism as the central justifying argument for his decisions is difficult to dispute, to put it mildly. The overriding theme in the president's rhetorical arsenal, particularly with regard to his war and terrorism policies—but by no means only those—has been the purported need to fight against Evil and to defend the Good.

Ultimately, whether moralistic dualism is in fact what motivates the president or whether he manipulatively adopts its rhetoric to justify his actions has no bearing on the need to examine and, where necessary, refute the framework he (and his political allies) invoke in order to persuade Americans of the rightness of their actions. Put another way, when assessing the Bush presidency (or any political movement or political leader), one can undertake two entirely separate and independent tasks: (1) examine the justifications and arguments *proffered* by the president to justify his policies (in the case of Bush, Manichean moralism) and engage and refute those arguments at face value, or (2) attempt to expose the *genuine, underlying, concealed motives* fueling those policies, motives clouded or outright concealed by the dualistic rhetoric.

To engage, analyze, and refute the president's proffered justifications for his actions is neither to accept nor reject that they are sincerely held. In either case, those Manichean appeals have powerfully shaped the perceptions of many Americans and have been a potent tool in inducing Americans to support many of the president's most radical policies. And other influential political figures, including several who wish to succeed Bush, invoke the same worldview to advocate their own extremist policies, both domestically and abroad. That alone compels the need to examine the president's Manichean moralism and its underlying premises on their own merits, independent of the question of whether he really embraces it.

There is, of course, no shortage of theories as to the "true motives and objectives" of the Bush administration, particularly concerning matters of war and terrorism. And indeed, there is little doubt that the president is surrounded and heavily influenced by a constellation of aides, advisers, think tanks, supporters, and ideologues—many of whom have agendas and belief systems that are as far removed as can be from concerns of Good vs. Evil, to put it generously. (Chapter 4 critiques the Bush administration's conduct and thinking concerning Iran, and the potent influences and agendas that are brought to bear on the president's decision-making are examined and documented there.)

But independent of those matters, whether as a genuine belief system or cynical persuasive tool, Manichean theories play a vital role in American political discourse, and any meaningful assessment of the Bush presidency necessarily centers on those theories. Manichean moralism pervades our political dialogue.

ENDLESS NEED FOR ENEMIES

More policies have been justified, more government power expanded, more mischief enabled, and more perceptions manipulated by the Bush administration's invoking concepts of the enemy—the pure Evil enemy—than by any other tactic. Dualistic rhetoric has not been confined to the president. Indeed, at the heart of most political arguments and tactics of the Bush-led "conservative" movement is the identification of an Evil enemy, and a rage-driven perceived need to crush it. Bush followers are frequently most excited and enlivened by designating the enemy, followed by swarming, rabid attacks on it.

At its core, the Bush movement has defined itself by that which it is *not* rather than by identifiable, affirmative ideas. Its foreign policy objectives are identifiable by one overriding goal—destroy and/or kill the enemy, potential or suspected, often including everyone nearby. And it has come to view its domestic objectives through the same lens. It is a movement in a permanent state of war. All matters, foreign and domestic, are framed in terms of that war and ritualistic attacks on the enemy du jour—the terrorist, the Communist, the illegal immigrant, the secularist, and most of all, the "Liberal."

In his best-selling 2006 book, *Conservatives Without Conscience*, John Dean compares the conservative movement he joined in the late 1960s to today's Bush-led movement. Dean was attracted to the political conservatism of Barry Goldwater (whose 1960 book, *The Conscience of a Conservative*, inspired Dean's title), and, at the age of thirty-two, Dean became Richard Nixon's White House counsel.

Dean's central premise is that the current Bush-led "conservative" movement shares none of the core principles that attracted him to Goldwater conservatism. And indeed, scores of the country's most prominent voices on the right, such as Pat Buchanan, William Buckley, and George Will, also find that the Bush movement bears little resemblance to "traditional conservatism."

In July 2006, the so-called father of modern conservatism, *National Review* founder William Buckley, pronounced that Bush's "singular problem" is "the absence of effective conservative ideology." At roughly the same time, George Will condemned the so-called neoconservatism that has guided the Bush foreign policy as a "spectacularly misnamed radicalism." One of the president's most influential neoconservative supporters, Robert Kagan, echoed Will's view when he acknowledged, in his *Washington Post* column in January 2005, that although the vast majority of self-proclaimed "conservatives" have been loyally supportive of Bush's so-called neoconservative foreign policy, the Bush foreign policy is actually the very "antithesis of conservatism":

> The goal of American foreign policy is now to spread democracy, for its own sake, for reasons that transcend specific threats. In short, Bush has unmoored his foreign policy from the war on terrorism.
>
> This is where Bush may lose the support of most old-fashioned conservatives. His goals are now the antithesis of conservatism. They are revolutionary.

And before his death, Barry Goldwater himself frequently accused the "social conservative" wing of the party of assaulting core conservative principles.

Relatedly, Dean documents that the "conservative" movement Bush leads is composed of various factions that actually share very few political beliefs. With the exception of a handful of isolated examples (such as a fervent belief in tax-cutting), these groups could not come close to agreeing on a core set of political principles and specific policy goals that define their movement. In the absence of a unified policy agenda, what, then, binds them and maintains their allegiance to this political movement?

Dean's answer is that these disparate enclaves hold in common the need to wage war against perceived Evil, and the shared (related) hatred of common enemies. Their collective attacks on those enemies have become the Bush movement's defining attribute. That commonality is sufficient to maintain allegiance because, argues Dean, it provides a tonic to a morally ambiguous, uncertain, and complex world—a world they perceive to be filled with dangers in every facet of life. All of these factions, like the devotees of Manicheanism, are in thrall to promises of a comforting and liberating moral simplicity, a framework that provides refuge from a complex, confusing, and frightening world. A unified crusade against Evil enemies bestows purpose, excuses failure, alleviates confusion, and enables sensations of power.

Not only American political discourse but also American culture generally are suffused with an endless parade of fear-inducing images, of constant warnings of latent dangers—the terrorist "sleeper cells" lurking in every community, the sex predators living covertly on one's own street, drug gangs and violent criminals and online pedophiles, radical tyrants seeking nuclear weapons. Basic human nature dictates that a world that seems frightening and hopelessly complex always engenders a need for both protection and clarity.

Religion—a belief in an all-powerful, protective deity and a clear, absolute, and eternal moral code—powerfully satisfies those cravings. True faith in an all-powerful, benevolent God alleviates both fear and anxiety and produces an otherwise unattainable tranquillity and feeling of safety. Identically, a political movement built on a strong, powerful, protective leader—one who claims that the world is morally unambiguous, who insists that it can be cleanly divided into Good and Evil, and who promises "protection" from the lurking dangers of Evil—fulfills the same needs. Those who lead the group—the Protectors—will inspire great personal loyalty, while those who oppose it will be viewed as mortal enemies.

The Bush administration's political rhetoric and that of its supporters almost uniformly conforms to a binary framework that sustains allegiance and cohesion and justifies the actions of its leaders. As Dean writes:

> Important conservative opinion journals, like the *National Review* and Human Events, see the world as bipolar: conservative versus liberal. Right-wing talk radio could not survive without its endless bloviating about the horrors of liberalism. Trashing liberals is nothing short of a cottage industry for conservative authors. . . .
>
> The exaggerated hostility also apparently satisfies a psychological need for antagonism toward the "out group," reinforces the self-esteem of the conservative base, and increases solidarity within the ranks.

Many of these tactics, including the ongoing use of Manichean rhetoric, have been wielded by the American right wing for decades, but they became particularly effective as a result of the 9/11 attacks and the resulting political power bestowed on President Bush. The terrorist acts of 9/11 *were* evil, and they *were* perpetrated by those who truly are enemies of the United States. For that reason, the uncompromising nature of the president's condemnation of those attacks—and his vows of retribution against the Evil enemy—potently resonated among most Americans, including many who are typically unreceptive, even resistant, to Manichean appeals.

But the propriety and success of such rhetoric in the context of vowing vengeance against Al Qaeda led to its application in many morally ambiguous contexts increasingly removed from 9/11. Thus, *evil* and *enemy* became terms wielded not merely against the terrorists who sought to launch 9/11-like attacks on Americans but also against an ever-lengthening list of others—countries with no current or historical connection to Al Qaeda, groups that were vaguely opposed to U.S. interests but not guilty of anti-American terrorist acts, and finally, to those who, even by peaceful means, opposed the president—whether abroad or at home. As the *Los Angeles Times* editorialized in the beginning of 2007:

> The 9/11 attacks reinforced the White House's penchant for viewing the world in binary terms, and Bush's "with us or against us" mantra fit the moment. On issue after issue, from tax cuts to Iraq to its tactics against suspected terrorists, this administration has portrayed opponents as beyond the pale, while its own positions are crucial to the defense of Western civilization.

Those who were not squarely behind the president's crusade for Good were suspected, and frequently declared guilty, of siding with Evil. Attempting to impede the president's policies or, worse, the president himself, subjected one to accusations of harboring sympathy for terrorists, or at least of a reckless indifference to the danger the enemy presented. The binary view of Good and Evil came not merely to define every significant political issue but to engulf all political debate. One was presented with a false choice—embrace and actively support the president's policies to wage war on Evil or side with Evil, either deliberately or by default.

With these dualistic premises underlying virtually the entire national political discussion, Supreme Court justices who ruled against the president on national security matters were accused of being tyrants, traitors, and pro-terrorist. Journalists who uncovered legally dubious Bush administration conduct and policies—from illegal, warrantless eavesdropping to CIA "black sites"—were accused of being criminals who should be prosecuted. Virtually all significant political opponents of the president's—Howard Dean, Al Gore, John Kerry, the Clintons—were relentlessly branded as liars, mentally unstable, corrupt, seditious, and/or sympathetic to the Enemy.

Indeed, even those who had devoted much of their adult lives to military service (often in ways far more courageous and impressive than most Bush supporters), or even those who have been longtime Republicans and conservatives, have seen their characters relentlessly smeared and their motives and integrity impugned as soon as they have criticized the administration in any way that could significantly embarrass the president—Richard Clarke, Paul O'Neill, the war-critic generals, Joe Wilson, Scott Ritter, Wesley Clark, John Murtha, Max Cleland, John Paul Stevens, and on and on and on.

The Bush movement has been devoted to the destruction of its enemies wherever they might be found. That movement took as its inspiration the resolute commitment to battle a genuine threat—the terrorist networks that perpetrated the 9/11 and similar attacks on the United States—and moved it further and further outward from that event, to the point where invocation of Evil and Enemies became reflexive, regardless of the targets or the circumstances.

The president and his supporters locate new "enemies" continuously, in every corner and seemingly on a daily basis, and vow heightened wars against them, because they must. Enemies are the essential sustenance of all Manichean movements.

BUSH'S DIVINELY INSPIRED STRENGTH

No meaningful analysis of the Bush presidency is possible without a thorough examination of President Bush himself. His strong personal convictions and rigidly held approach to decision-making have shaped every aspect of his presidency. To explore the way in which the president's worldview has been shaped, the starting and ending point is his religious faith. Bush has made as explicitly clear as he can that his evangelical Christianity and absolute faith in God lie at the heart of everything he does, including the decisions he makes as president.

An important caveat is in order here. The claim that Bush's faith is the centerpiece of his persona frequently provokes objections, particularly among his critics, that Bush's religious beliefs are insincere and purely decorative. That claim is typically predicated on the argument that his decisions and actions are in conflict with Christian doctrine, and that his claimed Christianity must therefore be a sham.

Those arguing for the inauthenticity of Bush's evangelical faith often cite as inconsistencies between Bush's conduct and Christian morality his ordering of unnecessary wars, his condoning (if not ordering) torture, his willingness to deceive, or even his general lack of personal humility. The premise of this objection is typically that if a person acts contrary to Christian dictates with sufficient frequency, it is fair to conclude that his professed beliefs in Christianity are illusory.

Just from a strictly doctrinal perspective, there are numerous flaws with that reasoning. The belief in original sin and mankind's fallen nature, for instance, means that all humans, even the most devout and faithful, will personally sin, and do so repeatedly. Independently, many evangelicals hold that a person who truly accepts Jesus as savior is saved permanently and irrevocably, without regard to the goodness of their subsequent acts.

But for purposes of understanding the president, all of those theological issues and questions as to whether he is a "true Christian" can be set aside. What matters is the president's own understanding of his faith, not whether by the metrics of others he falls short of being "Christian." Put another way, whether the president's behavior is consistent with Christianity in some objective sense is an entirely different question from whether he *believes* that he is acting in accordance with God's will and pursuant to the mandates of his religion as he understands them. To show that Bush's behavior as president is "un-Christian"—as measured against some objective barometer of piety—is not to demonstrate that Bush touts his Christianity cynically.

What is relevant for understanding the president's mind-set is that he himself believes that he is mandated to act in accordance with God's will, that he is able (at least with respect to certain critical matters) to discern that will, and that he is, in fact, acting in accordance with it by virtue of the course he has chosen. These *subjective* beliefs the president holds have guided his presidency and governed the course of his administration and our country.

To his credit, Bush has always been quite up front and explicit that there is nothing that he thinks or does that is independent of his evangelical beliefs. For example, when he identified Jesus as his "favorite philosopher" in a 1999 debate against other Republican presidential candidates, Bush evinced unabashed candor and no hesitation in declaring the central role his Christian faith plays in his life. Most presidents and those who sought to be president—particularly in modern times—have indicated a belief in God and an embrace of some form of Christian faith, but few, if any, have so explicitly and continuously emphasized the central role that religious belief plays in their decision-making.

Bush has never spoken publicly in any detail about his born-again conversion, though he has recounted that he was first "pointed to the path of God" in 1985, by the evangelical minister Billy Graham. In his 1999 campaign autobiography entitled *A Charge to Keep,* then-Governor Bush wrote: "Over the course of that weekend, Reverend Graham planted a mustard seed in my soul, a seed that grew over the next year."

Moreover, Bush has spoken extensively about his religious awakening when describing the circumstances that enabled him to stop drinking. A 1999 campaign interview with the *Washington Post* contained this exchange:

Why did you quit drinking?
A couple of things happened. One, you know, the Billy Graham visit in 1985. I met with Billy, but it's like a mustard seed. You know, he planted a seed in my heart and I began to change. . . . I realized that alcohol was beginning to crowd out my energies and could crowd, eventually, my affections for other people.

You quit drinking and you became more spiritual. Talk about that a little bit.
To put it in spiritual terms, I accepted Christ. What influenced me was the spirituality, sure, which led me to believe that if you change your heart, you can change your behavior. There's a lot of drug rehabilitation

programs and some that are based upon exactly what I went through, which is spiritually based—that's what AA is really based upon.

Though Bush has denied throughout his presidency that he receives specific instructions from God, he did believe that his running for president was an event that God specifically willed. In *The Faith of George W. Bush,* author Stephen Mansfield—relying on televangelist James Robison as his source—reported that when Bush decided to run for president, "he spoke to various evangelical groups that he felt God had called him to run for president in 2000: 'I know it won't be easy on me or my family, but God wants me to do it.'"

Similarly, Jackson Lears reported in a March 2003 *New York Times* article: "From the outset he has been convinced that his presidency is part of a divine plan, even telling a friend while he was governor of Texas, 'I believe God wants me to run for president.'" And in a December 2005 Fox News interview with Brit Hume, the president was asked about the role faith played in his life, and he emphasized its core function: "I think once faith is central in your life, it stays central in your life. I read the Bible every day."

Bush's emphasis on the primacy of his faith and his corresponding certainty that he is acting in accordance with God's will, even with respect to the decisions he makes as president, have led to some unfair caricatures of his religiosity. Unlike, say, Pat Robertson, who claims to be the beneficiary of one-on-one, literal conversations with the deity, the president generally makes no such grandiose claims.

To the contrary, he has repeatedly stated that God does not "instruct" him on what decisions to make. The president emphatically repudiates the notion that he carries on direct conversations with God in which he receives specific instructions as to what to do. In an October 2006 interview, Fox's Bill O'Reilly queried the president regarding the claim that "God tells you what to do and you go out and do it." The president replied: "I guess that I have pity for people who believe that. They don't understand the relationship between man and the Almighty, then."

Nevertheless, the president does commonly invoke the will of God as to specific issues in order to justify the decisions he has made as president. When Bob Woodward asked Bush if he consulted with his father about whether to invade Iraq, Bush—according to Woodward—responded that he did not, but instead appealed to "a higher father." And during secretly recorded discussions in June 2003, between Palestinian prime minister Mahmoud Abbas (who had previously met with President Bush) and various Palestinian factions—recordings obtained and then disclosed by the Israeli newspaper *Haaretz*—the following exchange occurred:

> Abbas said that at Aqaba, Bush promised to speak with Sharon about the siege on Arafat. He said nobody can speak to or pressure Sharon except the Americans.
>
> According to Abbas, immediately thereafter Bush said: "God told me to strike at al Qaida and I struck them, and then he instructed me to strike at Saddam, which I did, and now I am determined to solve the problem in the Middle East. If you help me I will act, and if not, the elections will come and I will have to focus on them."

Moreover, the president has repeatedly contended that the aspiration of the country should be to divine God's sense of "justice" and act accordingly, i.e., *that* is how one can be "on the side of" God. Thus, as the president sees it, though God does not send him literal instructions, God does have preferences for the nation that the president can and ought to discern and obey. At a 2004 ceremony commemorating the Day of Prayer, the president put it this way:

> God is not on the side of any nation, yet we know He is on the side of justice. . . . Our finest moments [as a nation] have come when we have faithfully served the cause of justice for our own citizens, and for the people of other lands.

Bush's evangelical fervor outweighs all other impulses and principles, including political conservatism. In that regard—and well prior to 9/11—Bush is a *fundamentally* different conservative, in both belief and temperament, than was Ronald Reagan. Whereas a belief in limited government was (at least ostensibly) Reagan's overarching principle, Bush entirely subordinates political conservatism to (at most) a secondary consideration, endowing his faith with unchallengeable primacy. When those two belief systems clash, Bush's religious convictions prevail. As Bush speechwriter David Frum described in his 2003 book, *The Right Man:*

Goodness had been one of the main themes of Bush's campaign speeches. He often observed that if the government could ever write a law that could make people love their neighbors, he would be glad to sign it. This was, when you think about it, an odd thing for a Republican president to say. If Congress had sent Ronald Reagan a law obliging people to love their neighbors, he would have vetoed it as an impertinent infringement of personal liberty, and unconstitutional besides.

But Bush came from and spoke for a very different culture from that of the individualistic Ronald Reagan: the culture of modern Evangelicalism. To understand the Bush White House you must understand its predominant creed. It was a kindly faith, practical and unmystical.

Whenever any competing considerations—including political conservatism—conflict with the imperatives of Bush's theology, his moralistic conceptions prevail. And indeed, placing limitations on government has never been a priority for Bush. To the contrary, he has been committed to an expansion of government power as a means of coercing his conception of the moral Good. In this regard, one can describe Bush's political philosophy much more accurately as a theory of evangelical governance than as conservatism, reflected by his commitment to use government power as a force to promote his conception of God's will.

In his book *The Conservative Soul*, Andrew Sullivan—once a leading, vocal supporter of the president and the invasion of Iraq—describes the process by which he renounced his support for the Bush presidency. Sullivan came to believe that Bush's conservatism was a fundamental departure from, and not just a modification of, the Reagan/Thatcher theories of conservatism which attracted him to that movement in the 1980s. To demonstrate this point, Sullivan highlights, as did Frum, the evangelical mission at the heart of the Bush presidency:

> President Reagan's most famous quote from his 1981 Inaugural Address was the following: "In this present crisis, government is not the solution to our problem. Government is the problem." President George W. Bush explained a markedly different philosophy in September, 2003: "We have a responsibility when somebody hurts, government has to move."

According to the president, seeking God's will and acting in accordance with it drives each of his decisions, particularly the most consequential ones. Bush himself described his mission to Bob Woodward as such:

> "Going into this period [when he ordered the invasion of Iraq], I was praying for strength to do the Lord's will. . . . I'm surely not going to justify war based upon God. Understand that. Nevertheless, in my case I pray that I be as good a messenger of His will as possible. And then, of course, I pray for personal strength and for forgiveness."

Thus are all of the president's most significant and most controversial policy decisions grounded in his convictions about God's will and, in particular, his understanding of what approach to the world God's will fundamentally requires. The following chapters examine specifically how these Manichean imperatives have been used to justify (both *to* the president and then *by* him) the militarism in Iraq, Iran, and the broader Middle East. For instance, the imperative of spreading democracy—no matter the necessary means (including brutal wars) and even in the absence of a connection to anti-American terrorism—is inherently Good and just, because it is in accordance with God's will; God wills that every man, woman, and child be free, and any measures in pursuit of that ultimate end, including wars, are just and necessary. These policies are not subject to debate or uncertainty in Bush's mind any more than his faith in God is, because the former stems directly from—is compelled by—the latter.

These premises operate within a broader belief system whereby Bush has become convinced that his presidency is part of, perhaps the catalyst for, a religious reawakening in the United States and a reemerging religious purpose for the country. And we know that because, among other reasons, the president has said so. In September 2006, the president met with a group of right-wing pundits in the White House. According to their published reports, he spoke extensively of his religious fervor, and particularly of his belief that America was in the midst of what he called a "Third Awakening." One of the pundits who was present, *National Review* editor Rich Lowry, wrote:

> The President mentioned that he is struck by the number of people he meets who tell him they are praying for him. He jokingly noted, "Now

maybe the only people who pray in America come to my events," but he wonders if there is evidence of a Third Awakening saying, *"It feels like it to me"* [emphasis added].

The First Great Awakening was a wave of Christian fervor that raged in colonial America from about 1730 to 1760; the Second Great Awakening generally refers to a similar religious revival that swept the nation from 1800 to 1830. For the president to predict not merely the imminence of a Third Great Awakening but to proclaim that it is already under way is to posit that religious passion is the predominant attribute of contemporary American life, shaping the thought processes and priorities of most Americans.

In the same September 2006 meeting, Bush claimed that the most intense support for Abraham Lincoln's bid to end slavery came from Christians who were the by-product of the Second Awakening and who therefore "saw life in terms of good and evil." According to Lowry:

> He talked about the two constituencies that faithfully supported President Lincoln, noting that he had recently read extensively about the former President and his own policies aren't based on his insights (nor obviously does he consider himself another Lincoln). Bush explained that Lincoln's strongest supporters were religious people from the Second Awakening "who saw life in terms of good and evil" and who agreed with Lincoln that slavery was evil, and the Union soldiers who Lincoln had "great affection and admiration for."

Following on those observations, Bush elaborated on his Third Awakening supporters and their similar view—as well as his own—that life should be viewed "in terms of good and evil":

> A lot of people in America see this as a confrontation between good and evil, including me. . . . There was a stark change between the culture of the '50's and the '60's—boom—and I think there's change happening here. It seems to me that there's a Third Awakening.

The president's proclamation of a new religious awakening in America came at a time when his popularity was at a low point and the war in

Iraq was increasingly seen to be a debacle. Opposition to the president was so intense before the looming midterm election that Democrats had settled on a strategy of transforming that vote into a specific referendum on the highly unpopular president.

That the president would take solace in the extraordinary belief that he was presiding over a Third Great Awakening at the very moment he was most under siege is not surprising. He could comfort himself with the assurance that there was such strident opposition to him *not* because he had done anything wrong or because he had erred, but precisely because he *had not erred*, because he had unyieldingly devoted himself to Good, and was hated for that reason. In an October 2006 Fox interview with Bill O'Reilly, Bush seemed to make exactly that point. He agreed with O'Reilly that many opponents "hate" him because he is "a man of faith":

> **O'REILLY:** The secular progressives don't like you because you're a man of faith.
> **BUSH:** Yes.
> **O'REILLY:** You know that.
> **BUSH:** Yes. That causes me to be sad for people who don't like somebody because he happens to believe in the Almighty.
> **O'REILLY:** Absolutely. They think you are some kind of evangelical. God tells you what to do and you go out and do it. And they hate that.
> **BUSH:** I guess that I have pity for people who believe that. They don't understand the relationship between man and the Almighty, then.

On several other occasions, the president has similarly suggested that his unpopularity was *not* a sign that he had gone astray and should change, but rather, that he was on a righteous course, and resistance to his policies and presidency were a by-product of his unyielding commitment to battling Evil. He began casting the dissatisfaction with his presidency as a challenge he must overcome—by steadfastly remaining on the moral course.

Further, and subsequent to the massive Democratic gains in the 2006 midterm election, the president increasingly began invoking the legacy of Harry Truman and claiming that, like Truman, his unpopularity would ultimately lead to his historical vindication. In December 2006, McClatchy's Washington bureau reported on a tense meeting between the president and various Congressional Democrats poised to take over control of the Congress. Democrats expected the president to explore a new path in Iraq:

> Instead, Bush began his talk by comparing himself to President Harry S. Truman, who launched the Truman Doctrine to fight communism, got bogged down in the Korean War and left office unpopular.
>
> Bush said that "in years to come they realized he was right and then his doctrine became the standard for America," recalled Senate Majority Whip-elect Richard Durbin, D-Ill. "He's trying to position himself in history and to justify those who continue to stand by him, saying sometimes if you're right you're unpopular, and be prepared for criticism."
>
> Durbin said he challenged Bush's analogy, reminding him that Truman had the NATO alliance behind him and negotiated with his enemies at the United Nations. Durbin said that's what the Iraq Study Group is recommending that Bush do now—work more with allies and negotiate with adversaries on Iraq.
>
> Bush, Durbin said, "reacted very strongly. He got very animated in his response" and emphasized that he is "the commander in chief."

This incident strikingly illustrates a pattern seen throughout the president's tenure. The more the president is challenged, the more his policies are deemed to be failures, the more rigidly he digs in and becomes less open and receptive to change.

The president's reaction to the 2006 Democratic sweep was also highly illustrative. Virtually all political analysts attributed the election results to the public's deep dissatisfaction with the Iraq War, yet the president's response was to order an *escalation* of the war. He did so despite—or perhaps because of—pervasive opposition to such escalation among virtually all Democrats, the overwhelming majority of most Americans, and even substantial numbers in his own party. As opposition to escalation became overwhelming, the president's reaction was to *dig in further* in order to underscore the certainty of his rightness and to emphasize that his war was a moral imperative and would therefore never be subject to compromise.

Beyond Contemporary Judgment

That the president would dismiss the importance of contemporary public opinion in favor of vindication by "history" seemed particularly confounding in light of the president's prior claims that historical judgment was irrelevant, or at least unknowable. When promoting his second Bush book, *Plan of Attack*, Bob Woodward recounted a December 2003 discussion he had had with the president, by which point it was widely assumed that there were no WMDs in Iraq:

> After the second interview with him on Dec. 11, we got up and walked over to one of the doors. There are all of these doors in the Oval Office that lead outside. And he had his hands in his pocket, and I just asked, "Well, how is history likely to judge your Iraq war," says Woodward.
>
> And he said, "History," and then he took his hands out of his pocket and kind of shrugged and extended his hands as if this is a way off. And then he said, "History, we won't know. We'll all be dead."

When the president enjoyed soaring personal approval and his policies were overwhelmingly popular, he could not have been more indifferent, even scornful, toward the notion that history's verdict on him was worthy of consideration. But once Americans turned against both him and his war, the president sought solace in historical judgment to lend support for his chosen course—support that was so plainly lacking among the citizens of the country he led.

The shifting, self-contradictory rationales offered by the president as to *why* he refuses to change course suggest that the justifications for remaining in place do not matter much. When the standard of judgment he uses shifts from affirming his actions to undermining them, he simply seeks out a new, more hospitable standard. The one option he will never consider is that he erred, that his chosen course was wrong. That is because his decisions are rooted in, and dictated by, his faith, and that—by definition—can never be wrong. Thus, anything or anyone that suggests that it is wrong must, for that reason alone, be discarded.

• • •

During the height of Bush's popularity, in 2002 and 2003, there was very little discussion of the role the president's evangelical beliefs played in his political and foreign policy decisions. In fact, in a nation that had placed itself squarely and loyally behind the president in the wake of the 9/11 attacks, there was little questioning about any of the president's decisions and virtually no scrutiny of his attributes. The political and journalistic elites in the United States, as well as a solid majority of Americans, had placed their faith in George W. Bush, and as usually is the case whenever faith is in play, there was very little skeptical examination of the president or his conduct.

But as the president refused to recognize (or, at least, publicly acknowledge) that severe problems were emerging in Iraq, and as his popularity consequently declined precipitously throughout 2004, far more attention was paid to the extent to which the president's evangelical certainty precluded him from changing course. Bruce Bartlett, a conservative official in both the Reagan and Bush 41 administrations, told Ron Suskind in the weeks before the 2004 election:

> Just in the past few months I think a light has gone off for people who've spent time up close to Bush: that this instinct he's always talking about is this sort of weird, Messianic idea of what he thinks God has told him to do.

After Bill O'Reilly interviewed the president in October 2006, he observed: "My theory about President Bush is that he is a true believer—he sincerely thinks he is looking out for America in the best ways possible and the polls be damned. That kind of certainty provides solace and calm."

In his book *The Conservative Soul*, Andrew Sullivan explores the differences between the epistemology embraced by religious fundamentalism and that of non-fundamentalist religious adherents (whether Christian, Muslim, Jewish, or of any other religion):

> The essential claim of the fundamentalist is that he knows the truth. It's a simple, short phrase, but it would be foolish to underestimate its power in today's unmoored West and developing world. The fundamentalist

doesn't guess or argue or wonder or question. He doesn't have to. He *knows*. . . . The distinction that others make in the modern world—that there is a difference between what we know empirically and what we believe normatively—is one the fundamentalist rejects.

And what the fundamentalist knows is true. It isn't a proposition, held provisionally, to be tested by further evidence. It isn't an argument from which he could be dissuaded by something we call reason. It isn't something that is ever subject to change: what is fundamentally true now, by definition, must be true for all time. For the fundamentalist, there is not a category of things called facts and a separate category called values. The values of the fundamentalist *are* facts. . . .

The president himself has explained that the certainty his faith brings liberates him from doubt and anxiety about the courses of action he pursues. He declared in his 1999 book, *A Charge to Keep:* "My faith frees me. . . . Frees me to make decisions others might not like. Frees me to do the right thing, even though it will not poll well. Frees me to enjoy life and not worry about what comes next."

The solace from such certitude is surely of great value to an individual at the spiritual level. As the president himself put it, it frees him to make even the most daunting and (literally) earth-shattering decisions without having to worry about public reaction, worry about whether the decision was the right one, or "worry about what comes next." Serenity flows and anxiety is eliminated by the conviction that one has found absolute truth.

But when pragmatic concerns are excluded from political and strategic deliberations, then, by definition, decisions become immune from re-examination in light of failed results. Such a mind-set is dangerous in elected officials as such, and especially so when the policy in question is the most monumental of all: war. As Garry Wills wrote in the November 2006 edition of *New York Review of Books* with regard to the evangelical Christians who continue to rank among the president's most loyal supporters:

There is a particular danger with a war that God commands. What if God should lose? That is unthinkable to the evangelicals. They cannot accept the idea of second-guessing God, and he was the one who led them into war. Thus, in 2006, when two thirds of the American people told pollsters that the war in Iraq was a mistake, the third of those still standing behind it were mainly evangelicals (who make up about one third of the population). It was a faith-based certitude.

The president's core belief in a Manichean world provides a template for those who wish to exert influence on his decision-making process. Those who seek to induce the president to view other nations as enemies of America can achieve that goal by invoking the Manichean worldview to persuade him that the targeted nation is pure Evil.

On February 28, 2007, President Bush hosted what he called "a literary luncheon" to honor right-wing "historian" Andrew Roberts. Accounts of that luncheon—which describe the "lessons" the guests taught the president (and they call them "lessons")—provide an amazing glimpse into the Bush mind-set and his relationship with neoconservatives.

The White House invited a tiny cohort, a total of fifteen guests, of standard neoconservatives and other Bush followers to the luncheon, including Norman Podhoretz (father of John and father-in-law of Iran-contra convict Elliot Abrams), Gertrude Himmelfarb (wife of Irving Kristol and mother of Bill), Mona Charen and Kate O'Beirne of *National Review*, and *Wall Street Journal* editorial page editor Paul Gigot. *The Weekly Standard*'s Irwin Stelzer was also invited, and he thereafter wrote about the luncheon in the most glowing terms.

Stelzer's account provides amazing, truly illuminating insight into what neoconservatives have been filling the president's head with for years now, and demonstrates how they have managed to keep him firmly on board with their agenda. Their most critical priority is to convince the president to continue to ignore the will of the American people and to maintain full-fledged loyalty to the neoconservative agenda, no matter how unpopular it becomes.

To do this, they have convinced the president that he has tapped into a much higher authority than the American people—namely, objective morality, mandated by God—and as long as he adheres to that (by continuing his militaristic policies in the Middle East, where he is fighting Evil and defending Good), God and history will vindicate him. As Stelzer wrote:

> On one subject the president needed no lessons from Roberts or anyone else in the room: how to handle pressure. "I just don't feel any," he says with the calm conviction of a man who believes *the constituency to which he must ultimately answer is the Divine Presence* [emphasis added]. Don't misunderstand: God didn't tell him to put troops in harm's way in Iraq; belief in Him only goes so far as to inform the president that there is good and evil. It is then his job to figure out how to promote the former and destroy the latter. And he is confident that his policies are doing just that.

Another luncheon attendee, Michael Novak of the American Enterprise Institute, recalled (also in *The Weekly Standard*) the president saying: "I want to have my conscience clear with Him. Then it doesn't matter so much what others think." Novak also revealingly marveled that "the president was not at all intimidated by his fifteen or so guests," even though the guests included Podhoretz, Himmelfarb, and "Irwin Stelzer himself." In Novak's world, one expects the president of the United States to be intimidated in the presence of such powerful neoconservative luminaries, not the other way around.

Stelzer recounts what he calls the multiple "lessons" they taught Bush at this luncheon. One of the key lessons is Roberts's view that the United States should be most concerned with its relationships with the other "English-speaking countries in the world," and not worry nearly as much about all those countries where they speak in foreign tongues ("Lesson Four: Cling to the alliance of the English-speaking peoples").

But that "lesson" led Bush to wonder bewilderedly why there was such rising anti-Americanism all over the world, even in English-speaking countries such as England ("'Is it due simply to my personality?' he wondered, half-seriously. 'Is it confined to intellectuals?' asked a guest"). Anti-Americanism, the neoconservatives instructed Bush, is something he should just ignore. As long as he continues to follow neoconservatism, that is all that matters:

> The combined Roberts-Stelzer response: The causes of rampant anti-Americanism do indeed include dislike of Bush. But there are others: the

war in Iraq; anti-Israel, pro-Palestinian sentiment, laced with some covert anti-Semitism; and resentment of American power. Roberts *urged the president not to concern himself with these anti-American feelings, since in a unipolar world the lone superpower cannot be loved. His advice: "Get your policies right and history will prove a kind muse"* [emphasis added].

Nothing matters—not the disapproval by the American people of the president's actions nor the rising anti-Americanism around the world. He should simply ignore all of that and continue to obey the mandates of neoconservatism because that is what is Good and his God will then be pleased.

Other "lessons" that Bush was taught that day: "First: Do not set a deadline for withdrawal. That led to the slaughter of 700,000 to 1 million people in India, with the killing beginning one minute after the midnight deadline." They also told the president to ignore the fact that other powerful countries and even empires that tried to dominate the world have all collapsed. Those monumental historical realities are irrelevant and teach us nothing because—unlike the Glorious Leader today—those people simply lacked the Will to Power. Thus:

> Second lesson: Will trumps wealth. The Romans, the tsars, and other rich world powers fell to poorer ones because they lacked the will to fight and survive. Whereas World War II was almost over before Americans saw the first picture of a dead soldier, today the steady drumbeat of media pessimism and television coverage are sapping the West's will.

They also instructed the president to continue his policies of indefinite imprisonment without charges: "Third lesson: Don't hesitate to intern our enemies for long, indefinite periods of time. That policy worked in Ireland and during World War II. Release should only follow victory." "Victory," of course, is decades away—it is a permanent war—so the "lesson" these neoconservatives are teaching is to imprison people forever with no charges and not to worry about all those petulant complaints from human-rights advocates that doing so is un-American. American values are no competition for the imperatives of neoconservative glory.

The lessons continued. "Appeasement," of course, is the ultimate Evil, the great French sin. Hence: "Fifth lesson: We are fighting an enemy that cannot be appeased; were that possible, the French would already have done it—a Roberts quip that elicited a loud chuckle from the president."

Finally, the neoconservatives left Bush with an overarching instruction—namely, the only thing that he should concern himself with, the only thing that really matters, is Iran. Forget every other issue—the welfare of the American people, every other region around the world—except the one that matters most:

> The closing note was a more serious one. Roberts said that *history would judge the president on whether he had prevented the nuclearization of the Middle East. If Iran gets the bomb,* Saudi Arabia, Egypt, and other countries will follow [emphasis added]. "That is why I am so pleased to be sitting here rather than in your chair, Mr. President." There was no response, other than a serious frown and a nod.

The president, concluded Stelzer with great satisfaction, "worries less about his 'legacy' than about his standing with the Almighty." And as a result of this luncheon, the president's standing—at least with the Almightys in the neoconservative circle—was as secure as ever.

The more unpopular the president becomes as a result of these failed policies, the more of a failure these policies are, the more emphatically they insist he ignore all of that, that none of it matters, that his God and history will conclude that he did the Right Thing. And the president believes that. The president's "lessons" in the moral righteousness of his actions, as preached by neoconservatives, continue, and he is as faithful an adherent to those beliefs as ever.

That these neoconservatives have adopted—or at least exploit—Manichean concepts to justify their agenda demonstrates that such a worldview by no means requires a belief in evangelical Christianity. Substantial numbers who view (or who claim to view) the United States as engaged in a supreme battle of Good vs. Evil are driven by a whole array of motives and beliefs.

Moreover, it bears emphasis that, like most other groups, evangelical Christians are far from monolithic, and, contrary to popular belief, it is not the case that they all support the president or the war. Not even close. In fact, the Pew poll referenced in the prior chapter—which found that 78 percent of self-identified "conservatives" continued to express approval for the president even as of March 2006—also showed that only 54 percent of "white Evangelicals" approve of the president's performance, a sharp decline from the 72 percent who approved of him even as late as February 2005. Clearly, substantial numbers of white evangelicals never shared the president's worldview, and many of those who initially did re-evaluated their assessment of him—almost uniformly for the worse—as the evidence of his ineptitude and untrustworthiness mounted.

Although Americans are a religious people, pragmatism—an emphasis on results, on success, on abandoning failed ways—has always been a significant aspect of their national character. A refusal to change or admit error comes to be seen as foolish, stubborn, arrogant, and hubristic. For that reason, even many of the president's most steadfast followers and loyal admirers—including many who are not alienated by his Manichean fervor, and even some who share it—have turned on him due to his manifestly failed policies and the inescapable realization of his ineptitude. In the ethos of most Americans, a core Goodness does not excuse recalcitrant ineptitude and failure, particularly in political leaders.

But for many evangelical Christians, their theological convictions are inextricably linked to and grounded in their political convictions. The lack of doubt and inerrant qualities in the former are equally present in the latter. Moral rightness trumps pragmatic success, and the imperatives of the crusade trump the constraints of reality.

The principal attribute of those who are true believers is that, by definition, they will not re-examine their core premises. Any evidence that cannot be interpreted in accordance with those premises will simply be steadfastly ignored or, when it cannot be ignored, discredited. News events that undermine such convictions must be the product of bias or intentional deceit. A failed course chosen on the basis of evangelical truths cannot fail. Failure simply means that there is insufficient resolve, or that the forces of Evil are impeding success and more efforts must be devoted to defeating them.

Emancipated from Doubt

Among the president's most supportive followers, one of the most common observations they make after meeting him is that he is free of doubt and—even as events *worsen*—unwaveringly certain about the rightness of his decisions. After he interviewed the president aboard Air Force One in September 2006, one of these supporters, Paul Gigot, editorial page editor of the *Wall Street Journal*, wrote:

> This is the fourth time I've interviewed Mr. Bush at length in the last eight years, going back to his time as Texas governor. One of the notable things about him is how similar he seems. He has always been supremely confident in his decisions and focused above all else on pushing forward, not looking back. If he is tortured by doubt, he doesn't show it to journalists. Some see this as obstinance, but he sees it as firmness of conviction.
>
> Whether or not he's right about the elections this fall, you have to respect his willingness to put that conviction on the line. "I said in my Inaugural Address, we should end tyranny in the 21st century," he says. "And I meant that."

At the same September meeting where Bush declared "a Third Awakening," the president led attendee Rich Lowry of *National Review* to make this observation (emphasis added):

> Bush's confidence goes well beyond comfort in his own skin. He exhibits a sincere, passionate, and uncompromising conviction in his principles. He is arguably losing a war in Iraq that could destroy his hopes for the Middle East and sink his party's hope in the midterm elections. But there's no wobble in Bush. If anything, the opposite.
>
> Basically right after "hello," the next words out of his mouth are: "Let me just first tell you that I've never been more convinced that the decisions I made are the right decisions. I firmly believe—I'm oftentimes asked about, well, you're stubborn and all this. If you believe in a strategy, in Washington, D.C. you've got to stick to that strategy, see. People want you to change. It's tactics that shift, but the strategic vision has not, and will not, shift."
>
> *Never been more convinced.*

Fundamentalism as a political doctrine is uniquely ill-suited to re-examination, compromise, or debate. For that reason, conservative icon Barry Goldwater warned of the dangers of basing political decisions upon evangelical certainty:

> Politics and governing demand compromise. But these Christians believe they are acting in the name of God, so they can't and won't compromise. I know, I've tried to deal with them. . . .
>
> There is no position on which people are so immovable as their religious beliefs. There is no more powerful ally one can claim in a debate than Jesus Christ, or God, or Allah, or whatever one calls this supreme being. But like any powerful weapon, the use of God's name on one's behalf should be used sparingly.

During the Bush presidency, numerous credible sources have reported discussions in which the president emphasized—proudly—that he relies upon his "gut" instinct more than an analysis of facts and empirical evidence. Ron Suskind recounts one such incident as reported by Senator Joe Biden:

> "I was in the Oval Office a few months after we swept into Baghdad and I was telling the president of my many concerns"—concerns about growing problems winning the peace, the explosive mix of Shiite and Sunni, the disbanding of the Iraqi Army and problems securing the oil fields. Bush, Biden recalled, just looked at him, unflappably sure that the United States was on the right course and that all was well. " 'Mr. President,' I finally said, 'How can you be so sure when you know you don't know the facts?' "
>
> Biden said that Bush stood up and put his hand on the senator's shoulder. "My instincts," he said. "My instincts." . . .
>
> The Delaware senator was, in fact, hearing what Bush's top deputies—from cabinet members like Paul O'Neill, Christine Todd Whitman and Colin Powell to generals fighting in Iraq—have been told for years when they requested explanations for many of the president's decisions, policies that often seemed to collide with accepted facts. The president would say that he relied on his "gut" or his "instinct" to guide the ship of state, and then he "prayed over it."

Precisely the same dynamic drove the president's approach to the 2006 midterm elections. For several months prior to those elections, virtually every public poll—every one—showed that Republicans were highly likely to lose control of the House. Particularly in the weeks before the election, the only real debate among pollsters and political analysts was how massive the Republican losses would be. Congressional Republicans were petrified at what appeared to be the certain doom approaching. Yet the president was convinced that all the polls were wrong and that Republicans would hold their majority.

All politicians publicly adopt optimistic poses. Candidates who are thirty points behind in polls will claim in the media that they expect to defy the polls and win. Outside of fringe political parties, no candidate can admit to an expectation of losing; such an admission would almost always become a self-fulfilling prophecy. Nobody is going to work to elect a political candidate who himself expects to lose, and in a country that venerates being a winner more than almost any other attribute, a politician who brands himself a likely loser is sure to become one quickly.

But the president was not contriving optimism about the midterms for public consumption. In private he was also emphatically insisting to Congressional Republicans and other trusted confidants that Republican success was assured. On October 15, Michael Abramowitz reported in the *Washington Post:* "Amid widespread panic in the Republican establishment about the coming midterm elections, there are two people whose confidence about GOP prospects strikes even their closest allies as almost inexplicably upbeat: President Bush and his top political adviser, Karl Rove."

That optimism, apparently based on nothing other than his own belief in his inevitable entitlement to victory, began to worry and even anger members of the president's own party. On October 13, 2006, Kenneth Walsh reported in *U.S. News & World Report:*

Some Republican strategists are increasingly upset with what they consider the overconfidence of President Bush and his senior advisers about the midterm elections on November 7—a concern aggravated by the president's news conference this week.

"They aren't even planning for if they lose," says a GOP insider who informally counsels the West Wing. If Democrats win control of the House, as many analysts expect, Republicans predict that Bush's final two years in office will be marked by multiple congressional investigations and gridlock.

Republican concern over the president's refusal to accept the evidence of this pending electoral devastation led to multiple press accounts in which prominent members of his party complained of Bush's apparent detachment from reality. The *Washington Post*'s Dan Froomkin wrote on October 16: "The question is whether this is a case of justified confidence—based on Bush's and Rove's electoral record and knowledge of the money, technology and other assets at their command—or of self-delusion. Even many Republicans suspect the latter." Froomkin added: "The notion that President Bush is not just in denial—but is *petulantly* in denial—is taking on greater credence."

The election results, of course, vindicated Republican fears that the president had, yet again, simply refused to accept unpleasant facts—i.e., reality—which were in conflict with his faith-based certitude. The day after the election, the president held a press conference and was asked: "You said you were surprised, you didn't see it coming, you were disappointed in the outcome. Does that indicate that after six years in the Oval Office, you're out of touch with America for something like this kind of wave to come and you not expect it?"

The president's reply was instructive: "Well, there was a—I read those same polls, and I believe that—I thought when it was all said and done, the American people would understand the importance of taxes and the importance of security." In his mind, Republicans lost the election *not* because Bush had embarked upon the wrong path or made the wrong choices—that is something that, by definition, cannot be—but because Americans failed to "understand the importance of taxes and the importance of security." Americans failed to recognize the Good and that Bush was fighting for it.

That "reasoning" was similar to the explanations issuing from the president prior to the 2006 election as to why he was certain, polls notwithstanding, that Republicans would win. Gigot interviewed the president in September and wrote in the *Wall Street Journal:*

ABOARD AIR FORCE ONE—SPEAKER NANCY PELOSI?

"That's not going to happen," snaps the president of the United States, leaning across his desk in his airborne office. He had been saying that he hoped to revisit Social Security reform next year, when he "will be able to drain the politics out of the issue," and I rudely interrupted by noting the polls predicting Ms. Pelosi's ascension.

"I just don't believe it," the president insists. "I believe the Republicans will end up being—running the House and the Senate. And the reason why I believe it is because when our candidates go out and talk about the strength of this economy, people will say their tax cuts worked, their plan worked. . . . And secondly, that this is a group of people that understand the stakes of the world in which we live and are willing to help this unity government in Iraq succeed for the sake of our children and grandchildren, and that we are steadfast in our belief in the capacity of liberty to bring peace."

"I just don't believe it"—it being the mountains of empirical data showing that Americans would remove his political party from power because of their profound dissatisfaction with his job performance generally, and with the Iraq War specifically. To the president, his decisions are so plainly and indisputably right, his course objectively grounded in what is Good, that it was literally inconceivable to him that Americans opposed his policies and would repudiate his party—notwithstanding massive and compelling evidence that they would. As always, empirical evidence was no match for his certitude.

The compulsion to ignore or deny the credibility of conviction-undermining facts is equally evident in the president's most mindlessly loyal followers. Hugh Hewitt is an evangelical Bush supporter with a popular talk radio show and blog. He also had the misfortune of writing a book in 2006—the same year, of course, when the Republicans suffered one of their worst electoral defeats in history—entitled *Painting the Map Red: The Fight to Create a Permanent Republican Majority.*

In the three weeks prior to the 2006 midterm election, Hewitt repeatedly insisted that Republican candidates were tied or ahead even when the consensus of polls showed those candidates were actually behind, sometimes by substantial margins. He was not merely predicting that the GOP candidate behind in the polls would win (there is nothing wrong with being hopeful). Rather, he was insisting that the GOP candidates who were behind in the polls were, in fact, *ahead in the polls*.

In response to e-mails he received objecting to his bizarre interpretation of the polling data, he explained his "thinking" behind this outright distortion of reality (emphasis added):

> I get a lot of e-mail asking me why I point to polls like the one favoring Steele when I discount some polls favoring some Democrats.
>
> Because this question comes mostly from lefties, I will pause to explain in as uncomplicated a fashion as possible.
>
> *Polling methodology and models favors Democrats. So polls that show Republicans tied or ahead I see as indicating a race in which the Republican is in the lead.*
>
> *Polls that show a Republican within striking distance I see as a poll indicating a dead heat.*
>
> *It shouldn't be that hard to grasp, even for a lefty.*

In Hewitt's world, polling data—like all other data, from war zone reports to intelligence assessments and everything in between—can be ignored and disregarded at will when it is unpleasant because it is unfairly biased against the Republicans. Hewitt took the data that he disliked, literally changed it in his own mind to make it more pleasant, and then embraced the fictitious data as his reality.

In fact, polling data for the 2006 midterm elections predicted results in the vast majority of races with almost complete accuracy. In the instances where there was a discrepancy, it was nearly in every case *favorable to the Republicans*—meaning the polling showed Democrats with a smaller lead than they ended up with (or behind by more than they actually lost by).

Following is a chart comparing the final polls of Rasmussen Reports for the eleven Senate races it (and the rest of the country) identified as the "Nation's Closest Senate Races" (Connecticut is the only race excluded here due to its confusing party breakdown). The table shows the final Rasmussen poll for each race, the actual election results, and the differential between the two and indicates whether the differential favored the Republican or the Democratic candidate:

STATE	RR FINAL POLL	ACTUAL RESULT	DIFFERENTIAL
MD	50–45 Cardin	54–44 Cardin	5% (against Dem.)
MI	56–40 Stabenow	57–41 Stabenow	0%
MO	49–48 McCaskill	49–47 McCaskill	1% (against Dem.)
MT	50–48 Tester	49–48 Tester	1% (for Dem.)
NJ	48–43 Menendez	53–45 Menendez	3% (against Dem.)
OH	54–43 Brown	56–44 Brown	1% (against Dem.)
PA	55–42 Casey	59–41 Casey	5% (against Dem.)
RI	52–44 Whitehouse	53–47 Whitehouse	2% (for Dem.)
TN	51–47 Corker	51–48 Corker	1% (against Dem.)
VA	49–49 Tie	49–49 Webb	0%
WA	54–42 Cantwell	58–39 Cantwell	7% (against Dem.)

In the eleven Senate races identified as "the closest Senate races" (excluding Connecticut), Rasmussen's polls predicted the exact outcome in two of them. For the nine races where there was a disparity, seven of the nine disparities *favored the Republicans.* Only two of the eleven races showed a gap in favor of Democrats, and in those two races (Montana and Rhode Island), the difference was minuscule—respectively, 1 percent and 2 percent.

And it was not just Rasmussen. Polls in general were either remarkably accurate or, to the extent they were wrong, largely skewed in favor of Republicans (at least in terms of what they predicted versus the actual result). The Real Clear Politics average final polls (which averaged the outcomes of multiple polls from around the country) show that for the same eleven Senate races, the polling disparities *favored Republicans in eight of the eleven races, often by considerable margins.* In the three races where the disparities favored Democrats, it was by very small margins, of 1 to 3 points.

The point here is not to criticize Hewitt for being wrong in virtually all of his prognostications about the midterm elections. It is natural for partisan desires to influence people's predictions, and predicting races even within the science of polling, let alone without it, is extremely difficult. But Hewitt was not merely inaccurate. As is so common among Bush supporters (including, as demonstrated above, the president himself), Hewitt ignored, indeed *consciously denied and rejected,* information that undercut his beliefs, and insisted that even the most objective facts were "biased." As Stephen Colbert put it during his highly controversial, satirical speech at the White House Correspondents Dinner in 2006:

> Now, I know there are some polls out there saying this man [the president] has a 32 percent approval rating. But guys like us, we don't pay attention to the polls. We know that polls are just a collection of statistics that reflect what people are thinking in "reality." And reality has a well-known liberal bias.

Though it was satire, Colbert's point captured exactly the manner in which Hewitt argued. And as noted, the president himself repeatedly insisted that the Republicans would win the election despite all of the data to the contrary (just as he continuously insisted that the United States was making progress and even "winning" in Iraq for years despite abundant evidence negating such a claim). The president, like his zealous supporter Hewitt, was not merely waxing optimistic. Rather, both decided that empirical evidence was meaningless, because it was unpleasant, because it conflicted with their convictions, and *it therefore could not be real.*

Among the most striking aspects of the Bush administration has been the extent to which loyalty has been demanded of, and received from, those who work near the president. The requisite loyalty is to George Bush the individual (and his decisions). In contrast to prior administrations, the Bush administration has marched in virtual lockstep. Leaks by senior White House officials unfavorable to the president have been almost unheard of, particularly when compared to past administrations. Dissident officials who stray from the president's views have been inexorably excised from power.

That such total fealty is expected in Bush circles is unsurprising. Political decisions grounded in pragmatism, with the paramount goal of reaching a certain outcome (i.e., "maximize American security"), are always subject, by their nature, to rational debate and examination. The mission is to find the optimal method for reaching the desired destination.

By contrast, policies that are determined on the basis of faith and/or a moral calculus ("God wants every human being to live in freedom, and America is called to the mission of spreading democracy") cannot be challenged because they stem from evangelical faith. As a result, faith-based decision-makers will accept input only from those who share the faith, and will ignore and even expel those who challenge or contest it. That can have the effect of reinforcing and, worse, creating perceptions of reality that are pleasing but fictitious. As Reagan and Bush 41 official Bruce Bartlett told journalist Ron Suskind in 2004,

> "This is why [Bush] dispenses with people who confront him with inconvenient facts," Bartlett went on to say. "He truly believes he's on a mission from God. Absolute faith like that overwhelms a need for analysis. The whole thing about faith is to believe things for which there is no empirical evidence." Bartlett paused, then said, "But you can't run the world on faith."
>
> The demand for loyalty is itself a by-product of his faith-based certainty. Certitude that one is right will naturally reduce, if not eliminate, a tolerance for those who question what has been accorded the status of unquestionable Truth.

Bush's moral conviction—his intractable certainty in his religious faith—even dictates the rules of behavior imposed on his staff. In his influential October 2004 article in the *New York Times Magazine*, Suskind examined the ways in which the Bush personality drives his presidency, and concluded:

> That a deep Christian faith illuminated the personal journey of George W. Bush is common knowledge. But faith has also shaped his presidency in profound, nonreligious ways. The president has demanded unquestioning faith from his followers, his staff, his senior aides and his kindred in the Republican Party. Once he makes a decision—often swiftly, based on a creed or moral position—he expects complete faith in its rightness.

The faith-based presidency is a with-us-or-against-us model that has been enormously effective at, among other things, keeping the workings and temperament of the Bush White House a kind of state secret.

The president's contempt for dissent is notorious. That he unleashes his temper at underlings is legendary and has generated a well-documented climate of fear in which his aides are highly reluctant to convey unpleasant news. David Frum described Bush in *The Right Man* as "impatient" and "quick to anger." In a November 2005 *Newsweek* article, Evan Thomas reported on the breakdown of the communication lines to the president concerning Hurricane Katrina:

> It's a standing joke among the president's top aides: who gets to deliver the bad news? Warm and hearty in public, Bush can be cold and snappish in private, and aides sometimes cringe before the displeasure of the president of the United States, or, as he is known in West Wing jargon, POTUS.

Thomas attributed the failure of the government's response to Katrina in large part to the atmosphere the president created, in which aides are meek and fearful of delivering bad news:

> Bush can be petulant about dissent; he equates disagreement with disloyalty. After five years in office, he is surrounded largely by people who agree with him. Bush can ask tough questions, but it's mostly a one-way street. Most presidents keep a devil's advocate around. Lyndon Johnson had George Ball on Vietnam; President Ronald Reagan and Bush's father, George H. W. Bush, grudgingly listened to the arguments of Budget Director Richard Darman, who told them what they didn't wish to hear: that they would have to raise taxes.
>
> When Hurricane Katrina struck, it appears there was no one to tell President Bush the plain truth: that the state and local governments had been overwhelmed, that the Federal Emergency Management Agency (FEMA) was not up to the job and that the military, the only institution with the resources to cope, couldn't act without a declaration from the president overriding all other authority.

Thomas's reference to the role played by the dissenting, highly intelligent Richard Darman in the Bush 41 administration is telling. According to David Frum, the president purposely staffs the White House with capable but less-than-brilliant individuals, precisely because he seeks those who will loyally carry out instructions rather than those who will prod, question, and deviate from his predetermined policies. In short, Bush affirmatively sought to prohibit Darman-like dissent:

> If you looked around the Bush cabinet, you saw very able, solid, and reliable people—but only one, Donald Rumsfeld, whose mind could truly be said to sparkle. If you looked at the White House staff, there was again a dearth of really high-powered brains. One seldom heard an unexpected thought or met someone who possessed unusual knowledge. Aside from Mitch Daniels in OMB & of course Karl Rove, *conspicuous intelligence seemed actively unwelcome in the Bush White House* [emphasis added].
>
> Clinton had brought in eccentrics, some of them, perhaps, but also powerful intelligences, open to new ideas. The country could trust the Bush administration not to cheat or lie. But could the administration cope with an unprecedented problem? That might be rather dicier.
>
> The reason for the bias toward the ordinary was Richard Darman, the most conspicuously brilliant person in Bush 41's White House. In the 1992 election, he attacked Bush 41 himself. And the lesson the younger Bush took from that experience was: no new Darmans.

As Christine Whitman told Suskind of her (predictably short-lived) tenure as Environmental Protection Agency administrator: "In meetings, I'd ask if there were any facts to support our case. And for that, I was accused of disloyalty!"

Demands of rigid loyalty, along with a "kill the messenger" attitude toward bearers of news that undermines beliefs, are particularly dangerous for a president such as George Bush, who, by his own reckoning, depends so heavily on aides—not only for advice and counsel but also for basic information about what is going on in the world. In a September 23, 2003, interview with Fox News' Brit Hume, the president boasted of the fact that he does not read newspapers, but instead forms his understanding of the world based upon what his closest aides tell him:

HUME: How do you get your news?
BUSH: I get briefed by Andy Card and Condi in the morning. They

come in and tell me. In all due respect, you've got a beautiful face and everything [*sic*].

I glance at the headlines just to kind of get a flavor for what's moving. I rarely read the stories, and get briefed by people who are [*sic*] probably read the news themselves. But like Condoleezza, in her case, the national security adviser is getting her news directly from the participants on the world stage.

HUME: Has that been your practice since day one, or is that a practice that you've . . .

BUSH: Practice since day one.

HUME: Really?

BUSH: Yes. You know, look, I have great respect for the media. I mean, our society is a good, solid democracy because of a good, solid media. But I also understand that a lot of times there's opinions mixed in with news. And I . . .

HUME: I won't disagree with that, sir.

BUSH: I appreciate people's opinions, but I'm more interested in news. And the best way to get the news is from objective sources. And the most objective sources I have are people on my staff who tell me what's happening in the world.

Over time, the president's staff has become increasingly monolithic and loyal to the president's worldview and core convictions, and correspondingly less burdened by dissent. Thus, the great paradox of the Bush presidency is that as his presidency and his war in Iraq have collapsed around him, the world he occupies has been designed to affirm unceasingly that he is on the side of Good and is thus entitled—even obligated—to remain on the path of righteousness even as opposition to that course grows and evidence of its failure expands.

DESIRES FULFILLED

That the president is accustomed to an environment that caters to his beliefs and desires is to be expected, in light of his upbringing as the eldest son in a powerful and wealthy political family. While the president was growing up, his father was a congressman, U.N. ambassador, Senate nominee, Republican National Committee chair, and CIA director, and he was thus accustomed to having others create opportunities for him and grant his wishes, thereby being able to do what he wanted without much resistance from others. Perhaps most significantly, the power and prestige of his father enabled him to be saved from mistakes and disasters—including a series of failed business ventures—that created the expectation that no serious damage would ever result, even from reckless errors. Being repeatedly rescued—and continuing to thrive even in the face of repeated failures—can ultimately engender a sense of infallibility, or at the very least an implicit belief that one need not really fear, or even consider, the consequences of one's actions.

In the 1970s, one of the closest friends of the Bush family was Jimmy Allison, a Texas campaign consultant highly trusted by George H. W. Bush. Allison's widow, Linda, who had spent substantial time in the company of the Bush family, sat for several days of interviews with journalist Mary Jacoby. Jacoby then published a 2004 article based on those interviews in *Salon,* in which Linda Allison recounts incidents that capture the younger Bush's sense of entitlement, as well as his petulance and rage when told "no":

> The break [between Bush and his father] happened not long after a boozy election-night wake for Blount, who lost his Senate bid to the incumbent Democrat, John Sparkman. Leaving the election-night "celebration," Allison remembers encountering George W. Bush in the parking lot, urinating on a car, and hearing later about how he'd yelled obscenities at police officers that night. Bush left a house he'd rented in Montgomery trashed—the furniture broken, walls damaged and a chandelier destroyed, the *Birmingham News* reported in February.
>
> "He was just a rich kid who had no respect for other people's possessions," Mary Smith, a member of the family who rented the house, told the newspaper, adding that a bill sent to Bush for repairs was never paid.
>
> And a month later, in December, during a visit to his parents' home in Washington, Bush drunkenly challenged his father to go "mano a mano," as has often been reported.

To his credit, Bush has candidly acknowledged the disregard for responsibilities and the welfare of others that drove his life until he found God in 1985, at the age of almost forty. In one sense, the authenticity of

Bush's evangelical conversion seems beyond doubt, given the profound life changes it facilitated, most particularly the abrupt and total cessation of what was, by all accounts (including his own), a rather severe addiction to alcohol. But in another, equally significant sense, replacing an alcohol-fueled life of unbridled hedonism with a fervent evangelical certainty can be seen as a lateral, rather than a vertical, move. Both before and after the conversion, Bush evinced a strong sense of certainty, superiority, and elite piety. Pre- and postconversion, Bush's place in the world was clear, right, secure, unquestioned, and unquestionable. And in both phases, there was little space or tolerance for those who opposed or contradicted him.

Even now, the president's own statements frequently reveal this insatiable sense of inborn entitlement—an expectation that his will can and should be transformed into reality without opposition or obstruction. In a December 2001 press conference, the president admonished American citizens as follows:

> The American people must understand when I said that we need to be patient, *that I meant it.* And we're going to be there for a while. I don't know the exact moment when we leave, David, but it's not until the mission is complete. The world must know that this administration will not blink in the face of danger and will not tire when it comes to completing the missions that we said we would do. The world will learn that when the United States is harmed, we will follow through. The world will see that when we put a coalition together that says "Join us," I mean it. And *when I ask others to participate, I mean it* [emphasis added].

There is a parental, even bullying, tone that pervades the president's outlook. He decrees. Everyone else accepts that he "means it." And so it will be.

This self-centered mentality—whereby Bush expects his desires to be fulfilled immediately—has repeatedly manifested in how he governs. After the president announced his "surge" plan for Iraq in early 2007, CBS News recounted the conversation about the plan that ensued between President Bush and newly inaugurated House Speaker Nancy Pelosi:

> In an interview, Pelosi also said she was puzzled by what she considered the president's minimalist explanation for his confidence in the new

surge of 21,500 U.S. troops that he has presented as the crux of a new "way forward" for U.S. forces in Iraq.

"He's tried this two times—it's failed twice," the California Democrat said. "I asked him at the White House, 'Mr. President, why do you think this time it's going to work?' And he said, 'Because I told them it had to.'"

Asked if the president had elaborated, she added that he simply said, " 'I told them that they had to.' That was the end of it. That's the way it is."

Even after four years of complete chaos and uncontrolled violence in Iraq, Bush expects that his plan will work. Why? Because he *ordered* his generals to make it work, and so it shall be.

Similarly, in the middle of the raging Israel-Hezbollah War of 2006, Bush, unbeknownst to him, was tape recorded while speaking privately to Tony Blair at a dinner of European leaders. Bush, in between bites of food, made clear what the solution was to the war: "What they need to do is get Syria to get Hezbollah to stop doing this shit and it's over." The Decider issues orders. Everyone complies. And problems are solved for the Good, regardless of complexities, obstacles, or realities.

True to form, Bush's presidency evinces a pattern whereby he reacts most aggressively when he is challenged or feels powerless. What Bush the president detests most is a feeling of weakness, being told there are limits on his will, on his power as the Decider. In 2000, after being elected only after a 5–4 Supreme Court vote in a judicial battle to resolve one of the closest elections in U.S. history, it was conventional wisdom that Bush would need to be exceedingly restrained and modest in his governance. In light of his precarious claim to the presidency, Bush would have to be more bipartisan than most prior presidents. But Bush did precisely the opposite.

Vehemently rejecting the notion that his presidency began with questionable legitimacy or on weak footing, he governed as if he had won by a landslide, pursuing his agenda without much restraint and appointing some of the most extreme ideologues to key cabinet posts, including John Ashcroft as attorney general and Donald Rumsfeld as defense secretary. Bush's response to the conventional assumption that he would be a weak president was to exert maximum power.

Demands that Donald Rumsfeld be fired ensured that Rumsfeld ended up being just days away from becoming the longest-serving defense secretary in history. Complaints, primarily from his own supporters, that Bush had deployed insufficient numbers of troops in Iraq, and that this mistake was the principal cause of the chaos, meant that Bush steadfastly refused *for years* to send more troops. After Bush squeaked out a victory in the 2004 election, he replaced those officials who had exhibited even minimal independence of mind, such as Colin Powell and John Ashcroft, with the supremely loyal Condoleezza Rice and Alberto Gonzales. And when Bush's Republican Party lost its House and Senate majorities in the 2006 elections, Bush quickly acted *not* by seeking out different counsel, but by further purging dissent from his inner circle.

In December 2006, the *Washington Post's* Dan Froomkin reviewed the post–midterm elections ouster of several key Bush officials and concluded that there was yet another "purge of the unbelievers." Froomkin cited Harriet Miers as White House counsel ("never a true believer in Vice President Cheney's views of a nearly unrestrained executive branch"), Iraq Ambassador Zalmay Khalilzad ("considered by Cheney to be too soft on the Sunnis"), John Negroponte as national intelligence director ("not alarmist enough about the Iranian nuclear threat"), and Generals George Casey and John Abizaid ("jettisoned for having shown a little backbone in their opposition to Cheney and Bush's politically-motivated insistence on throwing more troops into the Iraqi conflagration").

As demonstrated in the prior chapter, the collapse of the Bush presidency—in both its magnitude and its intensity—has been truly historic. Yet remarkably, this collapse has not really weakened the president himself. Before the ink was even dry on the story of the 2006 midterm elections, the president unveiled his plan for a troop "surge"—escalation—in Iraq, which ensured that he continued to dominate the American political discussion.

In early 2007, the president remained the dominant figure in American politics, notwithstanding the stinging rejection by the electorate, the Democratic takeover of Congress, and his extreme unpopularity, to say nothing of his officially commenced status as a lame duck. His bellicose language toward Iran began to be matched by overtly hostile actions—examined fully in chapter 4—thus bolstering his position as the focal point of political debate. The weaker and more unpopular the president becomes—the more he hears that his presidency has become impotent—the more aggressive and extreme he is with his assertions of his power.

Jeffrey Smith, in an October 2006 *Washington Post* article, detailed the dramatic increase in what is known as "intolerance" rhetoric from the president—exactly at the time he has become weakened both by historic levels of unpopularity and world events:

> President Bush finds the world around him increasingly "unacceptable."
>
> In speeches, statements and news conferences this year, the president has repeatedly declared a range of problems "unacceptable," including rising health costs, immigrants who live outside the law, North Korea's claimed nuclear test, genocide in Sudan and Iran's nuclear ambitions.
>
> Bush's decision to lay down blunt new markers about the things he deems intolerable comes at an odd time, a phase of his presidency in which all manner of circumstances are not bending to his will: national security setbacks in North Korea and Iraq, a Congress that has shrugged its shoulders at his top domestic initiatives, a favorability rating mired below 40 percent.
>
> But a survey of transcripts from Bush's public remarks over the past seven years shows the president's worsening political predicament has actually stoked, rather than diminished, his desire to proclaim what he cannot abide. Some presidential scholars and psychologists describe the trend as a signpost of Bush's rising frustration with his declining influence.

Employing such categorical intolerance language in the wake of such a stinging rebuke is easily understood. For the *Post* article documenting Bush's increasingly aggressive rhetoric, Smith interviewed Steven Kull, a political psychologist who directs the University of Maryland's Program on International Policy Attitudes. Kull explained that some individuals respond to failure "by intensifying an authoritarian posture and insisting that their preferences are equivalent to a moral imperative." Moisés Naím, the editor in chief of *Foreign Policy* magazine, said there is a relationship between "how strident and extreme" the language of many leaders is and how limited their options are. For Bush, Naím said, "this comes at a time when the world is convinced he is weaker than ever."

ENTITLEMENT TO POWER

From the president's overarching conviction that he is on the side of Good and is waging a vital battle against Evil emerges a relentless pursuit of maximum power and an accompanying sense of entitlement to that power. Because Bush is on the right side of the Manichean battle—the more power he has, the better, given the vital and just ends to which it is applied.

In a January 2007 op-ed in the *Washington Post*, Dahlia Lithwick examined several of the most extreme Bush actions—such as José Padilla's detention, the Guantánamo abuses, and omnipotence-declaring signing statements—and concluded:

> I once believed that the common thread here is presidential blindness—an extreme executive-branch myopia that leads the chief executive to believe that these futile measures are integral to combating terrorism; a self-delusion that precludes Bush and his advisers from recognizing that Padilla is a chump and Guantanamo Bay is just a holding pen for a jumble of innocent or half-guilty wretches.
>
> But it has finally become clear that the goal of these efforts isn't to win the war against terrorism; indeed, nothing about Padilla, Guantanamo Bay or signing statements moves the country an inch closer to eradicating terrorism. The object is a larger one: expanding executive power, for its own sake.

As Lithwick explains, the allegation against U.S. citizen Padilla that he was a "Dirty Bomber" who sought to detonate a radiological weapon has been abandoned long ago, but Padilla continued to be held without charges as an "enemy combatant." And though Donald Rumsfeld insisted that Guantánamo was necessary to detain and try "the worst of the worst," more than half of the detainees have been released and very few of them will ever be tried. Yet Guantánamo, despite being one of the preeminent symbolic engines of anti-American resentment around the world, remains open. Lithwick explains why:

> But Guantanamo Bay stays open for the same reason that Padilla stays on trial. Having claimed the right to label enemy combatants and detain them indefinitely without charges, the Bush administration cannot re-

treat from that position without ceding ground. The president is as much a prisoner of Guantanamo Bay as the detainees are. Having gone nose to nose with Congress over his authority to craft stripped-down courts, guaranteed to produce guilty verdicts, Bush cannot call off the trials. The endgame in the war against terrorism isn't holding the line against terrorists. It's holding the line on hard-fought claims to limitless presidential authority.

In December 2005, I began writing on an almost daily basis about the Bush administration's deliberate violations of the Foreign Intelligence Surveillance Act (FISA). That lawbreaking was revealed when the *New York Times* reported that the president had ordered the National Security Agency to eavesdrop on the telephone calls of Americans without obtaining warrants from the FISA court, notwithstanding the fact that warrantless eavesdropping is a criminal offense—a felony—pursuant to FISA. What confounded me at first was the sheer *pointlessness* of the lawbreaking. It was not merely that the FISA court has always allowed the president—all presidents—to do almost any eavesdropping he wanted, and that bypassing FISA was therefore unnecessary.

That is true. But more significantly, if the president wanted FISA amended, even radically, to vest him with still greater eavesdropping powers, the boundlessly compliant post-9/11 Congress was as eager as could be to grant all of his wishes and to give him whatever new powers he requested. In fact, Congress *did* amend FISA to grant expanded eavesdropping authority—in complete accordance with the president's request—at the very same time Bush ordered illegal eavesdropping (in October 2001). As I wrote in my previous book, *How Would a Patriot Act?:*

> The picture that emerged [from the *Times* story on NSA eavesdropping] presented a sharply contradictory set of circumstances. A president who commanded the support and loyalty of national politicians in both parties. A president who sought, and was given, expanded powers by Congress to combat terrorism. A Congress that, in the aftermath of the 9/11 attacks, repeatedly and with virtual unanimity agreed to every request the president made. And yet a president who chose to secretly order eavesdropping on American citizens, on U.S. soil, in violation of the very law he had just requested.

Bush violated FISA for the same reason that Lithwick cites to explain his other lawless and extremist measures—because he *wanted to violate the law* in order to establish the general "principle" that he was not bound by the law, to show that he has the power to break the law, that he is more powerful than the law. This is a president and an administration that are obsessed first and foremost with their own power and with constant demonstrations of their own strength. Conversely, what they fear and hate the most is their own weakness and submission to limitations.

In May 2006, the Cato Institute, a think tank devoted to limited government, published an extremely well-documented condemnation of the Bush administration's multiple abuses of power. Its Executive Summary described the Bush administration's driving "principle"—radical expansion of its own power in every area:

> Unfortunately, far from defending the Constitution, President Bush has repeatedly sought to strip out the limits the document places on federal power.
>
> In its official legal briefs and public actions, the Bush administration has advanced a view of federal power that is astonishingly broad, a view that includes:
>
> - a federal government empowered to regulate core political speech—and restrict it greatly when it counts the most: in the days before a federal election;
> - a president who cannot be restrained, through validly enacted statutes, from pursuing any tactic he believes to be effective in the war on terror;
> - a president who has the inherent constitutional authority to designate American citizens suspected of terrorist activity as "enemy combatants," strip them of any constitutional protection, and lock them up without charges for the duration of the war on terror—in other words, perhaps forever; and,
> - a federal government with the power to supervise virtually every aspect of American life, from kindergarten, to marriage, to the grave. President Bush's constitutional vision is, in short, sharply at odds with the text, history, and structure of our Constitution, which authorizes a government of limited powers.

The driving philosophy and ultimate goal of the administration has been a virtually limitless expansion of its own power. For that reason, the weaker and more besieged the administration feels, the more compelled it will be to make a showing of its power.

Lashing out in response to feelings of weakness is a temptation most human beings have, but for George Bush, it is a primary dynamic driving his behavior. His party suffered historic losses in the 2006 midterm elections as a result of profound dissatisfaction with his presidency and with his war, and his reaction was *to escalate* the war, despite (really, because of) the extreme unpopularity of that option. And as Iraq rapidly unraveled, he even issued orders, as discussed at length in chapter 4, that pose a high risk of expanding the war to include Iran. When Bush feels weak and restrained, that is when he acts most extremely.

Bush officials and their followers talk incessantly about things like power, weakness, domination, and humiliation. Their objectives—both foreign and domestic—are always to show their enemies that they are stronger and more powerful and the enemies are weaker and thus must submit ("shock and awe"). It is a twisted worldview but it dominates their thinking. As John Dean, in reliance on extensive social science, demonstrated in *Conservatives Without Conscience*, a perception of one's weakness and the resulting fears it inspires are almost always what drive people to create or embrace empowering Manichean movements and the group-based comforts of moral certitude that such movements provide.

The most dangerous George Bush is one who feels weak, impotent, and under attack. Those perceptions are intolerable for him and it is doubtful if there are many limits, if any, on what he would be willing to do in order to restore a feeling of potency and to rid himself of the sensations of his own weakness and defeat. As he has made repeatedly and unambiguously clear, he is an instrument of the Good and is faced with true Evil. His mission is just and necessary, and he will therefore pursue it without constraints. That is the Manichean mind, and it—more than anything else—is what has propelled America along a radical, tumultuous path throughout the Bush presidency.

CHAPTER THREE

The Manichean Road to Baghdad

We clearly know that there were in the past and have been contacts between senior Iraqi officials and members of al Qaeda going back for actually quite a long time. . . . No one is trying to make an argument at this point that Saddam Hussein somehow had operational control of what happened on September 11, so we don't want to push this too far, *but this is a story that is unfolding, and it is getting clearer, and we're learning more* [emphasis added].

—**CONDOLEEZZA RICE,** then national security adviser, September 25, 2002
(shortly before Congress voted to authorize military force against Iraq)

In September 2002, Bush White House Chief of Staff Andy Card infamously told the *New York Times* that the Bush administration had waited until September to advocate an attack on Iraq because "[f]rom a marketing point of view, you don't introduce new products in August." But in point of fact, the groundwork for the arguments that ultimately persuaded Americans to support the invasion was laid well before that September. Almost immediately after the 9/11 attacks, as the World Trade Center lay in rubble, President Bush introduced the principles, rhetoric, and themes that ultimately enabled him to lead the country in waging war against Iraq.

Though the country has since debated extensively whether any rational connection exists between the 9/11 attacks and the invasion of Iraq, the president, as early as September of 2001, floated the argument those two events are not only connected, but that the latter flows directly and proximately from—and is even compelled by—the former. The premises underpinning the president's decision to invade Iraq are not uniquely applicable to that nation, and cannot meaningfully be examined standing alone. Instead, it was the president's general moralistic principles he enunciated almost immediately after 9/11 that led directly to the invasion.

From the outset, the president depicted the 9/11 attacks not merely as an act of Evil perpetrated by Evil men but rather as evidence of a much more consequential and all-consuming phenomenon. He immediately depicted a broader, overarching battle between the forces of Good and the forces of Evil. The day after September 11, Bush addressed the nation and articulated a very clear and simple worldview, one which would guide his entire presidency: "This will be a monumental struggle of good versus evil, but good will prevail."

Cast in theological terms, the president's belief that America had embarked upon a binary struggle of Good vs. Evil came to be the predominant theme of his presidency. The president and his administration invoked this starkly dualistic theme repeatedly to defend and justify a whole host of controversial actions. On September 20, 2001, the president addressed a Joint Session of Congress and made clear that not only was the conflict America faced one between pure Good and pure Evil, but further, everyone was compelled to choose one side or the other: "Every nation, in every region, now has a decision to make. Either you are with us, or you are with the terrorists."

President Bush underscored the rigidly binary nature of the challenge facing America and the world again in his October 7, 2001, televised address to the nation: "Today we focus on Afghanistan. But the battle is broader. Every nation has a choice to make. In this conflict there is no neutral ground."

And in his January 29, 2002, State of the Union speech, the president expressly extended this Good-Evil dichotomy beyond Afghanistan and Al Qaeda, and thus announced to the world that henceforth, U.S.

foreign policy would be devoted principally to combating the threats posed by an "axis of evil" threatening the world:

> North Korea is a regime arming with missiles and weapons of mass destruction, while starving its citizens. Iran aggressively pursues these weapons and exports terror, while an unelected few repress the Iranian people's hope for freedom.
>
> Iraq continues to flaunt its hostility toward America and to support terror. The Iraqi regime has plotted to develop anthrax, and nerve gas, and nuclear weapons for over a decade. This is a regime that has already used poison gas to murder thousands of its own citizens—leaving the bodies of mothers huddled over their dead children. This is a regime that agreed to international inspections—then kicked out the inspectors. This is a regime that has something to hide from the civilized world.
>
> States like these, and their terrorist allies, constitute an axis of evil, arming to threaten the peace of the world. . . .
>
> We'll be deliberate, yet time is not on our side. I will not wait on events, while dangers gather. I will not stand by, as peril draws closer and closer. The United States of America will not permit the world's most dangerous regimes to threaten us with the world's most destructive weapons. . . .
>
> History has called America and our allies to action, and it is both our responsibility and our privilege to fight freedom's fight.

In a nation still recovering from the trauma of the 9/11 attacks only four months prior; with anxiety-heightening, unsolved anthrax attacks via mail fresh in Americans' minds; and with a trusting citizenry standing behind George Bush, the president's accusations against Iraq, delivered in such a dramatic setting, were both potent and stirring. For Americans to hear from their president that Iraq "supports terror" and that it "plotted to develop anthrax" had the effect, surely by design, of powerfully linking the Saddam regime with the terrorists who flew the planes into American office buildings.

To accuse Iraq of working with its "terrorist allies" and attempting to "threaten us with the world's most destructive weapons" was, to understate the case, highly provocative rhetoric. Any American who had confidence in the president—and, in January 2002, the overwhelming majority of Americans did—was highly likely to come away from that speech with the distinct impression that Iraq was at least connected to, if not responsible for, the 9/11 attacks and even the recent anthrax attacks.

By the conclusion of the president's speech, he had made emphatically clear that America's enemies were not merely hostile to the United States and threatening to its interests but rather were pure Evil. They did not operate in isolation but as an "axis," the historically familiar term designating Hitler's Germany and its allies. Our enemies were intent on our total destruction—by nuclear weapons if possible—and they were all part of one undifferentiated mass. Above all, America was to be governed by an absolute truth: "We've come to know truths that we will never question: Evil is real, and it must be opposed." That proclamation came near the end of the president's speech, and it provided the framework for all the statements preceding it. That "evil is real" and "must be opposed" is a truth—the president avowed—"that we will never question."

That the administration attempted almost immediately to connect the 9/11 attacks to Iraq is hardly surprising. Former Bush treasury secretary Paul O'Neill reported that finding a way to invade Iraq was high on the Bush agenda long *before* 9/11. O'Neill said in a 2004 interview with *60 Minutes:* "From the very beginning, there was a conviction that Saddam Hussein was a bad person and that he needed to go." In Ron Suskind's book, *The Price of Loyalty*, Suskind quotes O'Neill as describing a pre-9/11 National Security Council meeting where the invasion of Iraq was discussed with virtually no dissent. Said O'Neill: "It was all about finding a way to do it. That was the tone of it. The president saying 'Go find me a way to do this.'"

Moreover, numerous key Bush officials—including the top three Pentagon officials (Donald Rumsfeld, Paul Wolfowitz, and Douglas Feith) and the national security adviser for Middle East policy (Elliot Abrams)—were advocating an invasion of Iraq in order to depose Saddam for *years prior to* 9/11, and they simply seized on the terrorist attack as the principal justification for a war they had long desired. Additionally, Bush's top terrorism official, Richard Clarke, disclosed that on the *day after* 9/11, Rumsfeld was expressly urging a military attack on Iraq. On the same day, Bush himself instructed Clarke to search for links between Iraq and Al Qaeda: "Iraq! Saddam! Find out if there's a connection," Clarke quotes Bush as ordering.

In light of those facts, there is little doubt that many of the speeches delivered in the immediate aftermath of 9/11 were crafted with Iraq in mind. In retrospect, those early speeches were plainly preparing the American citizenry to view Iraq as a grave threat that was part and parcel of the threat posed by Al Qaeda.

The day following his State of the Union address, the president delivered a thirty-minute speech to a boisterous and cheering crowd in Winston-Salem, North Carolina. He employed the word *evil* ten times to describe the enemies of the United States—vowing, for instance, that "the evil won't stand," proclaiming that "the people we fight are evil people," and declaring that a principal cause for the 9/11 attacks was that "the evil ones thought that we were weak." The president appeared deliberately to highlight the crowd-pleasing simplicity and uncomplicated purity of his down-home approach: "We haven't forgot [*sic*] our other objective, and that's bad news for Al Qaeda. Our other objective is to run them down wherever they hide and bring them to justice. Or, as I like to say, get 'em."

The president's speech that day was filled with folksy platitudes and repeated invocations of the all-encompassing battle between Good vs. Evil. But his rhetoric was also breezy, at times even joking, setting a tone that masked the deadly serious nature of his threats:

> We're making good progress. We put together a great coalition of nations around the world, with this message: Either you're with us or you're against us. Either you're on the side of freedom and justice, or you aren't.
>
> And the good news is most people are beginning to see the wisdom of being on the side of freedom and justice. (*Laughter and applause.*)
>
> We're after them. But the good news to report for our side, and the bad news for the evil, is that we're patient, and we're determined, and we will not stop until we achieve all our objectives.

After articulating a stark framework in which there were two sides and only two in the conflicts America faced—one Good, the other Evil—the president summarized his presidential mission as follows: "You know, you've heard me talk about this probably, but I really, truly view this as a conflict between good and evil. And there really isn't much middle ground—like none. (*Laughter.*) The people we fight are evil people.

"Either you're with us or you're against us. Either you're on the side of freedom and justice or you aren't."

Despite the seemingly grave subject matter and threatening nature of the president's remarks, a good time was apparently had by all, or at least many, who attended his address. The official White House transcript proudly indicates sixteen different instances in which the president's speech was interrupted by "Laughter" or "Laughter and applause"—including when an audience member interrupted the president's statement that the terrorists in caves "better not think they can hide forever" by yelling: "Give 'em what-for, G!" *(Laughter.)*

The president's rhetoric was suffused with swaggering informalisms of this sort, plainly designed to invoke the image of a brave and macho cowboy, or a borderline lawless (when necessary to fight Evil) nineteenth-century sheriff. At a press briefing less than a week after the 9/11 attacks, the president was proudly issuing threats in the language of the Old West: "I want justice . . . And there's an old poster out West I recall, that said, 'Wanted, Dead or Alive.'"

Thus was conveyed a man driven at his core by Goodness, by a resulting resolute commitment to protect those who are Good from the menace of terrorist Evil, a commitment so overarching and absolute that every other consideration—from the formalities of language to the formalities of law—was subordinate to the imperative of his mission. Like the American iconic film hero who breaks rules, steals cars, and defies every stifling convention when necessary to apprehend the bad guys, the president continuously evoked the language and struck the pose of the crusading cowboy on a mission. And that image resonated deeply with a nation full of angry, violated citizens who were hungry for aggressive retaliation.

But as was typically the case for that time period, there was much decency and even noble sentiments included in the president's speech to temper the Manichean chest-beating. With images of their fellow citizens leaping from the ninety-second floor of a collapsing office building in Manhattan still fresh in Americans' minds, it was easy and simple for the president to depict America's enemies as Evil. The Evil reflected by the attacks of 9/11 spoke for itself.

But exactly why America was the personification of Good was not a lesson one could infer from the terrorist attacks. More conceptual reasoning was required to support that conclusion. In his speeches, the president balanced his threatening and Manichean posturing with an often eloquent appeal to America's ideals. As noted in the first chapter, President Bush aggressively distinguished Muslims, including American Muslims, from the terrorist fanatics who exploit their religion, and sternly warned of the severe consequences for anyone attacking or otherwise harassing Muslim Americans. In his North Carolina speech, the president closed on this note:

> And, obviously, if you want to fight evil, we've figured out a way to do so militarily. That's one way. But at home, you fight evil with acts of goodness. You overcome the evil in society by doing something to help somebody. . . .
>
> Not only will our country be better, but we'll show the world—we will show the world that values, universal values must be respected, and must be adhered to. And as a result, the world will be more peaceful. History has called us to action, and action we will take. *(Applause.)*

Back in those early post-9/11 days, according to the president, America was Good not merely because it opposed nations and attacked groups designated as Evil, nor merely because it was attacked by Evil. America was Good for reasons wholly independent of the violent actions and depraved values of its enemies. America was Good in its own right—not inherently, but because of the values and principles to which it aspired, for which it stood in the world, and which it sought to inspire.

At least as the president typically expressed it in the post-9/11 months, America would demonstrate itself to be a force for Good, standing in contrast to the Evil of the terrorists, not principally with the potency of its bombs and invading armies (which few doubted), but instead—as the president said in North Carolina—by "show[ing] the world that values, universal values must be respected, and must be adhered to. And as a result, the world will be more peaceful." While the president's aggressive rhetoric in the wake of the 9/11 attacks was assuredly a primary cause for much of his popularity during that period, he did not single-mindedly tout an unrestrained or indiscriminate warpath.

Many Americans supported him in reliance upon his accompanying commitments that whatever aggression might be necessary, America would never abandon the values defining the country, nor would he degrade America's standing. The president vowed repeatedly that the nation would adhere to its political values and principles even when battling enemies who did not embrace those principles—both because doing so was the morally superior course, and because adherence to those values would enhance America's strength and security by maintaining its influence and prestige in the world. The initial post-9/11 George Bush was one who claimed to recognize that long-standing American values were what made the country not only better than the enemies that had attacked us but also a stronger and more secure nation.

Certainly in the hours and days following the shocking events of 9/11, many Americans—perhaps most—were understandably fueled by pure, unbridled fury and by a war-hungry desire to avenge the attacks. But as the weeks passed, that rage simmered down to a more focused and restrained anger. Many Americans were resolute about the need to pursue Al Qaeda aggressively but were not seeking maniacal, reckless warmongering.

The president's most loyal electoral base would likely have stood behind him even had he exclusively emphasized the "Destroy Evil" side of the Manichean equation. But the towering, transpartisan approval ratings the president enjoyed were the result of a *balanced* rather than bloodthirsty approach to the threat of terrorism. President Bush attracted widespread support by delivering convincing assurances that our nation's principles would preclude our descending to the lawless and barbaric level of the terrorists in order to defeat them.

Although initial speeches confined the Good-Evil dichotomy to the choice that America posed to the other nations of the world—either cooperate with the United States in its battle or be deemed to be on the side of Evil—application of this dichotomy would soon come to include domestic political debates as well. The simple, binary rhetoric of Good vs. Evil was increasingly invoked in order to depict Americans who opposed the president's policies—particularly in the areas of national security, war, and terrorism—as opponents not merely of the president's policies but of the United States itself, as enemies of the Good.

SADDAM OSAMA ADOLF HUSSEIN

By mid-2002, it had become increasingly apparent that President Bush was intent upon forcing a conflict with Iraq, using as his principal rhetorical tactic the assertion that confronting that nation was a critical component of fighting terrorism and combating Evil. Once the White House unveiled its "Iraq marketing project" with full force, the effort to equate an attack on Iraq with defense against terrorism intensified. In virtually every speech the president delivered, and in nearly all interviews he gave, Bush repeatedly linked Iraq with terrorism.

As a result of that refrain, those who merely raised concerns about invading Iraq—let alone those who emphatically opposed it—were accused by the president's supporters, first implicitly and then overtly, of opposing efforts to stop terrorism and even of siding with the terrorists and acting as their allies. And though the war with Afghanistan was on the president's immediate agenda when he first enunciated this dualistic framework, he made crystal clear that the choice all were called upon to make was by no means applicable only to *that* war, but also to the "broader battle": "Today we focus on Afghanistan. But the battle is broader. . . . In this conflict there is no neutral ground."

The president and his allies devoted considerable efforts to not only detailing the threat posed by Saddam Hussein but also depicting him as pure Evil, thus justifying any and all attacks on him regardless of what actual threat he posed to the United States. Central to this depiction was the administration's repeatedly equating Saddam Hussein with the Ultimate Historical Evil, Adolf Hitler. Dr. Rafael Medoff, director of the David S. Wyman Institute for Holocaust Studies, published a 2003 article documenting the increasingly common reliance of Bush officials on comparisons between Saddam Hussein and Adolf Hitler and/or Iraq and Nazi Germany:

> Appearing on "Meet the Press" on February 23, Bush administration official Richard Perle compared the charade of visits by United Nations weapons inspectors to Iraq with the infamous 1944 visit by Red Cross officials to the Nazis' Theresienstadt ghetto, where the performance of

the prisoners' orchestra helped lull the visitors into believing that Nazi treatment of the Jews was not so terrible after all. Perle was referring to Saddam Hussein's systematic effort to hide Iraq's weapons of mass destruction. . . .

Perle's remark was the latest in a series of statements by U.S. officials drawing analogies between current events and those of the Nazi era. President Bush, in his speech after the September 11 attacks, said that Muslim terrorists "follow in the path of Nazism." Other U.S. officials have compared European reluctance to confront Saddam with Europe's reluctance to confront Hitler in the 1930s.

In the public dialogue, the notion of "Pure Evil"—which most Americans agreed was applicable to the 9/11 attackers and to the Taliban radicals who harbored them—quickly and dramatically expanded. Suddenly that designation included a whole range of leaders and countries that had not attacked the U.S. and had almost nothing in common with the Sunni religious extremists of Al Qaeda—most prominently Saddam Hussein. In February 2003, one of the president's most influential supporters, evangelical leader James Dobson, appeared on CNN, where Larry King engaged him in respectful and solemn dialogue about the Evil posed by Saddam:

> KING: What do you make of going into Iraq? Does any part of that question your Christian values about going to war?
>
> DOBSON: No, not at all. It doesn't. No, I—you know Saddam Hussein is a tyrant, and he is out of the mold of Hitler and Stalin and others. And you can't negotiate with a tyrant. One who is bloodthirsty, one who's willing to kill innocent people. You can't do that. And he'll take your shorts if you try. And I think there's only one thing to do, and that's go in there and confront him. I just can't imagine Adolf Hitler negotiating in good faith or Stalin or Pol Pot or any of the other tyrants.
>
> KING: And if the world had moved against them, but there was no U.N.
>
> DOBSON: There was no U.N. and the British tried appeasement, which never works. It just never works. It just encourages a tyrant to be more bloody. And so, I think that we really do need to do what we need to do there.

For Dobson, the impact of 9/11 on America was primarily spiritual: "We had this resurgence of patriotism and this renewed religious faith, belief in God," he said in the interview, and it was that "renewed religious faith" that drove him to urge that the U.S. wage war on the Evil tyrant.

Cast in those terms—the invasion of Iraq as a necessary prong in the defeat of Evil, Saddam Hussein as Adolf Hitler, Iraq as Nazi Germany—whether the United States should invade Iraq and change its government was a simple choice, both politically and morally. With those premises in place, it became true, by logical necessity, that those who favored the invasion were devoted to the defense of Good against Evil. Those who opposed the invasion wanted to do nothing in the face of Evil, sided with terrorism, and perhaps were even in confederation with Evil itself.

By itself, the Good vs. Evil paradigm persuaded many, if not most, Americans to support the invasion. The demonization of Saddam as pure Evil was so effective in precluding rational debate that, according to a *USA Today* poll in September 2003 (a full six months after the U.S. invaded Iraq), almost *70 percent of the country*—a truly astonishing number—embraced the false belief that Saddam personally participated in the planning of the 9/11 attacks. While Americans continue through today to debate whether the administration and its followers deliberately "misled" the nation with respect to WMDs, there can be no reasonable debate that the president's all-consuming Manichean rhetoric planted a falsehood in the minds of most Americans—namely, that Iraq was connected to the 9/11 attacks.

Indeed, inducing a belief that Saddam had WMDs was probably less important than deploying a rhetorical strategem that caused the overwhelming majority of Americans to assume that Saddam played an active role in planning the 9/11 attacks. As but one of countless examples where top administration officials coyly suggested a link between 9/11 and Saddam, the following CBS News report from September 2002 (exactly the time when Congress was preparing to vote on the Authorization to Use Military Force [AUMF], and *long after it was established* that Saddam had no role whatsoever in 9/11) highlights just how culpable the administration was in disseminating that total fiction:

Condoleezza Rice's statements, aired Wednesday in a broadcast interview, are the strongest yet alleging contacts between Al Qaeda and the Iraqi government. . . .

"There clearly are contacts between al Qaeda and Iraq that can be documented; there clearly is testimony that some of the contacts have been important contacts and that there's a relationship here," Rice said.

"We clearly know that there were in the past and have been contacts between senior Iraqi officials and members of al Qaeda going back for actually quite a long time," Rice said. "We know too that several of the [al Qaeda] detainees, in particular some high-ranking detainees, have said that Iraq provided some training to al Qaeda in chemical weapons development." . . .

"No one is trying to make an argument at this point that Saddam Hussein somehow had operational control of what happened on September 11, so we don't want to push this too far, *but this is a story that is unfolding, and it is getting clearer, and we're learning more,*" Rice said [emphasis added].

No top administration official ever came out and expressly said they could prove that Saddam planned 9/11. But such definitive claims were unnecessary. The implied meaning of Rice's statements is manifest. The Saddam-9/11 connection "is getting clearer, and we're learning more," she said—as if there was a mountain of evidence that was just missing one or two tiny pieces to seal the deal. And all the momentum was moving toward that inevitable conclusion.

THE DOCILE "WATCHDOGS"

The uncompromisingly moralistic framing of the Iraqi conflict caused a substantial portion of Americans and, worse, the national media, to relinquish their critical faculties and—in the case of journalists— to abdicate their defining role as an *adversarial* watchdog over claims and actions by the government. Fearful of being cast as an ally of Evil, and subscribing to the president's worldview that U.S. security required bold preemptive military attacks in the Middle East, the media not only passively accepted but aggressively promoted the president's claims with regard to the threats posed by Saddam.

The front pages of the nation's major newspapers and lead stories on its network news programs touted Saddam's purported weapons programs and fueled the image of Saddam as Evil. With virtually unswerving fidelity to the administration's narrative, the American media depicted the proposed invasion as necessary in order to defend America from the forces of Evil.

And whatever else may be true, the media indisputably failed to disabuse the vast majority of Americans of the myth that Saddam had planned the 9/11 attacks. It is difficult to imagine a more potent indictment of the dysfunction of the American press than the fact that journalists, cowed by the president's dualistic rhetoric, all but stood by while the government convinced Americans of a "fact" that, as was well known even at the time, lacked a shred of evidence, then led the country *to war* based on that patent falsehood.

Even though it is more than four years old now, President Bush's infamous October 2002 pre–Iraq War speech, delivered in Cincinnati, Ohio, is a staggering read. That oration contained virtually every false assertion that was used to convince Americans to support the invasion of Iraq.

For it was in that Cincinnati speech that President Bush told the country:

- that Iraq "possesses and produces chemical and biological weapons";
- that—like the 9/11 terrorists—Iraq "could bring sudden terror and suffering to America" and it "is seeking nuclear weapons";
- that "the Iraqi dictator must not be permitted to threaten America and the world with horrible poisons and diseases and gases and atomic weapons";
- that "we know Saddam Hussein has dangerous weapons today";
- that "Iraq has trained al Qaeda members in bomb-making and poisons and deadly gases";
- that "Saddam Hussein is harboring terrorists and the instruments of terror, the instruments of mass death and destruction";
- that the United States had "urgent concern about Saddam Hussein's links to international terrorist groups";

- that "despite his public promises, Saddam Hussein had ordered his nuclear program to continue";
- that we must ask ourselves: "If we know Saddam Hussein has dangerous weapons today—and we do—does it make any sense for the world to wait to confront him as he grows even stronger and develops even more dangerous weapons?"
- that "the lives of Iraqi citizens would improve dramatically if Saddam Hussein were no longer in power";
- that "surveillance photos reveal that the regime is rebuilding facilities that it had used to produce chemical and biological weapons";
- that "Saddam Hussein has held numerous meetings with Iraqi nuclear scientists, a group he calls his nuclear mujahideen— his nuclear holy warriors";
- that Iraq "could have a nuclear weapon in less than a year"; and
- that "we cannot wait for the final proof—the smoking gun— that could come in the form of a mushroom cloud."

Dismissing the fundamental differences between the secular Hussein and the Muslim fanatic bin Laden, the president contended that they were merely "different faces of the same evil." In sum, the president said the central objective of his speech was to document "a grave threat to peace"—"the threat comes from Iraq."

A mere one week after the president made these dramatic claims in Cincinnati, the Congress overwhelmingly enacted the Authorization to Use Military Force in Iraq. Almost all Republicans and roughly half of the Democrats in the Senate voted in favor of the authorization, and with it, the invasion of Iraq became a fait accompli.

In the climate of heightened urgency which the administration worked very hard to maintain, most national journalists were petrified of aggressively challenging the "commander in chief" during this "time of war." They feared they would be pelted with all sorts of accusations from the president's followers that they were allies of Evil. Independently, many media stars, living largely in New York and Washington, had themselves been swept up by the fear of terrorism and, finding comfort in promises of "protection," they were accordingly marching in lockstep with the president's worldview.

Literally on a daily basis, the administration's highly dubious and even disputed assertions proffered to justify an attack on Iraq were published on the front pages of American newspapers *as though they were uncontested facts*. Further, the substantial bulk of the reporting on Iraq relied primarily, often exclusively, on anonymous "administration officials" or their designated intelligence "sources." In a national climate where the decision to go to war was cast as a moral imperative first, and as a policy decision a distant second, our country's most influential media outlets turned into little more than glorified megaphones for amplifying government claims, uncritically reciting them as though they were the by-product of diligent investigative journalism.

Many of those false government claims were amplified most loudly and influentially by the *New York Times*, often (though by no means only) in articles by plainly prowar (or at least war-enabling) reporters such as Judith Miller and Michael Gordon. That the *Times* bestowed credence on the Bush administration's rhetoric about the threats posed by Saddam played an influential role in persuading many Americans of the need to attack Iraq. The central role of newspapers is to examine the government's claims critically *and skeptically*, not to merely recite them as fact. But in the run-up to the war, the *Times* demonstrated all the critical spirit of *Pravda* rather than that of a trusted American newspaper, and thus convinced its readers of one false government claim after the next concerning the "Iraqi threat."

In May 2004—long after it was apparent that the "facts" continuously reported on its front page were false—the *Times* published a so-called Editor's Note that was part acknowledgment but also part justification of its errors. That mea culpa, though extraordinary for a large media outlet on such a significant matter, was woefully incomplete. The abdication of journalism's core function—not just by the *Times* but by the national media as a whole—was hardly confined to the issue of whether Saddam had WMDs; nor was it (as the Editor's Note suggested) purely the by-product of some narrow failure to examine the credibility of certain Iraqi exiles. The failure was broad, systemic, and decidedly ignoble.

At the heart of all of this was an arguably understandable—though still incomparably harmful—cowardice. The country was led by a powerful, popular War President, and the *Times* capitulated to him as cravenly and completely as did numerous other American institutions and political figures.

Despite Democratic control of the Senate, the president cowed the Congress into unprecedented submission, as it handed him every new power he requested and eagerly endorsed every decision he made, with little or no scrutiny. Despite the overwhelming capitulation of Congressional Democrats to the president's will, in the lead-up to the 2002 election many of the president's supporters still mocked even prowar Democrats as weak appeasers of the terrorists who were too spineless to fight Evil, and even as tainted with questionable and suspect loyalty to the United States. Wounded Vietnam veteran and Georgia senator Max Cleland voted *in favor* of the 2002 Authorization to Use Military Force against Iraq, yet was still defeated for re-election after the president's party ran commercials featuring photographs of Osama bin Laden and Saddam Hussein and accusing Cleland of being soft on terrorism. And with those effective tactics of mockery and demonization rolling over the submissive Democrats, the president rode his burgeoning popularity and Manichean warrior pose to a historic victory into those elections, resulting in the full-scale control of the Congress by the loyal supporters in his party.

The administration created a powerful framework that drove the nation. One could stand loyally behind the president and thus be powerful and strong and on the side of Good. Or one could oppose him, and thereby reveal oneself to be weak, spineless, and of questionable morality and loyalties—even subversive and on the side of Evil. Like most Americans, national journalists heard from the president that everyone was compelled to choose sides—Good or Evil—and one cannot overstate the impact of journalists' fear of being perceived as, and accused of, being on the wrong side.

Moreover, the relationship between official Washington and the permanent Beltway media class has become infinitely closer and more cooperative than ever before. Rather than acting as adversarial to one another, the most powerful political officials in Washington and the most influential media stars are part of the same system and nearly all are abundant beneficiaries of it. Many elite national journalists are incentivized to protect and defend powerful political leaders with whom they so frequently interact and on whom they depend for their access and their "scoops."

They have come instinctively to believe that Washington officials are intrinsically good people. Journalists live in the same social and socioeconomic circles, and the most powerful Washington figures are thus their colleagues and friends, not their investigative targets. Thus, many journalists have become implacably resistant to the idea that these political leaders are lying about profoundly important matters, let alone engaging in serious or illegal misconduct. Many journalists have come reflexively to believe what their closest government associates say and to refrain from searching for or trying to uncover serious wrongdoing, because they simply do not believe it is there or, if it is there, have no desire or incentive to expose it. Anyone who doubts any of these observations need merely consider the conduct of our national media in reporting on Iraq—not only in the run-up to the Iraq War but for a substantial period of time after the invasion.

Times reporter Elisabeth Bumiller, who covered the Bush White House during the lead-up to the Iraq War and attended the president's press conferences on behalf of the *Times,* made one of the most extraordinary—and certainly one of the most revealing—admissions about the media's prewar failures. After the invasion, Bumiller confessed that she and her colleagues were afraid—*afraid*—to ask the president questions about the justifications for our invasion of Iraq because they did not want to be too antagonistic:

> I think we were very deferential because . . . it's live, it's very intense, it's frightening to stand up there. Think about it, you're standing up on prime-time live TV asking the president of the United States a question when the country's about to go to war. There was a very serious, somber tone that evening, and no one wanted to get into an argument with the president at this very serious time.

The image described by Bumiller—national journalists paralyzed by fear, literally afraid to "get into an argument with the president"—seems like one that has prevailed in many countries during many time periods in history—but (with some exceptions) not in America. Yet that is the climate that the president succeeded in imposing on the nation, all by depicting the world in dualistic terms.

Accusations that the media works subversively against America have been a staple of the Bush presidency. Even as late as 2006, the vice president's wife, Lynne Cheney, went on CNN with Wolf Blitzer and, after complaining about CNN's broadcast of video showing insurgents shooting at American troops (which Cheney described as "terrorist propaganda"), she demanded to know of Blitzer: *"Do you want us to win?"* Blitzer thereafter eagerly sought to assure her: "We want the United States to win. We are Americans. There's no doubt about that." The attempt to force the media to choose to be "on the side of the Bush administration"—upon pain of being accused of being on the "other side," i.e., the side of the Evil terrorists—has been an effective weapon in putting the media in a defensive and even compliant posture.

Bumiller's confession revealed nothing new to anyone observing the behavior of national journalists throughout 2002 and 2003. They treated the president with an uncritical respect so great that it can only be described, without hyperbole, as reverence.

This overwhelming respect for Bush led journalists to renounce their role as adversarial watchdogs over government statements and instead become virtual propaganda arms of the Bush presidency. And it was the media, at times even more effectively than the president himself, that depicted our most complex and challenging foreign policy matters as little more than the trite battles against Bad Guys which one finds in League of Justice cartoons.

No matter how many times one thinks or writes about it, for instance, it never ceases to amaze, or to horrify, that our national media outlets actually disseminated playing cards—*playing cards*—with pictures of the Bad, Wanted Iraqis underneath their comic book villain nicknames. To this day, one can go to the websites of newspapers and explore the many interactive features of the card deck. Samir Abd Al-Aziz was the four of clubs, Kamal Mustafa Abdallah the Queen of Clubs, and Abid Hamid Mahmud was the Ace of Diamonds (Saddam, of course, was the Ace of Spades). Headlines and articles such as the following, on CNN's website, were commonplace:

U.S. MILITARY HOLDING DR. GERM, MRS. ANTHRAX

The U.S. military says women are not held at the two prisons named—the notorious Abu Ghraib in Baghdad and Umm Qasr near Basra—cited by the group known as Unification and Jihad but has acknowledged it is holding two female "security prisoners" elsewhere.

They are Dr. Rihab Rashid Taha, a scientist whom some American officials called "Dr. Germ" for helping Iraq make weapons out of anthrax, and Huda Salih Mahdi Ammash, a biological weapons researcher known as "Mrs. Anthrax."

When the women were seized in May 2003, U.S. officials told CNN they were optimistic that Taha's apprehension would prove to be extremely significant, given the scope of her work with biological agents.

The article went on to note that Mrs. Anthrax was listed as "the five of hearts in the deck." It bears repeating that while these playing cards were prepared by the Bush administration, they were disseminated and used as tools to "report" on the situation in Iraq.

The term *propaganda* rings melodramatic and exaggerated, but a press that—whether from fear, careerism, or conviction—uncritically recites false government claims and reports them as fact, or treats elected officials with a reverence reserved for royalty, cannot be accurately described as engaged in any other function. The nation suffered from a profound failure of its journalistic institutions throughout the Bush presidency; a principal cause of that failure has been the intimidating Manichean framework, in which there exists no middle ground between fighting the terrorists on George Bush's terms or being one of them.

ANTIWAR "RADICALS"

Conventional Beltway wisdom now insists, as established fact, that with respect to the issue of Saddam's WMDs "everyone" was fooled. We were all—the president included—victimized by bad intelligence.

After all, the whole world thought Saddam had WMDs. Who, then, could blame the press or the president for favoring the war? That exculpatory position has become the prevailing orthodoxy of the political and media establishment, which sponsored and urged on this war and now seeks to excuse itself for having done so.

But the claim at the heart of this excuse-making is patently false. There most assuredly *were* individuals who were not fooled by "bad intelligence." They *questioned* the evidence presented as being sketchy and unconvincing, rather than blindly believing the administration's assertions. Others urged that the U.N. inspection process be allowed to verify the president's assurances that Saddam possessed WMDs. Moreover, many war opponents emphatically warned that invading Iraq would spawn uncontrollable violence and sectarian warfare, engulf the United States in a protracted and brutal occupation, and weaken the ability of the U.S. military to confront greater threats. They insisted that there was no connection between Saddam and the terrorists responsible for the 9/11 attacks, and they warned that waging war on Saddam would drain away resources vital to finding and apprehending the actual terrorists. War opponents insisted that there were far more urgent threats to U.S. security than a contained, weakened dictator who had never attacked the U.S., never threatened to attack the U.S., and lacked the capacity to do so.

But those anti-invasion views were barely acknowledged by the mainstream political and journalistic forces that controlled the terms of the prewar "debate," and when they were acknowledged, it was usually for the purpose of mocking and deriding them. Individuals who made such arguments—arguments that turned out to be *completely right, as a pure and demonstrable matter of fact*—were scorned and demonized by the all-knowing pundit class, by our nation's media stars, and by the president's core supporters. Because they opposed the president and his crusade against Evil, individuals urging caution and deliberation were weak and unserious; they were pacifistic, borderline subversive losers who, like the hippies in the generation before them, were not even worth listening to. Saddam was Evil and had to be stopped; and, by definition, no serious person could deny that. Those who did immediately stood revealed as fringe, radical figures who were at least indifferent to threats posed by the terrorists, if not actually on the terrorists' side.

One of the most prominent—and most pilloried—preinvasion opponents of the war was Howard Dean. Dean is a medical doctor and was the governor of Vermont, having been elected five consecutive times by the citizens of that state. During his ten years governing Vermont, Dean was best known for his extreme frugality with taxpayers' money and his unyielding refusal to present anything other than a perfectly balanced budget, which is what Vermont enjoyed for his entire governorship. He battled endlessly with the progressives of his state over his relentless budget cutting.

Dean was also one of the most favored political officials of the National Rifle Association due to his steadfast opposition to gun control laws—a view that was grounded in his unusually firm commitment to states' rights, i.e., if hunters in Vermont want to live without gun control but residents of a state with high urban crime rates (such as New York or California) want such restrictions, the autonomy of both states should be respected. Prior to becoming governor, Dean had a small-town medical practice, and he and his wife raised their two children in the Green Mountain State. Until he exploded onto the national political scene in 2002, Howard Dean had lived as a typical American, and there had been nothing *remotely* radical about him, his life, or anything he had said or done.

In 2002, Dean witnessed the entire country, the president's loyal supporters, the national media, and even a sizable bulk of Dean's own party, sycophantically joining in, or standing meekly by, as the president marched the country to a preemptive, offensive war against a sovereign country that had not attacked us. He saw that there was virtually no opposition to this war march, and almost no questioning of the president's highly precarious claims. Worse, there was little evident concern for both the foreseeable and unintended consequences of this invasion—a blithe indifference to what a physician would see as "side effects." As a result, this previously unremarkable doctor and always-mainstream, small-state governor stood up and objected to the uncritical national war dance. And he voiced these objections at a time when very few individuals of any political prominence were doing so.

Because of his questioning of the president's assertions and his opposition to Bush's insistence that we attack Iraq—and because his candidacy was consequently opposed to the entire war-supporting Beltway political and media establishment—Dean was immediately depicted as a wild-eyed, fringe radical who was so far "to the left" that he was even outside the mainstream ideological spectrum. Almost overnight, this moderate, completely nonideological figure became demonized—by Republicans, prowar Democrats, and the mindlessly Bush-adoring press—as some sort of unholy, unhinged mix of Ward Churchill, Joan Baez, and Fidel Castro. Dean was the new Abbie Hoffman, a freakish creature whose insanity and emotional instability were matched only by his rabid affection for socialism, Saddam Hussein, and Islamic terrorism. That vilification project proved so potent that even now when Dean has been proven *right* about virtually every geopolitical issue with respect to Iraq, the stigma persists today and will likely never be expunged from many minds.

The issues Dean raised in defending his objections to the war were of vital importance, yet they were barely discussed. Instead, those highly pragmatic concerns were steamrolled by Manichean depictions of the Evil Nazi-like terrorist dictator about to create mushroom clouds over American cities. Only those who were weak or indifferent to the fate of Americans would oppose invading Iraq. As a result, not only was Dean himself demonized, but the arguments he attempted to make—with the objective of galvanizing a debate that the country needed to have before embarking on such a dangerous war—were utterly distorted, caricatured, then safely ignored.

To review Dean's speeches against the war is to read, in essence, an almost exact roadmap of what has happened, a predictive list of the now-realized consequences of invading Iraq that have made it one of the worst strategic disasters in our nation's history. By stark and tragic contrast, those who pilloried Dean (and urged that we start a war with Iraq because of the threats posed by Dr. Germ and Mrs. Anthrax), those who scorned him as an unserious radical who was weak, naïve, and lacking even limited credibility, were wrong about virtually everything they predicted—not only about whether Saddam had WMDs but about the consequences of removing his regime.

As but one example of his prescience, Dean gave a speech at Drake

University in February 2003, a month before the invasion, in which he explained why he opposed the president's imminent decision to invade Iraq. Reviewing that speech, and similar ones, provides an abject lesson in the dangers of replacing free and rational debate with moralistic certainty and borderline-religious reverence for political leaders. Dean explained why he had spoken up:

> I am worried that many of the policies the Bush Administration is pursuing today do not provide the best means of defending our interests, and do not reflect the fundamental values of our people. . . . I would not be doing my job as a citizen if I did not state my own conviction about where I believe we could do better. . . . The stakes are so high, this is not a time for holding back or sheepishly going along with the herd.
>
> I believe it is my patriotic duty to urge a different path to protecting America's security: To focus on Al Qaeda, which is an imminent threat, and to use our resources to improve and strengthen the security and safety of our home front and our people while working with the other nations of the world to contain Saddam Hussein.
>
> Had I been a member of the Senate, I would have voted against the resolution that authorized the president to use unilateral force against Iraq—unlike others in that body now seeking the presidency.

Dean was a steadfast supporter of the invasion of Afghanistan. He thus opposed the war on Iraq *not* because he was opposed to use of the military to defend America, but precisely because invading Iraq would drain our military resources and thus *prevent* the use of the military to defend against actual, imminent threats. As Dean asked: "What happened to the war against Al Qaeda? Why has this Administration taken us so far off track?"

For Dean, it was never in doubt that Saddam was a brutal, homicidal tyrant. Nobody doubted that. As Dean readily acknowledged: "I agree with President Bush—he has said that Saddam Hussein is evil. And he is. He is a vicious dictator and a documented deceiver." But many dictators around the world have always been, are now, and always will be brutal, tyrannical, and evil. That Saddam was these things was beyond dispute, but not remotely sufficient to justify starting a war. A whole slew of other considerations—which the president and most of the media systematically ignored—compelled Dean to warn about the dangerous and ill-advised course the country was about to undertake:

> As a doctor, I was trained to treat illness, and to examine a variety of options before deciding which to prescribe. I worried about side effects and took the time to see what else might work before proceeding to high-risk measures.
>
> We have been told over and over again what the risks will be if we do not go to war.
>
> We have been told little about what the risks will be if we do go to war.
>
> If we go to war, I certainly hope the Administration's assumptions are realized, and the conflict is swift, successful and clean.
>
> I certainly hope our armed forces will be welcomed like heroes and liberators in the streets of Baghdad.
>
> I certainly hope Iraq emerges from the war stable, united, and democratic.
>
> I certainly hope terrorists around the world conclude it is a mistake to defy America and cease, thereafter, to be terrorists.
>
> It is possible, however, that events could go differently, and that the Iraqi Republican Guard will not sit out in the desert where they can be destroyed easily from the air. It is possible that Iraq will try to force our troops to fight house to house in the middle of cities—on its turf, not ours—where precision-guided missiles are of little use. . . .
>
> There are other risks.
>
> Iraq is a divided country, with Sunni, Shia, and Kurdish factions that share both bitter rivalries and access to large quantities of arms.
>
> Iran and Turkey each have interests in Iraq they will be tempted to protect with or without our approval. . . .
>
> And, perhaps most importantly, there is a very real danger that war in Iraq will fuel the fires of international terror.
>
> Anti-American feelings will surely be inflamed among the misguided who choose to see an assault on Iraq as an attack on Islam, or as a means of controlling Iraqi oil.
>
> And last week's tape by Osama bin Laden tells us that our enemies will seek relentlessly to transform a war into a tool for inspiring and recruiting more terrorists.

And while it became virtually heretical to question the administration's WMD warnings once General Colin Powell appeared before the U.N. with his war-justifying slide show, Dean remained insightfully skeptical:

> Secretary Powell's recent presentation at the UN showed the extent to which we have Iraq under an audio and visual microscope. Given that, I was impressed not by the vastness of evidence presented by the Secretary, *but rather by its sketchiness.*

And though Dean was depicted as an unserious, weak-willed pacifist who required a "permission slip" from the U.N. before he would even consider defending the United States, the opposite was true. Dean endorsed the right of America to act against imminent threats with or without U.N. approval. His point—almost never fairly presented or debated—was that there was *no need to incur the always mammoth risk of war or unleash its inevitable horrors,* given that the inspection process would reveal soon enough whether the intelligence touted by the president was really true, i.e., whether Saddam really did pose the threat which the president claimed compelled us to invade that country:

> Now, I am not among those who say that America should never use its armed forces unilaterally. In some circumstances, we have no choice. In Iraq, I would be prepared to go ahead without further Security Council backing if it were clear the threat posed to us by Saddam Hussein was imminent, and could neither be contained nor deterred.

That a person speaking in such language was transformed into a fringe, crazed, soft-on-defense socialist-leftist, and that his posture was distorted by our national press into a radical symbol of anti-American weakness, oozing spineless and even subversive indifference toward U.S. security, is a testament to the effectiveness with which the administration imposed a Manichean worldview as the national political orthodoxy.

This demonization of Dean as an out-of-the-mainstream radical was fueled not even so much by the content of Dean's opposition to the president as it was by his unapologetic *tone.* He became the leading war opponent at a time of the almost-unanimously and hastily passed Patriot Act, of anthrax attacks, a paramilitary presence in many of our nation's cities, Homeland Security alerts, and sky-high popularity ratings for Bush. Most Democrats were cowed into submission, virtually endorsing every Bush desire and offering only the meekest and most apologetic resistance when they resisted at all.

The president was no longer a mere public servant nor even still a politician. He became far more epic and glorious than that. He was the *Commander in Chief in a time of war*. And though the United States Constitution makes clear that the president is vested with that role only with respect to members of the armed forces—most assuredly *not* vis-à-vis American civilians—his supporters frequently insisted that to undermine Bush was to weaken the United States and to aid America's enemies. As Joe Lieberman once put it, "In matters of war, we undermine presidential credibility at our nation's peril." During the 2004 campaign, President Bush said that John Kerry's criticisms of the war in Iraq "can embolden an enemy." He thereafter warned, as he and his administration have emphasized many times, "In a time of war, we have a responsibility to show that whatever our political differences at home, our nation is united and determined to prevail."

Dean is but one prominent example of how rational debate in the United States over whether to invade Iraq was trampled on by the president's emotion-inducing sermons that the U.S. had been called to fight Evil. Jim Webb, the former Reagan secretary of the Navy and decorated Marine combat hero, was equally as prescient as Dean, and just as tenacious in the lead-up to the war in trying to induce a reasoned examination of the serious risks entailed in an invasion. In September 2002, Webb authored an op-ed in the *Washington Post* arguing vehemently against invading Iraq. As with Dean's speeches, it is striking just how right Webb was about virtually everything he warned of and it is tragic that his arguments were all but ignored by a war-hungry political and media elite, intoxicated by an exhilarating Manichean mission:

> Meanwhile, American military leaders have been trying to bring a wider focus to the band of neoconservatives that began beating the war drums on Iraq before the dust had even settled on the World Trade Center. Despite the efforts of the neocons to shut them up or to dismiss them as un-

qualified to deal in policy issues, these leaders, both active-duty and retired, have been nearly unanimous in their concerns.

Is there an absolutely vital national interest that should lead us from containment to unilateral war and a long-term occupation of Iraq? And would such a war and its aftermath actually increase our ability to win the war against international terrorism? . . .

America's best military leaders know that they are accountable to history not only for how they fight wars, but also for how they prevent them. The greatest military victory of our time—bringing an expansionist Soviet Union in from the cold while averting a nuclear holocaust—was accomplished not by an invasion but through decades of intense maneuvering and continuous operations. With respect to the situation in Iraq, they are conscious of two realities that seem to have been lost in the narrow debate about Saddam Hussein himself.

The first reality is that wars often have unintended consequences—ask the Germans, who in World War I were convinced that they would defeat the French in exactly 42 days. The second is that a long-term occupation of Iraq would beyond doubt require an adjustment of force levels elsewhere, and could eventually diminish American influence in other parts of the world.

Other than the flippant criticisms of our "failure" to take Baghdad during the Persian Gulf War, one sees little discussion of an occupation of Iraq, but it is the key element of the current debate. The issue before us is not simply whether the United States should end the regime of Saddam Hussein, but whether we as a nation are prepared to physically occupy territory in the Middle East for the next 30 to 50 years. Those who are pushing for a unilateral war in Iraq know full well that there is no exit strategy if we invade and stay. . . .

These concerns, and others like them, are the reasons that many with long experience in U.S. national security issues remain unconvinced by the arguments for a unilateral invasion of Iraq. Unilateral wars designed to bring about regime change and a long-term occupation should be undertaken only when a nation's existence is clearly at stake.

Every dangerous and costly consequence Webb warned of has come to fruition. Yet the tough-guy political and pundit classes arrogantly derided Webb's thoughtful, sophisticated, rational, and—as it turns out—

prescient analysis, notwithstanding his status as combat hero and military expert. Instead, those shrilly warning about Iraqi mushroom clouds detonating over our cities and offering rosy-eyed assurances about invading Iraq were deemed to be the serious, responsible, and strong national security leaders.

In a January 2007 hearing before the Senate Committee on Foreign Relations, the newly elected senator from Virginia, Jim Webb, reminded Robert Gates, President Bush's new defense secretary, how individuals who had warned of the tragic results that have come to pass in postinvasion and occupied Iraq were treated:

> I also want to say something about my longtime friend Senator McCain's comments when he was talking about the consequences of pulling out of Iraq and in your statement, Secretary Gates, you list some of these as an emboldened and strengthened Iran, a base of operations for jihadist networks in the heart of the Middle East, an undermining of the credibility of the United States. In many ways, quite frankly, those have been the results of the invasion and occupation.
>
> There's really nothing that's occurred since the invasion and occupation that was not predictable and in fact, most of it was predicted. *It was predicted in many cases by people with long backgrounds in national security . . . and in many cases there were people who saw their military careers destroyed and who were personally demeaned by people who opposed them on the issues, including members of this administration.* And they are people in my judgment, who will be remembered in history as having had a moral conscience [emphasis added].

Senator Webb's description of the consequences befalling critics prior to the invasion captures the *reason* the president was able to lead a largely passive country to war with virtually no meaningful consideration of the consequences and costs. Those who have been proven almost entirely wrong in their starry-eyed prognostications clung tightly to the president's Manichean sermonizing as a means for evading debate. The president was strong and Good and must be trusted. War opponents were demonized and dismissed as guilty, not only of poor judgment but also of poor character.

As the country struggles desperately to find a way to minimize the damage wrought by the catastrophe in Iraq, the same people who are responsible for convincing Americans of the wisdom of that invasion, through an endless series of monumental errors of judgment and debate-squelching campaigns against critics, continue to hold sway. That they were wrong about virtually everything prior to the invasion of Iraq has not diminished their status as wise foreign policy experts.

And the converse endures with equal strength. Those who were right about Iraq—specifically, war opponents and those who challenged and resisted the rhetoric and manipulative tactics of the president and his followers—are *still* treated by the political and journalistic establishment as unserious and "weak on defense" radicals who are unfit to be trusted with the national defense. The mere mention of the names Howard Dean or Nancy Pelosi or Russ Feingold or Barack Obama or even Jack Murtha in the context of national security debate provokes knowing and condescending smirks among many of the most influential members of the pundit class. Astoundingly, even now, only those eager to send the nation to war—and who launched the country on its strategically disastrous course in Iraq—retain sufficient cachet to pontificate credibly on national security matters.

Few people were as consistently prescient—or as viciously demonized—as Scott Ritter was. Back in September 2002, Ritter was telling anyone who would listen that there was no convincing evidence showing Iraq had WMDs. He is a former U.S. Marine officer and was a top aide to Gen. Norman Schwarzkopf during the first Gulf War against Iraq, when he had built a reputation as a tenacious weapons inspector working for the U.N. It is difficult to imagine someone with stronger credentials and credibility and thus whose views on Iraq's WMD program—or lack thereof—ought to have been seriously considered.

At the time George Bush and his loyal supporters were assuring Americans that Saddam unquestionably had WMDs and that an invasion of Iraq was urgent, Ritter was desperately warning his fellow citizens of the dangers. In the fall of 2002, Ritter went to Iraq in an effort to forge an agreement that would save his country from making a horrendous mistake, and while there he addressed the Iraqi Parliament, warning:

My country seems on the verge of making an historic mistake. . . . My government is making a case for war against Iraq that is built upon fear and ignorance, as opposed to the reality of truth and fact.

As someone who counts himself as a fervent patriot and a good citizen of the United States of America, I feel I cannot stand by idly, while my country behaves in such a fashion. . . .

We, the people of the United States, are told repeatedly that we face a grave and imminent risk to our national security from a combination of past irresponsible behavior on the part of Iraq and ongoing efforts by Iraq to reacquire chemical, biological, and nuclear weapons and long-range ballistic weapons . . . which have been banned since 1991 by a Security Council resolution.

The truth of the matter is that Iraq is not a sponsor of the kind of terror perpetrated against the United States on 11 September, and in fact is active in suppressing the sort of fundamentalist extremism that characterizes those who attacked the United States on that horrible day.

This is the truth, and once the American people become familiar with and accept this truth, the politics of fear will be defeated and the prospect of war between our two countries greatly diminished. . . .

The truth of the matter is that Iraq has not been shown to possess weapons of mass destruction, either in terms of having retained prohibited capability from the past, or by seeking to reacquire such capability today. . . .

Iraq must loudly reject any intention of possessing these weapons and then work within the framework of international law to demonstrate this is a reality.

The only way that Iraq can achieve this is with the unconditional return of U.N. weapons inspectors, allowing such inspectors unfettered access to sites inside Iraq in order to complete the disarmament tasks as set forth in Security Council resolutions. . . .

Except when television pundits were convened to smear Ritter's character and attack his credibility, the mainstream American press all but ignored these warnings. On January 26, 2003, CNN's Wolf Blitzer held a panel discussion about Ritter's war opposition. Ritter was not present, but Peter Beinart, the prowar editor of *The New Republic,* and Jonah Goldberg, the prowar pundit from *National Review*, were invited to urge the invasion of Iraq, mock Ritter's antiwar arguments, and hurl personal attacks at him.

In stark contrast to Ritter, neither of these young, great "experts" who were urging the country to war had any experience with the military, the weapons inspection process, or Iraq. Joining them were Democratic strategist Donna Brazile and *New York Post* columnist Robert George, whose level of expertise on these matters was equal to Beinart's and Goldberg's.

Blitzer began the segment by describing Ritter as "an outspoken critic of a possible war against Iraq [who] was arrested in 2001 for allegedly communicating over the Internet with an undercover police officer who was posing as a sixteen-year-old girl." His question for the panel: "Is Scott Ritter's credibility now destroyed?" Brazile's answer: "Absolutely. It shows that he has poor judgment." Blitzer was referring to Ritter's arrest almost two years earlier, which ended with a dismissal of the charges against him, charges that Ritter has always denied.

George then accused Ritter of having been paid "hundreds of thousands of dollars from Saddam Hussein's regime," so everyone could safely ignore anything Ritter said because he was Saddam's agent—"a pro-Saddam guy." George referred to a documentary Ritter had produced that was financed by an American citizen of Iraqi descent and that contended, correctly as it turns out, that the U.N. inspection process had "defanged" Iraq's weapons program. But war supporters deceitfully depicted Ritter's film as being financed by the Iraqi government and claimed that Ritter himself had been paid by Saddam—complete falsehoods, disgustingly deployed to smear the former Marine and then–war critic as an enemy agent.

Thus, with attacks on Ritter's loyalty and character carrying the day, his convincing arguments that the inspection process would demonstrate that Iraq possessed no WMDs could be and were easily ignored. Beinart followed George on the CNN panel and said about George's smears of Ritter: "Yes, I agree." He continued:

> I think that he didn't have any credibility to begin with. I mean, this is the guy who never really explained, as Jonah said, why he flipped a hundred and eighty degrees and became a Saddam mouthpiece. So for me it's irrelevant. I never listened to what he had to say on Iraq to begin with.

After the Great Iraq expert Beinart was done eviscerating Ritter's credibility, Goldberg announced, "[Y]es, I agree with everybody," and then added:

He's now just basically joined Pete Townsend on the Magic School Bus. . . . Pete Townsend of the Who has also been implicated in child porn and things of that nature. But as everybody said, Ritter's credibility, just on the basics of Iraq, was completely shot and now there's even less reason to listen to him.

The brilliant "analysis" of this expert panel thereby completed, Blitzer then decreed: "Let's move on now." Ritter's arguments did not require engagement because these panelists—intoxicated by war rhetoric, Manichean imperatives, and the smug sense of their own rightness—had pronounced the ex-Marine and U.N. weapons inspector utterly lacking in credibility. Literally in a matter of minutes on CNN, Ritter—one of the nation's preeminent experts on the subject of the Iraqi weapons program—was transformed by a television cast of know-nothing war cheerleaders into a grotesque cartoon, a pro-Saddam propagandist, a liar, a child molester, and an integrity-free subversive whose loyalty was very much in question.

That Ritter was right about everything he said, and Beinart, Goldberg, and company profoundly wrong means nothing. To this day, it is almost impossible to avoid hearing from Peter Beinart and Jonah Goldberg in the nation's most influential media outlets (Beinart was recently given a column in the *Washington Post* and *Time*, and Goldberg went on to become a twice-weekly columnist for the *Los Angeles Times*). If, however, one wants to know what Ritter thinks about, say, whether the nation should wage war on Iran, one would have to search for small niche magazines, obscure websites, or alternative weekly newspapers.

Indeed, to discern what the U.S. should do about the Middle East or any other complex, grave national security matter, the national media hears from Bill Kristol, Fred Barnes, Charles Krauthammer, Fred Kagan, Joe Lieberman, John McCain, Tom Friedman, Rudy Giuliani, Rich Lowry, Newt Gingrich, and all the other "serious" tough guys who may have been wrong about nearly everything they predicted about Iraq but who are held out as foreign policy sages who possess credibility on these questions—*still*. But under no circumstances should one heed Howard Dean, Jack Murtha, Scott Ritter, Nancy Pelosi, various antiwar groups (including antiwar paleoconservatives), or anyone of that ilk, because they remain "unserious" about national defense.

When assessing the catastrophe that has been wrought from our invasion of Iraq, one can draw a straight line from the "debates" beforehand—and to those who were presented as credible experts—to the incalculable damage that has been done. And those experts are still thought of as such today, because even though they were profoundly wrong, they were on the side of Good. And in a Manichean world, that is far more important.

NORMALIZATION OF WAR

The Bush presidency has fundamentally transformed the way we speak about our country and its responsibilities, entitlements, and role in the world. In reviewing the pre–Iraq War "debate" this country had both on television and in print, one of the most striking aspects in retrospect is the casual and even breezy tone with which America collectively discusses and thinks about *war* as a foreign policy option, standing inconspicuously next to all of the other options. There is really no strong resistance to it, little anguish over it, no sense that it is a supremely horrible and tragic course to undertake—and particularly to *start*. Gone almost completely from our mainstream political discourse is *horror* over war. The most one hears is some cursory and transparently insincere—almost bored—lip service to its being a "last resort."

There are probably numerous reasons for this. Many claim that the senseless Vietnam disaster instilled in Americans an exaggerated resistance to war, a refusal to recognize it as necessary even when it really was. Whether that is true or not, the wars the United States fought in the 1980s and 1990s seem to have led Americans to the opposite extreme. The wars fought by the Reagan administration were covert (in Central America) or absurdly easy and bloodless (in Grenada). But, in all likelihood, the first Persian Gulf war—the war that has come to be seen as the all-Good, pure war—most fully explains the erosion of America's resistance to war. It was the first fully managed, expertly staged televised war, and it made war seem like nothing more significant than killing bad people, the forces of Evil, by crisply zapping them from the sky with super high-tech, precision weaponry that risked nothing—war as video game, cheered on safely and clinically from a distance.

Presented in this manner, war enables us to feel the power and strength that comes from triumph with none of the costs (the fact that *war* is the word we use for almost everything—on terrorism, drugs, even poverty—has certainly helped to desensitize us to its invocation; if we wage wars on everything, how bad can they be?). The things that make war tragic and horrific have been whitewashed away. The American media almost never show truly graphic photos of carnage in Iraq. The Bush administration bars the photographing of American war coffins. And that is why the few truly brutal though commonplace events that were captured partially on film or video—Abu Ghraib or the Saddam hanging—resonated so strongly. We are able to forget or pretend that those things are the consequences of the wars we cheer except when we are forced to confront them.

In our political discourse, there is no longer a strong presumption against war. In fact, it is almost as though there is a reverse presumption—that we should proceed to wage wars on whatever countries we dislike or which are defying our orders in some way unless someone can find compelling reasons not to. The burden is now on those who would like not to engage in a series of endless wars to demonstrate why we should not. And much of the presumption stems from viewing the world through a Manichean lens—we are inherently Good; those who oppose us are, by definition, Evil; large numbers of civilian deaths in other countries are mere collateral damage that may be a regrettable though tolerable by-product; and there is therefore nothing that ought to constrain us from using our full strength to destroy the new Enemy of the moment. War now is merely another tool to achieve epic and glorious Manichean victory—selected not reluctantly but eagerly, at times even excitedly, and the choice to wage war—in many corners—seems to generate far less torment and sorrow than it does excitement and pulsating feelings of purpose and power.

During the 2004 presidential campaign, meaningful debate over the terrorism threat remained repressed by tactics of mockery and the still potent and pervasive Manichean mind-set. Presidential campaigns are one of the few occasions when the nation collectively concentrates its energies on debating critical political questions. Yet George Bush's 2004 victory was marked not by a triumph in political debate, but rather by the repeated invocation of Manichean slogans in order to preclude debate altogether.

Though John Kerry voted back in 2002 to authorize an invasion of Iraq, his campaign was grounded in the argument that the key to preventing terrorism lay not in invading and occupying countries which have not attacked us, but instead, in improving our intelligence-gathering capabilities, strengthening law enforcement cooperation with other countries, increasing counterterrorism resources, and solidifying border security. Kerry told the *New York Times Magazine* that endless warfare could not ever end the Evil of terrorism because terrorism is a *tactic* used to advance a political and religious ideology, and thus cannot be eradicated solely through the use of military force.

But Kerry's advocacy of an alternative course to Bush's failing militarism provoked wild controversy and great derision, from the Bush campaign as well as journalists and pundits across the ideological spectrum. Kerry's approach lacked—indeed, it rejected—the fulfilling, reassuring simplicity of cheering on wars. The Bush campaign and the tough-guy media pundits wildly distorted, then caricatured, and then scornfully laughed away Kerry's point; it provoked everything except a substantive response and meaningful debate about how best to handle terrorism: Oh, how hilarious—weak little John Kerry wants to treat terrorism like a law enforcement problem! He wants to protect against Al Qaeda attacks with police methods! He would "protect us" by serving subpoenas on Osama bin Laden! He wants to surrender to the terrorists and give them therapy! He only wants to defend America if he first gets a permission slip from the U.N. That is so so funny.

By contrast, the president repeatedly invoked moralistic tales to defend his position on Iraq and to depict those who opposed it as suffering from an indifference to Evil. During his 2004 acceptance speech at the Republican National Convention, Bush offered this "justification" for the invasion:

The people we have freed won't forget either. Not long ago, seven Iraqi men came to see me in the Oval Office. They had X's branded into their foreheads, and their right hands had been cut off, by Saddam Hussein's secret police, the sadistic punishment for imaginary crimes. During our emotional visit one of the Iraqi men used his new prosthetic hand to slowly write out, in Arabic, a prayer for God to bless America. *(Applause.)* I am proud that our country remains the hope of the oppressed, and the greatest force for good on this earth. *(Applause.)*

And even as Iraq spiraled out of control, and the core pretext used to invade that country had been entirely discredited, the president continued to insist that the war was justified because we were Good and were waging war against the Evil Terrorists. From the same speech:

> Others understand the historic importance of our work. The terrorists know. They know that a vibrant, successful democracy at the heart of the Middle East will discredit their radical ideology of hate. *(Applause.)* They know that men and women with hope and purpose and dignity do not strap bombs on their bodies and kill the innocent. *(Applause.)* The terrorists are fighting freedom with all their cunning and cruelty because freedom is their greatest fear—and they should be afraid, because freedom is on the march. *(Applause.)*

Manichean imperatives and rank fear-mongering similarly pervaded Dick Cheney's RNC speech:

> Just as surely as the Nazis during World War II and the Soviets during the Cold War, the enemy we face today is bent on our destruction.
>
> As in other times, we are in a war we did not start, and have no choice but to win. *(Applause.)*
>
> Firm in our resolve, focused on our mission, and led by a superb commander-in-chief, we will prevail. *(Applause.)*
>
> The fanatics who killed some three thousand of our fellow Americans may have thought they could attack us with impunity, because terrorists had done so previously.
>
> But if the killers of September eleventh thought we had lost the will to defend our freedom, they did not know America, and they did not know George W. Bush. . . . *(Applause.)*
>
> In Iraq, we dealt with a gathering threat and removed the regime of Saddam Hussein. *(Applause.)*

Seventeen months ago, he controlled the lives and fortunes of 25 million people. Tonight he sits in jail.

And, most of all, Cheney mocked Kerry for his weak—and implicitly effeminate—unwillingness to fight the Terrorists:

CHENEY: Even in this post-9/11 period, Senator Kerry doesn't appear to understand how the world has changed. He talks about leading a "more sensitive war on terror" . . . *(Laughter.)* . . . as though Al Qaeda will be impressed with our softer side. *(Laughter and applause.)* He declared at the Democratic convention that he will forcefully defend America after we have been attacked. My fellow Americans, we have already been attacked . . . *(Applause.)*

AUDIENCE: U.S.A. U.S.A. U.S.A. . . .

CHENEY: George W. Bush will never seek a permission slip to defend the American people.

That was, and still is, the essence of the Bush worldview—one either recognizes the grave threat posed by Evil and thus supports maximum militarism and war-making, or one fails to recognize the threat (or even supported Evil) by opposing such measures. There is simply no other alternative to full-scale war ostensibly against the Evil enemies—no matter the complexities or risks involved, the constraints on resources, or the superiority of war-avoiding alternatives.

Kerry's attempt to expand beyond those two choices was not merely rejected; it was not comprehended. In the prevailing dualistic framework, an "alternative course" to war against the evildoers can only be understood, *by definition,* to constitute surrender and to declare oneself an ally of the Terrorist.

In an extraordinary August 2006 column, longtime conservative George Will wrote that the Bush administration had "denied the obvious, that Kerry had a point." In defending (two years after the fact) Kerry's arguments about terrorism, Will specifically cited this:

In a candidates' debate in South Carolina (Jan. 29, 2004), Kerry said that although the war on terror will be "occasionally military," it is "primarily an intelligence and law enforcement operation that requires cooperation around the world."

Will was specifically responding to a Bush official who was anonymously quoted that week in *The Weekly Standard* expressing the typical tough-guy derision that has long been used to preclude meaningful debate about terrorism:

The idea that the jihadists would all be peaceful, warm, lovable, God-fearing people if it weren't for U.S. policies strikes me as not a valid idea. [Democrats] do not have the understanding or the commitment to take on these forces. It's like John Kerry. The law enforcement approach doesn't work.

In response to that quote, Will declared:

This farrago of caricature and non sequitur makes the administration seem eager to repel all but the delusional. But perhaps such rhetoric reflects the intellectual contortions required to sustain the illusion that the war in Iraq is central to the war on terrorism, and that the war, unlike "the law enforcement approach," does "work."

It is critical to note the circumstances in which Will argued that Kerry had been right about terrorism, and that the militaristic rhetoric of Bush followers with regard to terrorism consists of pure "caricature and non sequitur" which should "repel all but the delusional."

Two highly illustrative events were dominating the news that week: the intense, brutal (and ultimately unsuccessful) Israeli bombing campaign of Lebanon with the ostensible aim of eliminating the Hezbollah threat, and the announcement by the British government that it had disrupted a plot by Islamic extremists in England to blow up ten commercial jets over the Atlantic Ocean. Bush supporters were touting both events to underscore the necessity of waging war in the Middle East as a means for fighting terrorism, even though—as Will noted—they each proved exactly the opposite.

The president himself, as he always does whenever it comes to news of alleged terrorist plots, was excitedly hyping the dramatic "U.K. airline" plot to claim that it vindicated his approach to terrorism. During a brief press conference that week, the president argued:

The recent arrests that our fellow citizens are now learning about are a stark reminder that this nation is at war with Islamic fascists who will use any means to destroy those of us who love freedom, to hurt our nation.

Manichean war cries of this type are, as one would expect, politically effective. Glorious crusades to crush Evil with violence will always be more intuitively exciting and emotionally satisfying than less flamboyant means for defeating it. But in the case of terrorism, this mind-set is incoherent, dangerous, and—worst of all—entirely counterproductive, because nothing fuels the anti-America resentment at the heart of terrorism more than invasions and bombing campaigns in Muslim countries.

For that reason, such rhetoric ought to—as Will put it—"repel all but the delusional." After all, as Will noted in his column, the U.K. terrorist plot was disrupted *not* by invading other countries or dropping bombs on Middle Eastern neighborhoods, but through diligent, legal, and patient law enforcement efforts, i.e., the measures advocated by Kerry that prompted such mockery in the press:

> The London plot against civil aviation confirmed a theme of an illuminating new book, Lawrence Wright's *The Looming Tower: Al-Qaeda and the Road to 9/11*. The theme is that better law enforcement, which probably could have prevented Sept. 11, is central to combating terrorism. F-16s are not useful tools against terrorism that issues from places such as Hamburg (where Mohamed Atta lived before dying in the North Tower of the World Trade Center) and High Wycombe, England.
>
> Cooperation between Pakistani and British law enforcement (the British draw upon useful experience combating IRA terrorism) has validated John Kerry's belief (as paraphrased by the *New York Times Magazine* of Oct. 10, 2004) that "many of the interdiction tactics that cripple drug lords, including governments working jointly to share intelligence, patrol borders and force banks to identify suspicious customers, can also be some of the most useful tools in the war on terror."

The Bush administration and/or its supporters unabashedly exploit terrorist threats for political gain every time a new plot is revealed—no matter how serious or frivolous, how advanced or preliminary, the particular plot might be. Bush followers squeeze such events for every last drop of political gain they can. As the president stated when the U.K.

conspiracy was revealed, this was "a stark reminder that this nation is at war with Islamic fascists who will use any means to destroy those of us who love freedom." Put another way, the president's use of terrorist plots such as this one is designed to convey this message: Those who oppose my policies forget that there are Evil people in the world and these plots therefore show that I have been right all along.

But that argument is as incoherent as it is manipulative. Nobody doubts that there are Muslim extremists who would like to commit acts of violence against the United States and the West. No political disputes are premised, nor have they ever been premised, on a conflict over whether terrorism *exists* or whether it ought to be taken seriously. Nor does anyone of consequence doubt that terrorists are malicious and dangerous. Thus, events such as the U.K. plot reveal *what everyone already knows,* and do nothing to vindicate the Bush administration's militaristic foreign policy or its radical lawlessness at home.

Above all, the existence of Evil terrorists and the fact that some want to attack the United States certainly does nothing to vindicate the president's invasion of Iraq. Opposition to the war in Iraq is not and never was based upon the premise that no terrorist threat exists. Among other arguments, it was based on the premise that the invasion of Iraq *undermines,* rather than *strengthens,* the American campaign to protect itself against terrorism.

Most of the participants in the U.K. bomb conspiracy were British citizens, born in England. They had nothing to do with Iraq or Saddam Hussein or Iranian mullahs or the ruling Assad family in Syria. They were motivated by hatred for the United States, hatred which could not possibly be anything other than *inflamed,* and certainly not diffused, as a result of watching the U.S. attack a sovereign oil-rich country filled with Muslim holy sites. The ongoing occupation of Iraq spawns daily video of corpses of Muslim children, pictures of bombed marketplaces, and tales of American abuses against Muslims inside torture prisons formerly used by Saddam Hussein. All of that is continuously broadcast by Al Jazeera and other Middle East media outlets. That such conduct by the U.S. would heighten the risk of terrorism and spread Islamic radicalism is self-evident.

The president and his supporters love to speak of Osama bin Laden

and his terrorist allies as hiding in fear of the president's militarism—
or even hoping that Democrats win elections because terrorists so dislike George Bush's war-making. Yet the exact opposite is true. Nothing
has aided the cause of Islamic terrorism more than George Bush's brutal
and endless acts of aggression in the Middle East; nothing has ignited
the fuel of terrorism—anti-American anger—more than that. And it is
hard to imagine a more ardent fan of the president's embrace of a Manichean worldview than Osama bin Laden, who shares that Manichean
mentality and expressly sought, with the 9/11 attacks, to provoke exactly
the split between the U.S. and the Muslim world that the Bush policies
have wrought. As James Fallows reported in a 2006 article in *The Atlantic Monthly:*

> Documents captured after 9/11 showed that bin Laden hoped to provoke
> the United States into an invasion and occupation that would entail all
> the complications that have arisen in Iraq. His only error was to think
> that the place where Americans would get stuck would be Afghanistan.
>   Bin Laden also hoped that such an entrapment would drain the
> United States financially. Many al-Qaeda documents refer to the impor-
> tance of sapping American economic strength as a step toward reducing
> America's ability to throw its weight around in the Middle East.

The more military and intelligence resources we are forced to pour
into waging wars against countries that have not attacked us—Iraq has
consumed the vast bulk of American military force, intelligence resources,
and political attention, to say nothing of its financial drain—the weaker
we become, the *less able* we are to track and combat Al Qaeda and the
other terrorist groups that actually seek to harm us. Turning Iraq into a
chaotic caldron of anarchy and violence filled with seething anger toward
the United States is exactly the environment in which Al Qaeda thrives.

Other than the very rare circumstance where there is a state that is
actively aiding a terrorist group devoted to attacks on the U.S.—as the
Taliban government in Afghanistan was aiding Al Qaeda—conventional
war-making as a tool to combat terrorism is entirely *counterproductive.*
War cannot possibly have any effect on anti-American Islamic fanati-
cism other than to *inflame, increase, and strengthen* it.

And, indeed, by the beginning of January 2007, it became almost universally recognized that the threat posed by the terrorists was *not* a justification for invading Iraq; rather, that threat was an argument *against* doing so. In January 2007, *Newsweek*'s Mike Isikoff reported:

> Intel director John Negroponte gave Congress a sobering assessment last week of the continued threats from groups like Al Qaeda and Hizbullah. But even gloomier comments came from Henry Crumpton, the outgoing State Department terror coordinator. An ex-CIA operative, Crumpton told *Newsweek* that a worldwide surge in Islamic radicalism has worsened recently, increasing the number of potential terrorists and setting back U.S. efforts in the terror war. "Certainly, we haven't made any progress," said Crumpton. "In fact, we've lost ground." He cites Iraq as a factor; the war has fueled resentment against the United States.

That assessment merely confirmed a prior, definitive report *from the Bush administration*, described by the *New York Times* in September 2006:

> A stark assessment of terrorism trends by American intelligence agencies has found that the American invasion and occupation of Iraq has helped spawn a new generation of Islamic radicalism and that the overall terrorist threat has grown since the Sept. 11 attacks.
>
> The classified National Intelligence Estimate [NIE] attributes a more direct role to the Iraq war in fueling radicalism than that presented either in recent White House documents or in a report released Wednesday by the House Intelligence Committee, according to several officials in Washington involved in preparing the assessment or who have read the final document.
>
> The intelligence estimate, completed in April, is the first formal appraisal of global terrorism by United States intelligence agencies since the Iraq war began, and represents *a consensus view of the 16 disparate spy services inside government* [emphasis added]. Titled "Trends in Global Terrorism: Implications for the United States," it asserts that Islamic radicalism, rather than being in retreat, has metastasized and spread across the globe.
>
> The report "says that the Iraq war has made the overall terrorism problem worse," said one American intelligence official.

Numerous sources had told the *Times* about the contents of the NIE, which "are the most authoritative documents that the intelligence community produces on a specific national security issue, and are approved by John D. Negroponte, director of national intelligence." Thus, these conclusions emanated from the Bush administration, and are the consensus of the same intelligence community that the administration had spent the last several years purging of all dissidents.

Fueling the Engine of Terrorism

The most effective weapon wielded by George Bush for bludgeoning any possibility of rational debate has been the all-purpose, all-justifying label *terrorist*. Despite the ongoing existence of a serious terrorist threat, that term has been so crassly and transparently manipulated for political purposes by the president and his supporters that it has become virtually impoverished of real meaning.

Throughout the 2004 presidential election, the Bush campaign endlessly wielded this rhetorical tactic by defining the Iraqi insurgents not as Iraqis resisting foreign occupation but as "terrorists." With that premise in place, those who favored the war in Iraq *by definition* favored fighting the terrorists, while those who opposed the war *by definition* wanted to "surrender" to the terrorists—and as a result, real debate over the war, as intended, became impossible. After all, terrorists are the people who flew those planes into our buildings. Who could oppose waging war on them—the terrorists?

But once safely re-elected, the president in 2005 gave one of the types of speeches he delivers periodically that seems designed to pass along to Americans the tutorial he received about what is going on in Iraq. In doing so, he clearly acknowledged that the vast, vast majority of people whom we are fighting in Iraq are not terrorists at all, but merely Sunni "rejectionists" who favor a system of government that preserves long-standing Sunni privileges:

> A clear strategy begins with a clear understanding of the enemy we face. The enemy in Iraq is a combination of rejectionists, Saddamists, and terrorists. The rejectionists are by far the largest group. These are ordinary Iraqis, mostly Sunni Arabs, who miss the privileged status they had under the regime of Saddam Hussein—and they reject an Iraq in which they are no longer the dominant group.

The president is right, of course, that "a clear strategy begins with a clear understanding of the enemy we face." That is precisely why the constant invocation of "fighting terrorists" as a justification for invading Iraq was such a deceitful rhetorical tool, and it is why America was led so astray. Astonishingly, even into 2007, war supporters continue to manipulate the terrorist threat in brazenly dishonest ways in order to justify their conduct. Joe Lieberman appeared on *Meet the Press* after the president's January 2007 "surge" speech, looked into the cameras, and told Americans:

> I think the consequences for the Middle East, which has been so important to our international stability over the years, and to the American people, *who have been attacked on 9/11 by the same enemy that we're fighting in Iraq today,* supported by a rising Islamist radical super-powered government in Iran, the consequences for us, for—I want to be personal—for my children and grandchildren, I fear will be disastrous. That's why I want to do everything I can to win in Iraq [emphasis added].

By January 2007, it was unfathomable to hear anyone telling Americans that in Iraq we were fighting "the same enemy" who perpetrated the 9/11 attacks. As the president himself acknowledged two years earlier, the anti-U.S. insurgency is composed predominantly of Iraqis who want to eject the United States from their country. And the civil war that has been raging in Iraq has been a sectarian conflict between Iraqi Shiites and Sunnis. Yet Senator Lieberman knows that this sort of deceitful rhetoric has successfully precluded rational debate about our country's most pressing issues, and he thus continues to cling to the hope that Manichean invocations of the terrorists will obscure the catastrophe that he and his Bush-supporting comrades have unleashed.

But there is, at long last, a growing recognition that waging more wars does not make us stronger or more secure. It does exactly the opposite. Those who want to pursue our failed policy in Iraq indefinitely or who want to attack more countries are not people who are "strong on security." They are gradually, though inexorably, destroying our security through a mindless militarism that becomes more reckless and crazed the more it fails. And this bloodthirsty militarism becomes more desperate as the sense of weakness and humiliation felt by its proponents—including those in the White House—intensifies.

If George Will can announce that John Kerry was right about how best to deal with terrorism and that the Bush approach does nothing but exacerbate it, then perhaps we can soon reach the point where national journalists will understand that there is nothing "strong" or "serious" about clamoring for more and more wars. Nor is there anything "weak" about opposing warmongering and instead advocating more substantive, rational, and responsible methods for combating terrorism.

Anyone rational can see that our invasion of Iraq did not make us more secure. Nor will attacking Syria and/or Iran or fueling more proxy wars in the Middle East make us any safer. Quite plainly, those measures have had, and will continue to have, the opposite effect. Meanwhile, we neglect the genuinely effective methods for protecting against terrorism because those methods are boring and unappealing and unexciting to the increasingly crazed neoconservative warriors looking for militaristic glory and slaughter for its own sake. Untold benefits will accrue if journalists can finally understand that whatever adjectives accurately describe such individuals, "strong" is not one of them.

The Manichean cartoons that overrode virtually all substantive and responsible debate during the Bush presidency obscured a fundamental contradiction at the heart of the president's approach to the world. Since the 9/11 attacks, the president has insisted upon two fundamentally inconsistent propositions, namely, that (a) we are called upon to spread democracy, because doing so is morally right, consistent with God's will, and an effective tool for eradicating terrorism, and (b) the imperative of the first proposition is so overwhelming that we pursue it regardless of international objections or world opinion.

Let us stipulate that this second principle is valid—i.e., that if a country is forced to choose between taking measures to protect its citizens or being popular in the world, its leaders have the obligation to choose the former over the latter. If there is but one way that a country can defend itself from external threats, negative world opinion engendered by such a course is an insufficient reason to forgo it. That is true not only for the United States, of course, but for all countries. A government's first obligation is to protect its citizens from genuine dangers posed by others, not to protect its international reputation. At a very high level of generality, that is all fair enough.

But in the specific case of the moralistic imperatives underlying the Bush worldview of national security, the twin pillars of that approach are plainly, and quite dangerously, in conflict. To spread democracy around the world, while at the same time inflaming anti-Americanism, is the very model of self-defeating behavior.

In December 2006, Venezuela's president Hugo Chávez was overwhelmingly re-elected. Opposition to the United States played a significant role in his successful campaign. According to the Associated Press account of Chávez's victory, Chávez repeatedly promised "a more radical version of socialism and [to] forge a wider front against the United States in Latin America." Chávez is one of the most anti-American leaders on the planet. He made world headlines months earlier when, during a speech before the United Nations and in violation of all diplomatic decorum, he referred to President Bush as Satan while pantomiming that he was waving away the smell of sulfur left by Bush, who had addressed the General Assembly from the same podium the day before. Chávez's flamboyant, indecorous attack on the U.S. president obviously did not impede his electoral prospects. To the contrary, his resolute anti-American rhetoric almost certainly bolstered his popularity among his citizens.

Over the last two years, anti-American factions, including those whom the president has identified as "terrorist groups," have become increasingly popular in their countries—even ascending to power as a result of victories in the precise democratic elections which the Bush administration worked to bring about. The Palestinians democratically elected Hamas leaders. The Lebanese have elected Hezbollah to play a major role in their parliamentary government. The Iranian-allied militias in Iraq are substantially represented in the democratically elected Iraqi government, and the so-called Iranian Hitler, the stridently anti-American president Mahmoud Ahmadinejad, was himself democratically elected.

If the leaders whom we are supposed to hate so much—including even those we are told are the terrorists—continue to be elected democratically, that fact would seem to negate the ostensible premise of the

Bush foreign policy—namely, that America-loving allies will magically spring up all over the democratic world and help us fight terrorism.

More to the point, it is infinitely more likely that anti-American leaders will continue to be democratically elected if the U.S. persists in conduct seemingly designed to make much of the world resentful and suspicious of us. If we operate on the premise, as we have during the Bush presidency, that we must not be concerned with world opinion (as the president defiantly boasted during the 2004 State of the Union speech: "America will never seek a permission slip to defend the security of our country"), and if we continue to insist that our Crusade against Evil is so righteous and necessary that we are entitled to set our own rules, violate long-standing treaties, and trample on conventions we have long touted, then intense anti-Americanism is simply inevitable.

It is, after all, basic human nature for a person to become resentful toward those who explicitly and even boastfully disdain his opinions and concerns. And when arrogant behavior of that sort is systematically engaged in by a country that is the strongest military force on Earth—and therefore is incapable of being restrained—that antipathy will be exacerbated by magnitudes. Resentment by the weak toward the strong is also a natural human reaction, but it can be constrained and managed, even virtually eliminated, when strength is used responsibly and in accordance with agreed-upon principles. But when the strongest applies its strength to impose its will without regard either to the viewpoints of others or to any set of recognized conventions and norms, resentment will be at its maximum peak of intensity.

The results of this imperial mind-set are as predictable as they are threatening to U.S. security. The BBC's World Service commissioned a worldwide survey of attitudes toward twelve major nations, and its findings, released in March 2007, revealed the following:

> Israel, Iran and the United States were the countries with the most negative image in a globe-spanning survey of attitudes toward 12 major nations. Canada and Japan came out best in the poll, released Tuesday. . . .
>
> Israel was viewed negatively by 56 percent of respondents and positively by 17 percent; for Iran, the figures were 54 percent and 18 percent.

The United States had the third-highest negative ranking, with 51 percent citing it as a bad influence and 30 percent as a good one. Next was North Korea, which was viewed negatively by 48 percent and positively by 19 percent.

American standing in the world under the Bush presidency has tumbled so drastically that we are now sandwiched between Iran and North Korea in terms of how the world perceives us.

If the United States continues to be overtly belligerent and essentially indifferent to world opinion, then pro-American candidates will increasingly have difficulty getting elected anywhere in the world, thereby subverting the central goal we claim we have of eliminating anti-American resentment by spreading democracy. The president's homage to democracy has obscured this destructive contradiction at the heart of our national conduct since 2001. Certainly many additional issues account for Chávez's support in Venezuela, Hamas' electoral victory among the Palestinians, etc., but those whose foreign policy vision consists of alienating our allies, changing other countries' governments at will, and invading whomever we want should not really be that surprised when anti-American sentiment is a potent campaign tool.

Independently, engaging in such resentment-inducing behavior is almost certain to fuel the extremist beliefs that motivated the 9/11 attackers. Consider the president's own explanation for why 9/11 occurred: "anger and resentment grew, radicalism thrived, and terrorists found willing recruits." Similarly, the president himself said in a September 2006 interview with the *Wall Street Journal*'s Paul Gigot: "But in the long run the only way to make sure your grandchildren are protected, Paul, is to win the battle of ideas, is to defeat the ideology of hatred and resentment."

The president's own premises demonstrate that policies which alienate most human beings on the planet and inflame hatred toward the United States—such as invading and bombing other countries or making a flamboyant showing that the U.S. can and will do whatever it wants regardless of world opinion—seem guaranteed to exacerbate the threat of terrorism like virtually nothing else could.

Of course, this contradiction disappears if all we really mean by "democracy" is a country run by leaders who obey America's dictates even if their power has nothing to do with elections. And whatever it is that is driving our foreign policy, a premium on democracy does not seem, in reality, to be high on the list, given that some of our most important allies (Pakistan, Saudi Arabia, Egypt, Jordan, the UAE, arguably China) are profoundly undemocratic, while some of our worst enemies and even some of the "terrorist enemies" themselves have been democratically elected. But one thing that ought to be clear is that democratic elections do *not* inherently produce governments friendly to the U.S.

Numerous other irrational and even internally contradictory premises were simply overlooked, by consensus, during the war intoxication that drove the country to support invading Iraq. The Middle East is characterized by centuries-old conflicts, sectarian factions, and competing interests, yet all of that was dismissed by the president's simplistic embrace of the moralistic premise that Saddam was Evil and therefore had to be destroyed.

Iran, for instance, has long been the prime enemy of Iraq, and is now routinely cited by the president himself as the greatest threat to peace in the region, if not the world. Yet in the 1980s, Iraq and Iran waged vicious war for eight years, and they served to contain each other's regional ambitions. The greatest impediment to increased Iranian power was the Ba'athist regime in Iraq—the one that George Bush, driven by a moralistic mission rather than geopolitical considerations, removed. Predictably, as *Time*'s Joe Klein reported:

> The U.S. "has been Iran's very best friend," a diplomat from a predominantly Sunni nation told me recently. "You have eliminated its enemies, the Taliban and Saddam Hussein. You have even reduced yourselves as a threat to Iran because you have spent so much blood and treasure in Iraq."

Moreover, the Shiite Iraqi government that our military has fought to install and then protect has developed, as one would expect, extremely close ties with the Iranian government. Thus, we are essentially fighting *for* Iran. And the longer we stay and the more we fight and drain all of our resources in order to stabilize the Iraqi government, the more we promote the interests of the country that the administration now says is the greatest threat to American interests. Every time the administration or its supporters talk about the dangers posed by Iran, it ought to be immediately pointed out that nothing has strengthened Iran more than our invasion of Iraq.

It may not be entirely accurate to say that Iran is the *sole* beneficiary of our invasion of Iraq, since there may be one other. As Thomas Ricks reported in the *Washington Post* in September 2006:

> The chief of intelligence for the Marine Corps in Iraq [Peter Devlin] recently filed an unusual secret report concluding that the prospects for securing that country's western Anbar province are dim and that there is almost nothing the U.S. military can do to improve the political and social situation there, said several military officers and intelligence officials familiar with its contents. . . .
>
> One Army officer summarized it as arguing that in Anbar province, "We haven't been defeated militarily but we have been defeated politically—and that's where wars are won and lost." . . .
>
> Devlin reports that there are no functioning Iraqi government institutions in Anbar, leaving a vacuum that has been filled by the insurgent group al-Qaeda in Iraq, which has become the province's most significant political force, said the Army officer, who has read the report.

Al Qaeda thrives in anarchy. By throwing Iraq into chaos—about which our own military says: "there is almost nothing the U.S. military can do to improve the political and social situation there"—we have transformed Iraq from a place where Al Qaeda could not operate into territory plagued by the very anarchy in which it thrives. Put another way, the two largest beneficiaries of this war—likely the only two—are Iran and Al Qaeda.

So, to recap the Iraq War: There were never any WMDs. The proliferation of government death squads and militias in Iraq means that, even compared to the Saddam era, human rights violations and torture have increased to record levels. Iranian influence has risen massively, as a result of a Shiite fundamentalist government loyal to Tehran replacing the former anti-Iranian regime. Iraq was a country in which Al Qaeda could never operate, but now it holds virtually free rein over large swaths of that country. We have squandered hundreds of billions of dollars and thousands of lives. At least tens of thousands, and more likely hundreds of thousands, of innocent Iraqis have died as a result of our invasion. And we have—according to the consensus of our own intelligence community—directly worsened the terrorist problem, and continue to exacerbate it with our ongoing occupation. But those who objected to the war plans on the ground that it would result in precisely these outcomes were demonized as weak-willed allies of Evil and thus ignored.

BUSH'S MANICHEAN PRISON

A s the course the country has embarked upon in Iraq has yielded unmitigated disaster, the president's response, as examined in the prior chapter, is to redouble his commitment to that failed course. Even as the American electorate, the Washington Establishment (in the form of the Baker-Hamilton Commission/the Iraq Study Group), and even members of his own party urge him to re-examine and abandon the mind-set that has led the United States into this debacle, Bush insists that he was right all along and that he is more certain than ever that this is so.

Even as it became evident that our occupation of Iraq was a disaster, that that country was spiraling out of control and descending into uncontrollable chaos and civil war, the president continuously denied that reality, because it conflicted with his morally grounded convictions of the rightness of the invasion. Rather than accept facts that conflicted with his beliefs, he instead repeatedly blamed the media for distorting the situation in Iraq or even exaggerating the violence there. As early as October 2003, at a press appearance with the president of Kenya, President Bush began insisting that the situation in Iraq was better than it appeared from media reports:

> And, listen, we're making good progress in Iraq. Sometimes it's hard to tell it when you listen to the filter. We're making good progress. . . . The situation is improving on a daily basis inside Iraq. People are freer, the security situation is getting better. The infrastructure is getting better— the schools are opening, the hospitals are being modernized.

In one illustrative December 2005 press conference, Bush insisted, in the face of all evidence to the contrary, "This is quiet, steady progress. It doesn't always make the headlines in the evening news. But it is real and it is important. And it is unmistakable to those who see it close up."

In March 2006, as the civil war was exploding in full force, Donald Rumsfeld, during a Pentagon press briefing, accused the media of exaggerating the situation in Iraq:

> From what I've seen thus far, much of the reporting in the U.S. and abroad has exaggerated the situation, according to General Casey. . . . The number of attacks on mosques, as he pointed out, had been exaggerated. The number of Iraqi deaths had been exaggerated.

Once the president's party was voted out of the majority in Congress in 2006 due largely to the chaos in Iraq, the White House still persisted in this bizarre reality-denying exercise, even sending out Laura Bush to make the same claim on television: "I do know that there are a lot of good things that are happening that aren't covered. And I think that the drumbeat in the country from the media, from the only way people know what is happening is discouraging."

In fact, reports about Iraq were not excessively gloomy and pessimistic. The exact opposite was true. It was the administration which routinely distorted what was occurring in Iraq in order to prevent a recognition— on the part of the American public, the media, and perhaps even the president himself—of just how dire the situation there was. As the Iraq Study Group (ISG) documented in 2006:

> In addition, there is significant underreporting of the violence in Iraq. The standard for recording attacks acts as a filter to keep events out of reports and databases. . . . For example, on one day in July 2006 there were 93 attacks or significant acts of violence reported. Yet a careful review of the reports for that single day brought to light 1,100 acts of violence. Good policy is difficult to make when information is systematically collected in a way that minimizes its discrepancy with policy goals.

In an October 2006 interview with Fox's Sean Hannity, the president expressly stated that, for him, the war in Iraq is not mere policy, and is not a matter confined to geopolitical considerations. Instead, it is the centerpiece of the Manichean battle to which he has devoted himself:

BUSH: But, Sean, this is an ideological standoff between those of us who like liberty and freedom and have, you know, support a hopeful phi-

losophy versus extremists and radicals who, you know, hate everything we stand for. And this is going to be a long struggle. . . .

HANNITY: Is this a struggle literally between good and evil?

BUSH: I think it is.

HANNITY: This is what it is? Do you think most people understand that?
I mean, when you see the vacillating poll numbers, does it discour-
age you in that sense?

BUSH: Well, first of all, you can't make decisions on polls, Sean. You've
got to do what you think is right. The reason I say it's good versus
evil is that evil people kill innocent life to achieve political objectives. And that's what Al Qaeda and people like Al Qaeda do.

In the September 2006 interview he sat for with various right-wing
pundits, the president, according to *National Review*'s Rich Lowry and
Kate O'Beirne, emphasized: "A lot of people in America see this as a
confrontation between good and evil, including me." As Lowry wrote
subsequent to that interview:

Bush's faith in the rightness of his strategy in the broader war is deep-
seated—it is, indeed, a product of faith. "Freedom is universal," Bush
says. "And I recognize there's a debate around the world about the kind
of—whether that principle is real. I call it moral relativism, if people do
not believe that certain people can be free. I mean, I just cannot subscribe
to that. People—I know it upsets people when I ascribe that to my belief
in an Almighty, and that I believe a gift from that Almighty is universal
freedom. That's what I believe."

For the president, the war in Iraq specifically, and the war to install
democracy generally, is not a strategy subject to re-examination because
it is grounded in, and compelled by, the inerrant will of God and by the
mission that both Bush and the nation have been "called" to fulfill. As
he said in his 2004 State of the Union address:

God has planted in every human heart the desire to live in freedom. And
even when that desire is crushed by tyranny for decades, it will rise again.
(Applause.) . . . America is a nation with a mission, and that mission
comes from our most basic beliefs.

The president has repeatedly described the commitment to wage war in
order to bring democracy to the world not merely in terms of a strategy

to make America safe but also as a "calling"—the evangelical term for God's planned purpose for an individual or a country. In his 2004 speech at the Republican National Convention, the president stated his views as follows:

> I believe that America is called to lead the cause of freedom in a new century. I believe that millions in the Middle East plead in silence for their liberty. I believe that given the chance, they will embrace the most honorable form of government ever devised by man. I believe all these things because freedom is not America's gift to the world, it is the almighty God's gift to every man and woman in this world. *(Applause.)*

It is simply extraordinary that the president is committed to the continuation of a war not merely because it is purportedly in America's national interest, but more so, because the war and the goals he is pursuing are compelled by God's will, because Bush is, in essence, a warrior delivering God's gift of freedom to the world. The role of the U.S. president, traditionally and properly, is to use the force of the U.S. government to advance American interests in the world, not to follow a perceived "calling" from God to do Good in the world. That foundational principle led to this 2004 exchange between Mike Wallace and Bob Woodward on *60 Minutes:*

> **WOODWARD:** The president still believes, with some conviction, that this was absolutely the right thing, that he has the duty to free people, to liberate people, and this was his moment.
>
> **WALLACE:** Who gave George Bush the duty to free people around the world?
>
> **WOODWARD:** That's a really good question. The Constitution doesn't say that's part of the commander-in-chief's duties.
>
> **WALLACE:** The president of the United States, without a great deal of background in foreign policy, makes up his mind and believes he was sent by somebody to free the people, not just in Iraq, but around the world?
>
> **WOODWARD:** That's his stated purpose.
>
> **WALLACE:** Right.
>
> **WOODWARD:** It is far-reaching and ambitious, and I think will cause many people to tremble.

The president received a stinging rebuke in the form of the 2006 election disaster for the Republican Party. And the isolation he suffered became even more pronounced when the ISG shortly thereafter strongly repudiated the president's approach in Iraq. In the aftermath of those humiliations, many seemed to expect the president humbly to acknowledge error, or at least to concede that the United States must gradually search for a way to extricate itself from Iraq. But for the president, re-examination of his Manichean premises is, by definition, not an option, and he thus reacted wholly opposite to normal expectations—he re-emphasized his commitment to his war and even committed to escalation. That the president would never change course was placed further beyond doubt when Vice President Cheney appeared on Fox News on January 14, 2007, and proclaimed about Iraq, "We've made enormous progress."

And thus the president stands, widely repudiated across the political spectrum, yet more convinced than ever of the rightness of his actions and entirely steadfast in his rejection of change. On January 14, 2007, the Associated Press described the president's rigid commitment to his failed policies as follows:

> President Bush once said he was determined to stick with the Iraq war even if his wife and his dog were the only ones left at his side.
>
> It's moving in that direction.
>
> "He is as isolated as a president can be," said Julian Zelizer, a political historian at Boston University.

When a president makes foreign policy decisions based not upon strategic calculations or prudential considerations, but instead upon Manichean, moral imperatives, then he is precluded from re-examination and change. With two years left in office, the president is an isolated and intensely unpopular president. Yet the war in Iraq rages on, and will continue to do so, at least until he leaves office, because the president's core convictions allow no other course.

CHAPTER FOUR

Iran: The Next War?

President Mahmoud Ahmadinejad said on Friday Iran should not show weakness over its nuclear program, a day after Tehran ignored a United Nations deadline to stop nuclear work which the West says could be used for making bombs.

"If we show weakness in front of the enemy the expectations will increase but if we stand against them, because of this resistance, they will retreat."

—**REUTERS,** February 23, 2007

"Today, it should be clear that not only is weakness provocative," Mr. Rumsfeld said, standing at a lectern with President Bush and Vice President Dick Cheney at his side, "but the perception of weakness on our part can be provocative as well. . . .

"A conclusion by our enemies that the United States lacks the will or the resolve to carry out missions that demand sacrifice and demand patience is every bit as dangerous as an imbalance of conventional military power," Mr. Rumsfeld said in a buoyant but sometimes emotional speech.

—**NEW YORK TIMES,** on former secretary of defense Donald Rumsfeld's farewell speech to the Pentagon, December 15, 2006

The simplistic and moralistic Bush mind-set—by which even the most vexing problems and complex conflicts are reduced to a contest of "strength" in the face of Evil—can perhaps be seen most clearly in the president's treatment of Iran. Throughout 2006, the president's Iran policy became mindlessly antagonistic, and was reduced eventually to the point where it was shaped by a handful of absolutist and moralistic premises which bordered on the cartoonish. Bush's perspective amounts to this:

Iran is governed by Evil leaders. They are the moral and practical equivalent of Hitler's Nazis. They are intent on regional, perhaps even world, domination. They are so insane and so Evil that they will attack other countries with nuclear weapons even if it means that they would then be annihilated. Particularly if they acquire nuclear weapons, they would pose a grave, imminent, and undeterrable threat to the United States. Their leaders do not fear death, and in fact crave it as a result of their religious extremism. They cannot be negotiated with because they are both Evil and deranged. The only feasible course of action with Iran is to treat it as a Nazi-like enemy, refuse to negotiate, and stop it by any means necessary, which—due to its leaders' inability to be reasoned with—inevitably requires "regime change," by military confrontation if necessary.

With those premises bolted into place, the Bush administration has transformed what was—especially after the 9/11 attacks—a rapidly improving and cooperative relationship with the Iranians into a bellicose chest-beating exercise whereby the likelihood of military confrontation of some sort becomes increasingly likely every day. The two-dimensional Good vs. Evil framework that the president has applied to a complex and diverse Iran leaves virtually no other alternative.

Throughout 2006, it was unclear whether the president's increasingly antagonistic rhetoric toward Iran was a political ploy to satiate his warmongering political base or whether, notwithstanding our incapacitating occupation of Iraq, the president himself really believed that war with Iran might be inevitable. But the 2006 midterm elections did not put an end to the president's militarism toward the Iranians. Quite the contrary, once the elections were over—and even with a clear antiwar message delivered by voters—the president began sending signals that he would not only escalate America's military commitment to the war in Iraq but also intensify our hostile posture toward the Iranians.

Thus, by the end of the year, the only options presented to the Iranians were (a) submit to the president's demands by freezing their nuclear energy program as a precondition to any negotiations, or (b) accept the inevitability of some type of military strike by the United States and to prepare accordingly.

The mentality underlying the president's view of Iran has long been evident. In Bush's October 2002 Cincinnati speech discussed in the prior chapter, the president expressly denied the fundamental differences between competing factions in the Middle East and instead insisted that they were all "different faces of the same evil."

And as early as his January 2002 "axis of evil" speech, it has been apparent that the president views Iran as part of the same undifferentiated mass of "America's Enemies" that also includes Al Qaeda and included Iraq—notwithstanding Iran's Persian rather than Arab ethnicity, notwithstanding its Shiite rather than Sunni religion, and notwithstanding its intense and protracted hostilities with both Saddam Hussein and Al Qaeda. The president, who sees the world as one cleanly divided between Good and Evil, and who believes he has been called to the mission of battling Evil, is incapable of recognizing, let alone navigating and exploiting, the critical differences among the various factions that do not submit to America's will. Thus, our "enemy" is not one terrorist group or one country, but a whole host of heterogeneous groups and nations that have been grouped together as "Evil" and targeted with the same single-minded policies of aggression.

Yet, in his 2002 Cincinnati speech, the president—in addition to compiling all of that "evidence" demonstrating the "grave threat" posed by Iraq—sought to assure Americans that the underlying rationale for invading Iraq would not compel a series of new wars thereafter. Instead, the president argued, the threat posed by Saddam Hussein was unique in both nature and severity; it was unlike any other anywhere in the world:

> First, some ask why Iraq is different from other countries or regimes that also have terrible weapons. While there are many dangers in the world, *the threat from Iraq stands alone*—because it gathers the most serious dangers of our age in one place. Iraq's weapons of mass destruction are controlled by a murderous tyrant who has already used chemical weapons to

kill thousands of people. This same tyrant has tried to dominate the Middle East, has invaded and brutally occupied a small neighbor, has struck other nations without warning, and holds an unrelenting hostility toward the United States.

By its past and present actions, by its technological capabilities, by the merciless nature of its regime, *Iraq is unique*. As a former chief weapons inspector of the U.N. has said, "The fundamental problem with Iraq remains the nature of the regime, itself. Saddam Hussein is a homicidal dictator who is addicted to weapons of mass destruction" [emphasis added].

Despite those prior assurances to Americans of the "unique" threat posed by Iraq, the president, throughout 2006, has been applying almost identical language, and identical reasoning, to prepare the country for a potential military confrontation with Iran. His choice to depict Saddam as a Nazi-like Evil threat led inexorably to the U.S. invasion of Iraq, and his similar depiction of Iran and its leaders portend the same outcome.

Thus, as the president sees and describes the world, Iran has now replaced Iraq as a "grave threat" and "state sponsor of terrorism" and the ruling Iranian mullahs and the elected Iranian president Mahmoud Ahmadinejad have replaced Saddam Hussein as the new "Hitler," the current incarnation of pure Evil. Just as Saddam was allegedly too power-crazed and Evil to be reasoned with, so, too, is the Iranian government. And just as Saddam Hussein's alleged development of nuclear weapons was such an intolerable threat to American security that the United States was compelled to stop Iraq by any means necessary, the president spent much of 2006 and early 2007 making the same argument with respect to Iran.

Indeed, the administration seems to be intentionally repeating most of its rhetoric almost *verbatim*. As early as January 2006, the *Washington Post* noted the obvious:

President Bush declared Friday that a nuclear-armed Iran would pose "a grave threat to the security of the world" as he tried to rally support from other major powers for U.N. Security Council action unless a defiant Tehran abandons any aspirations for nuclear weapons.

In using the phrase "grave threat," Bush invoked the same language he used before launching the invasion of Iraq in 2003. . . .

That January press conference marked a serious and deliberate escalation of the saber-rattling rhetoric toward Iran:

> The "grave threat" language was not in any talking points prepared and distributed Friday across the U.S. government and surprised diplomats and even some of Bush's own aides.
>
> But by and large, he has shied away from those words regarding Iran.

In August 2006, the president delivered a speech at a fundraising event for Senator Orrin Hatch which left no doubt that, in his mind, there is nothing at all unique about Iraq. Instead, as he sees it, there is a whole host of other equally evil and threatening "state sponsors of terrorism" against which he is willing to wage war based on exactly the same reasoning he deployed to persuade the country of the need to invade and occupy the "uniquely" dangerous Iraq. The president explained:

> The enemies of liberty come from different parts of the world, and they take inspiration from different sources. Some are radicalized followers of the Sunni tradition, who swear allegiance to terrorist organizations like Al Qaeda. Others are radicalized followers of the Shia tradition, who join groups like Hezbollah and take guidance from state sponsors like Syria and Iran.

According to the president, Iran (and Syria) are "state sponsors" of terrorism, which are tantamount to—perhaps even teamed up with—Al Qaeda. What do we do with state sponsors such as Iran and Syria? In the president's worldview, the answer is obvious, as the president emphasized in the same speech: "If you harbor terrorists, you are just as guilty as the terrorists; you're an enemy of the United States, and you will be held to account." Under what he calls the Bush Doctrine, when the president labels another country a "state sponsor of international terrorism," it is the functional equivalent of a declaration of war; that is how they are "held to account."

In the president's August 2006 speech, the specific assertion that Iran is a "state sponsor of terrorism" was accompanied by this crystal-clear ultimatum to the Iranians, employing language virtually identical to that directed at Saddam Hussein in the fall of 2002:

This summer's crisis in Lebanon has made it clearer than ever that the world now faces a grave threat from the radical regime in Iran. . . . The Iranian regime denies basic human rights to millions of its people. And the Iranian regime is pursuing nuclear weapons in open defiance of its international obligations.

We know the death and suffering that Iran's sponsorship of terrorists has brought, and we can imagine how much worse it would be if Iran were allowed to acquire nuclear weapons. Many nations are working together to solve this problem. The United Nations passed a resolution demanding that Iran suspend its nuclear-enrichment activities. Today is the deadline for Iran's leaders to reply to the reasonable proposal the international community has made. If Iran's leaders accept this offer and abandon their nuclear weapons ambitions, they can set their country on a better course. Yet, so far, the Iranian regime has responded with further defiance and delay.

It is time for Iran to make a choice. We've made our choice: We will continue to work closely with our allies to find a diplomatic solution— but there must be consequences for Iran's defiance, and we must not allow Iran to develop a nuclear weapon.

These threats were issued with the same language as that used toward Iraq and are equally incoherent. If, for instance, Iran is such a crazed regime, how can we ever trust that they have given up nuclear weapons development? And even if they do that, they would still allegedly remain "state sponsors of terrorists," and thus must be "held to account" under the Bush Doctrine. That would mean that even a vigorous inspections and verification process or even a cessation of Iran's nuclear research activities would not alleviate Bush's perceived need for regime change (just as Saddam's capitulation to the U.N. weapons inspection process did not avert Bush's invasion of Iraq).

Indeed, just as was true with Iraq, the president's emphasis has been *not only* on Iran's alleged attempt to acquire nuclear weapons *but also* on its government's alleged connection to "the terrorists" as well as its repressive internal practices. Just as was true for Iraq, this formulation means that there is but one solution that would satisfy Bush—*not* merely a suspension of Iran's nuclear program, but *regime change*. And given that there is no chance that a "diplomatic solution" will result in "regime change," the president's claimed commitment to diplomacy is illusory, just as it was with Iraq.

The president himself has emphasized that his thought process with regard to Iran is virtually identical to that which guided him in the weeks prior to the invasion of Iraq—with the sole exception that he apparently views a diplomatic solution with the Iranians as being *less likely* than it was with Saddam's regime, and that war with Iran is therefore even more probable than it was with Iraq. *National Review* editor Rich Lowry was a member of a small group of conservative pundits to sit for an interview with President Bush in September 2006. On September 13, Lowry wrote about the president's remarks on Iran:

> Time is also something Bush emphasizes in the Iran crisis. But his language suggests that the Robert Kagan–thesis that the seemingly interminable Iran diplomacy *is the necessary run-up to a strike on Iran* has something to it. Bush says, "It is very important for the United States to try all diplomatic means."
>
> That's what we did in Iraq: "I'm often asked what's the difference between Iran and Iraq. We tried all diplomatic means in Iraq." *Iran, he seems to imply, might eventually prove impervious to diplomacy, but that's something we have to find out* [emphasis added].

The notion that the president "tried all diplomatic means in Iraq" before invading is as transparently insincere as is his claim that he is seeking to do the same in order to avoid war with Iran. And just as the president's threatening rhetoric toward Iran is identical to that which he adopted vis-à-vis Iraq, so, too, is the language he is using to deny the inevitability of military conflict with Iran.

Long after it was apparent that the president was intent on invading Iraq, he continued publicly to deny that fact, insisting instead that he was still committed to a diplomatic resolution. As *New York Times* reporter Michael Gordon and retired general Bernard Trainor documented in their book, *Cobra II—The Inside Story of the Invasion and Occupation of Iraq*, the president repeatedly insisted that he was not working on war plans to invade Iraq even when war was the option with the greatest claim on his attention.

In May 2002, for instance, the president went to Germany and sought to assure European allies that he was seeking to avoid war with Saddam: "I told the Chancellor that I have no war plans on my desk, which is the truth, and that we've got to use all means at our disposal to deal with Saddam Hussein." Three days later, in Paris at a news conference with French president Jacques Chirac, the president made a virtually identical statement: "The stated policy of my government is that we have a regime change. And as I told President Chirac, I have no war plans on my desk."

And later in May, when General Tommy Franks was asked how many troops would be needed to invade Iraq, he responded, "That's a great question and one for which I don't have an answer because my boss has not yet asked me to put together a plan to do that. They have not asked me for these kinds of numbers."

But as Gordon and Trainor document, all of those claims were highly misleading, if not outright dishonest, because the president was clearly intent on invading as the sole means to resolve the "grave threat" posed by Saddam:

> The president's statement was true in only the most literal but trivial sense. Bush had ordered the development of a new CENTCOM war plan, repeatedly met with Franks to hear its details, offered his own views on the schedule for deploying troops and on the military's effort to couch the invasion as a liberation, and sent his vice president halfway around the world to secure allies for the war. And as for Franks, even the cleverest hair-splitting could not reconcile his remarks with the activity of CENTCOM during the previous six months.

In like manner, throughout 2006 the president and then-Secretary Rumsfeld were employing almost identical language, and identical means of denial, with regard to their war planning against Iran. In April, for instance, they chided the media for what they both called "wild speculation" with regard to the president's preparation for military action against the Iranians.

And as the year progressed, the president, when asked about Iran, would respond almost exactly as he did when queried in mid-2002 about Iraq: by quickly expressing hope for a "diplomatic solution," cursorily noting that war is a "last resort," but then animatedly stressing that military action is an option and that, regardless of what else is true, it is "unacceptable" to allow Iran to acquire a nuclear weapon.

Indeed, throughout the year, the president repeatedly used the term *unacceptable* when speaking of Iran, a term which, as noted in October by the *Washington Post,* is one of the most bellicose and deliberate words a president can choose in the foreign policy context:

> Having a president call something "unacceptable" is not the same as having him order U.S. troops into action. But foreign policy experts say the word is one of the strongest any leader can deploy, since it both broadcasts a national position and conveys an implicit threat to take action if his warnings are disregarded.

When the president calls Iran a "state sponsor of international terrorism" and repeatedly proclaims its conduct "unacceptable," that is as unambiguous a threat of war as can be issued short of an ultimatum or promise to commence a bombing campaign on a specific date.

Worse, the president's own claims about Iran make diplomacy all but impossible from the start. When one embraces the view that a certain country is the equivalent of Nazi Germany and its leader tantamount to Adolf Hitler, diplomacy, by definition, is not occurring and is certain to fail, since one has preordained that the country, by definition, cannot be trusted and cannot be reasoned with. What rendered Hitler such a singular threat—his *defining* attribute—was that he *craved* war as a means for asserting dominion over other countries, and affirmatively did not want a "diplomatic solution." To equate Saddam, and now Iranian leaders, to Hitler, and to equate the threat posed by their countries to the one posed by Nazi Germany, is by definition to declare in advance that diplomacy is destined to fail and that—as was true with Hitler's Germany—war is the only viable option.

War-threatening allegations regarding Iran have not been confined to the president's speeches and interviews. On September 5, 2006, the White House unveiled its new National Strategy for Combating Terrorism. It is composed largely of empty rhetorical platitudes that are by now depressingly familiar. Its fundamental premise is that "the War on Terror will be a long war," but there is no need to worry, because we have a very specific and coherent strategy for winning:

There will continue to be challenges ahead, but along with our partners, we will attack terrorism and its ideology, and bring hope and freedom to the people of the world. This is how we will win the War on Terror.

That is the president's plan for "how we will win the War on Terror"—we are going to "bring hope and freedom to the people of the world."

But the strategy is not completely filled with moralistic platitudes of this sort. Just like the 2002 strategy that presaged the invasion of Iraq, the document contains some unquestionably meaningful pronouncements, the most significant being the emphasis on Iran and Syria as "state sponsors of terrorism." The strategy repeatedly makes the claim that those two countries are supporting terrorists: "Some states, such as Syria and Iran, continue to harbor terrorists at home and sponsor terrorist activity abroad." The strategy also notes that "the United States currently designates five state sponsors of terrorism: Iran, Syria, Sudan, North Korea, and Cuba," but pointedly asserts that "Iran remains the most active state sponsor of international terrorism."

This is the same claim the president made in a speech he delivered several days prior to the issuance of the strategy, in which he declared, "We know the death and suffering that Iran's sponsorship of terrorists has brought," and then ominously warned, "if you harbor terrorists, you are just as guilty as the terrorists; you're an enemy of the United States, and you will be held to account."

In September 2006, Paul Gigot, editor of the *Wall Street Journal* editorial page, asked the president about Iran. Gigot wrote on September 9:

> On the other hand, Mr. Bush remains as blunt as ever about the nature of the Iranian regime when I ask if one lesson of North Korea is that Iran must be stopped *before* it acquires a bomb. "North Korea doesn't teach us that lesson. The current government [in Iran] teaches that lesson," Mr. Bush says. "Their declared policies of destruction and their support for terror makes it clear they should not have a nuclear weapon."
>
> One way or another, Iran will be the major dilemma of the rest of his presidency, and Mr. Bush knows it.

While the emphasis on Iran is relatively new, the Bush mentality driving the administration's war-seeking posture was announced long ago and has not changed. As early as February 2002, for instance, Vice President Cheney gave a speech at the Nixon Library in California and accused Iran of being "a leading exporter of terror," and then pointedly added, "Under the Bush Doctrine, if you harbor a terrorist, you are a terrorist. If you feed or fund a terrorist, you are a terrorist, and you will be held accountable."

In early 2002, then-Secretary Rumsfeld was eager to underscore the newly threatening posture of the United States toward Iran, telling reporters,

> If I were in Iran or North Korea or Iraq and I heard the president of the United States say what he said last night about weapons of mass destruction and about terrorism and about terrorist networks and about nations that harbor terrorists, I don't think there would be a lot of ambiguity as to the view he holds of those problems and their behavior.

As Bush supporter and former CIA director James Woolsey said during a television appearance in January 2002 about the president's accusations that Iran is a "state sponsor of terror":

> It's very definitely a clear statement of the president's attitude and it leans—it seems to me—toward a policy of telling these governments that if they do not get out of the business of terror and developing weapons of mass destruction, they stand at risk of their regimes being deposed forcefully by the United States.

One of President Bush's closest and most influential aides during the first five years of his presidency, Michael Gerson, views military confrontation with Iran as highly likely and *imminent*, if not inevitable (not to mention noble and necessary). In an August 2006 *Newsweek* essay, Gerson revealed the type of counsel the president has been receiving for the last five years. "Cowboy diplomacy" is a virtue because it is the only approach that keeps Evil tyrants in line; operating from that premise, Gerson hopes for and all but predicts war with Iran:

> First, the nation may be tired, but history doesn't care. It is not fair that the challenge of Iran is rising with Iraq, bloody and unresolved. But, as President Kennedy used to say, "Life is not fair."
>
> Behind all the chaos and death in Lebanon and northern Israel,

Iran is the main cause of worry in the West Wing—the crisis with the highest stakes. . . . And despite other disagreements, all the factions in Iran—conservative, ultraconservative and "let's usher in the apocalypse" fanatics—seem united in a nuclear nationalism.

Some commentators say that America is too exhausted to confront this threat. But presidential decisions on national security are not primarily made by the divination of public sentiments; they are made by the determination of national interests. And the low blood-sugar level of pundits counts not at all. Here the choice is not easy, but it is simple: can America (and other nations) accept a nuclear Iran? . . .

There are still many steps of diplomacy, engagement and sanctions between today and a decision about military conflict with Iran—and there may yet be a peaceful solution.

But in this diplomatic dance, America should not mirror the infinite patience of Europe. There must be someone in the world capable of drawing a line—someone who says, "This much and no further." At some point, those who decide on aggression must pay a price, or aggression will be universal. If American "cowboy diplomacy" did not exist, it would be necessary to invent it.

By the end of 2006, even some Democrats—almost entirely confined to those who supported the U.S. invasion of Iraq (and were therefore wrong about the need for *that* war)—were openly suggesting that war with Iran may be both inevitable and necessary, for exactly the same reasons they told Americans that war with Iraq was. Indiana senator Evan Bayh, for instance, told *The New Yorker*'s Jeffrey Goldberg:

> "You just hope that we haven't soured an entire generation on the necessity, from time to time, of using force because Iraq has been such a debacle," he said. "That would be tragic, because Iran is a grave threat. They're everything we thought Iraq was but wasn't. They are seeking nuclear weapons, they do support terrorists, they have threatened to destroy Israel, and they've threatened us, too."

Some key Bush supporters in government who are particularly impatient for war with Iran take Gerson's aspirations a step or two further by proclaiming that the United States is *already* at war with Iran, and the only question is when the U.S. would begin fighting back. One of the most vocal supporters of the administration's militaristic Middle East policies, Senator Joseph Lieberman, ended 2006 with a *Washington Post* editorial in which he, in essence, declared that we are *already* at war with Iran, and that our task is to recognize them as our real Enemy (emphasis added):

> While we are naturally focused on Iraq, *a larger war is emerging.* On one side are extremists and terrorists *led and sponsored by Iran,* on the other moderates and democrats supported by the United States. Iraq is the most deadly battlefield on which that conflict is being fought. How we end the struggle there will affect not only the region but the worldwide war against the extremists who attacked us on Sept. 11, 2001.

According to Lieberman, all the chaos and violence in Iraq is the fault of Iran and Al Qaeda:

> This bloodshed, moreover, is not the inevitable product of ancient hatreds. It is the predictable consequence of a failure to ensure basic security and, equally important, of a conscious strategy by al-Qaeda and Iran, which have systematically aimed to undermine Iraq's fragile political center. . . .
>
> On this point, let there be no doubt: If Iraq descends into full-scale civil war, it will be a tremendous battlefield victory for al-Qaeda and Iran. Iraq is the central front in the global and regional war against Islamic extremism.

Perhaps most telling was the president's own January 2007 prime-time speech to the nation, the ostensible purpose of which was to unveil his "surge" strategy for Iraq. In the course of the speech, the president mentioned Iran no fewer than six times and included what the *New York Times* described as "some of his sharpest words of warning to Iran" yet. But those words could be described more accurately as a virtual declaration of war. Bush accused the Iranian government of "providing material support for attacks on American troops" and vowed to "seek out and destroy the networks providing advanced weaponry and training to our enemies." But those networks are located *in Iran*, which means that search-and-destroy missions on such networks might include some incursion into Iranian territory, whether by air or ground.

Hours before the speech, the White House released a PowerPoint presentation with details about the president's new policy. "Increase operations against Iranian actors" was listed in the "Key Tactical Shifts" section. As the *New York Times* reported: "One senior administration official said this evening that the omission of the usual wording about seeking a diplomatic solution [to the Iranian nuclear stand-off] 'was not accidental.'"

Notwithstanding a grossly depleted military bogged down in both Iraq and Afghanistan, the president's own worldview—his decision to treat Iran as a pure "Evil"—has boxed him into a corner composed exclusively of a military option against Iran. Yet Iran is a country with a population ten times as large as Iraq's, a military force that is more formidable, multiple means for inflicting real economic and even military damage on U.S. interests in the Middle East, and a cadre of allies that include some of the world's most important and powerful countries. The president's own cultivated Manicheanism, then, has propelled him toward an unsustainable and exceedingly dangerous confrontation with what he has come irrevocably to view as the "evil terrorist state" of Iran.

FIGHTING ALL THE HITLERS

Anyone, including the Iranians, paying even minimal attention to American political discourse over the past year or two would be keenly aware that a substantial portion of the president's supporters are eager for military confrontation with Iran. The president is quite explicit about his Manichean view of the world, and those who exert influence on him have long recognized that depicting political conflicts, particularly international ones, in a framework of Good vs. Evil is the key for capturing the president's attention and triggering his interest and passion.

The Manichean framework that has been manufactured and publicly disseminated is the enabling foundation for the president's policies. This framework is vividly illustrated by the ability of the president's most militaristic supporters to persuade him in early 2002 to include Iran as part of the "axis of evil," even in the midst of unprecedented U.S.-Iran rapprochement, and by their ongoing success in convincing the president to escalate hostilities with Iran. These enthusiasts for endless war simply ignore all subtleties and inconvenient facts, and substitute fact-free caricatures straight out of Saturday-morning League of Justice cartoons in which omnipotent superheroes invariably overcome all odds to defeat pure villains bent on world domination.

Shoving a complex world into a simplistic moralistic framework not only grossly contracts policy options but also, by design, stifles debate. By declaring Iran a Nazi-like Evil, the question of whether to wage war on it is transformed from a mere political question into a moral and even psychological one: By urging war, individuals can prove themselves opposed to Evil as well as strong, powerful, and resolute warriors. Conversely, by opposing war, one is revealed to be an appeaser of Evil and, worse, weak, spineless, and cowardly.

This manipulative formula can be, and often is, applied by war supporters to influence the president's own behavior. It is deployed to challenge the president's courage and manliness—will he prove that he is a brave and devoted warrior for Good by recognizing Iran as pure Evil and treating it accordingly, or will he back down and reveal himself as a coward, one who submits meekly to political pressures and crawls away from the epic challenge of his time?

Plainly, this binary formulation of the issue is intended to trigger the president's core view of himself as a warrior for Good, his evangelical belief that he is "called to" the battle against Evil. And if the president and the country he leads are to continue to be on the side of Good—and if history is to view the president as such—then there is no choice but to confront Iran regardless of the costs and irrespective of the opinion of the world or even of Americans themselves. The president's only other choice is to follow in the weak and amoral footsteps of Nazi-appeaser Neville Chamberlain.

Bush supporters eager for war with Iran have dramatically escalated their rhetoric in 2006 to all but challenge President Bush to decide whether he will confront this pure Evil or wear the shameful mantle of Chamberlain. Interviewed by *Human Events Magazine* in February 2006, Newt Gingrich stressed the equivalency between the threats posed by Iran and Nazi Germany and expressly challenged the president:

This is 1935 and [Iranian president] Mahmoud Ahmadinejad is as close to Adolf Hitler as we've seen. We now know who they are—the question is who we are. Are we Baldwin or Churchill? . . .

The current behavior of the bureaucracy is perfectly compatible with Stanley Baldwin and totally incompatible with Winston Churchill. My hope is that the President will impose his will. Short of the President's imposing his will, it is inconceivable that the current system would be prepared to take on the Iranian government.

Bill Kristol—the neoconservative pundit, Fox News contributor, and *Weekly Standard* editor who exerted great influence in persuading Americans to support an invasion of Iraq—is not the slightest bit deterred, or ashamed, by the fact that virtually every bit of prewar wisdom he offered led to disaster and every prognostication he made was dead wrong. To the contrary, like Gingrich, Kristol is again parading around with pretenses of great warrior nobility and military wisdom, this time leading the war dance against all of the new Hitlers in Iran.

In an April 2006 column in *The Weekly Standard*, Kristol issued an overt call to war against Iran, and he was unable to refrain from dredging up the only historical event that he knows in the first paragraph:

In the Spring of 1936, seventy years ago—Hitler's Germany occupied the Rhineland. France's Léon Blum denounced this as "unacceptable." But France did nothing. As did the British. And the United States.

Kristol argued that avoiding France's 1930s appeasement mistakes and those of other Western nations "would mean serious preparation for possible military action [against Iran]—including real and urgent operational planning for bombing strikes and for the consequences of such strikes." And not only must we go to war against Iran, we must do so quickly:

It is not "moral progress" to put off serious planning for military action to a later date, probably in less favorable circumstances, when the Iranian regime has been further emboldened, our friends in the region more disheartened, and allies more confused by years of fruitless diplomacy than they would be by greater clarity and resolution now.

For good measure, Kristol added that anyone who opposes his mindlessly militaristic approach toward Iran is guilty, of course, of seeking to "appease the mullahs." And indeed, ever since the invasion of Iraq, Kristol has been insisting that the United States is only at the beginning, not the end, of the list of countries it intends to attack. In an April 2003 *Weekly Standard* column, he pronounced:

> The battles of Afghanistan and Iraq have been won decisively and honorably. But these are only two battles. We are only at the end of the beginning in the war on terror and terrorist states.

Similarly, the American Enterprise Institute's Michael Rubin, on *National Review*'s blog in October 2006, wrote, "Clinton administration attempts to engage the Taliban and the North Korean regime were folly. Any attempt to do likewise with Iran would be equally inane. Certain regimes cannot be appeased." Equating "an attempt to avoid new wars" with "cowardly appeasement of Evil" is a constant theme among Bush supporters seeking to persuade the president to wage war on Iran.

This sort of cheap equivalence between Hitler and the tyrant du jour is, among other things, rather disorienting. One minute we are told that Hitler is a singular manifestation of unparalleled Evil to which nothing should ever be compared, lest the uniqueness of his atrocities be minimized. The next minute, though, there are nothing but Hitler spawns running around everywhere, and we need to wage war against each of them in order to avoid suffering the fate of 1938 Czechoslovakia and Neville Chamberlain. In a 2005 *National Review* article entitled "Nazi Nonsense," Jonah Goldberg wrote:

> Hitler holds our fascination because of his *singular* villainy. But this shouldn't crowd out our ability to make distinctions. Hitler is supposed to define the outer limits of evil, not the lowest threshold. Something can be very, very bad and be far "better" than the Holocaust.

This is the very same Jonah Goldberg who is soon to publish a book entitled *Liberal Fascism: The Totalitarian Temptation from Mussolini to Hillary Clinton*—with a cover showing a happy face marred by Adolf Hitler's mustache and which, according to his publisher, "draws striking parallels between historic fascism and contemporary liberal doctrines." But what would appear to a rational person to be a painfully glaring inconsistency actually illustrates the tactic used frequently by prowar Bush followers. In particular, many of the same people who appear to believe that they have proprietary rights over the invocation of Hitler and Nazism and who issue stern condemnations against its use by others, blithely proceed to wield Hitler and Nazi imagery, freely and recklessly, in order to manipulate public opinion and provoke new wars that they crave.

Charles Krauthammer—one of the most vocal cheerleaders in favor of invading Iraq who also threatened a war with Syria within less than two months after Iraq was invaded—has also now extended his warmongering rhetoric to Iran. In an April 2006 issue of *Time* magazine, Krauthammer claimed that the Iranian president believes that "the end of history is only two or three years away" and pronounced him to be "exceedingly dangerous." In his May 2006 *Washington Post* column, he described Iranian leaders as those "who would finish Hitler's work" and claimed that Hitler's "successors now reside in Tehran." Krauthammer dutifully raised the clichéd and plainly inapposite analogy that the U.S. is currently in 1938, facing the choice of whether to confront or appease the "new Hitlers":

> Last week Bernard Lewis, America's dean of Islamic studies, who just turned 90 and remembers the 20th century well, confessed that for the first time he feels it is 1938 again. He did not need to add that in 1938, in the face of the gathering storm—a fanatical, aggressive, openly declared enemy of the West, and most determinedly of the Jews—the world did nothing.

This single-minded equation of Iran with Nazi Germany falls from the mouths of some of our highest elected officials. On September 18, 2006, Ohio Republican senator George Voinovich said during a Foreign Relations committee meeting: "Ahmadinejad—I call him Ahmad-in-a-head—I think he's a Hitler type of person. . . . He's a, he's a—we all know what he is."

When war historian Victor Davis Hanson, an admired figure among the most hawkish components of the president's base, was interviewed by right-wing radio talk show host Hugh Hewitt in November 2006, he argued that those who fail to take a sufficiently militaristic stance against Iranians "don't have the ability to identify evil from good." On the weekend following the December 2006 hanging of Saddam Hussein, Hanson expressed his desire for more executions of leaders hostile to the United States, including those in Iran and Syria. "Their demise will come soon enough, and only the clips and outtakes of the appeasers will remain," the bloodthirsty Hanson predicted.

This is the lexicon invariably employed by the president's core supporters to attempt to persuade him that more war in general—and specifically war with Iran—is necessary. For the most deluded war cheer-leaders, it is always 1938. *Hitler* is any leader of another country whom we do not like. *The New Nazi Germany* is any country opposed to U.S. interests or that does not submit fully to American dictates. *Appease* means "a desire to avoid starting new wars." *Churchill* means "an eager-ness to wage wars without limitation or restraint on any country one does not like."

The leading neoconservative magazine *Commentary* published a series of essentially identical arguments throughout 2006 advocating war with Iran. The series culminated with a November 2006 all-out call for war by Arthur Herman, a history professor at George Mason University, entitled "Getting Serious About Iran—a Military Option"—a piece that Hewitt hailed as a "must-read." After reviewing all of the available short-of-war options for deterring Iranian nuclear proliferation, Herman declares, "all of these recommendations fly in the face of reality." For Herman, nothing short of war with Iran will do.

Copying the tactics that brought us to war with Iraq, Herman sounded the alarm that Iran may possess a nuclear weapon "within the next two to three years," and that the United States is amply justified in waging war now on Iran:

> Which brings us back to the military option. That there is plentiful warrant for the exercise of this option—in Iran's serial defiance of UN resolutions, in its declared genocidal intentions toward Israel, another member of the United Nations, and in the fact of its harboring, support-ing, and training of international terrorists—could not be clearer.

Like a teenager in the obsessive midst of an online video war game, Herman lays out a detailed fantasy plan for our massive military assault on Iran: "The attack could move to include Iran's nuclear facilities—not only the 'hard' sites but also infrastructure like bridges and tunnels in order to prevent the shifting of critical materials from one site to another. Above all, the air attack would concentrate on Iran's gasoline refineries."

With the air attack on Iran's industrial infrastructure, Herman is just warming up. After that, the real war begins:

> The scenario would not end here. With the systematic reduction of Iran's capacity to respond, an amphibious force of Marines and special-operations forces could seize key Iranian oil assets in the Gulf, the most important of which is a series of 100 offshore wells and platforms built on Iran's continental shelf.
>
> North and South Pars offshore fields, which represent the future of Iran's oil and natural-gas industry, could also be seized, while Kargh Island at the far western edge of the Persian Gulf, whose terminus pumps the oil from Iran's most mature and copiously producing fields (Ahwaz, Marun, and Gachsaran, among others), could be rendered virtually useless. By the time the campaign was over, the United States military would be in a position to control the flow of Iranian oil at the flick of a switch.

Once the United States controls Iran's oil, Herman envisions that we can then start dictating to Iran what form their government will take and what policies they should and should not undertake, basically putting them into complete submission to our national will. Herman argues that our war plan "must therefore be predicated not only on seizing the state's oil assets but on refusing to relinquish them unless and until there is credible evidence of regime change in Tehran or—what is all but inconceivable—a major change of direction by the reigning theocracy."

And what of the rather self-evident, towering risks of unilaterally attacking a country such as Iran and seizing its oil assets? Herman dismisses those as casually and cursorily as he drew up his grand war plans: "The tactical risks associated with a comprehensive war strategy of this sort are numerous. But they are outweighed by its key advantages."

The very idea that the United States is going to launch a unilateral bombing campaign against Iran, shatter its infrastructure, and then seize its oil assets is pure insanity of the highest order. There is no other way to describe that.

But it is worth underscoring here that Herman's grandiose war fantasy is published in a magazine edited by neoconservative icon Norman

Podhoretz—father of *New York Post* and *National Review* contributor John Podhoretz, and father-in-law of Elliot Abrams, the White House official in charge of Middle East policy for the National Security Council. Calls for war on Iran, on the grounds that it is an incorrigible Evil, issue not from the fringe back alleys of our political institutions but from its most influential core.

When it comes to operating within the minimum confines imposed by basic rationality and plain reality, those advocating a new war with Iran really are indistinguishable from, say, Lyndon LaRouche or Fred Phelps or any number of other deranged extremists who are radical in their ideology as well as so far removed from reality that they command no attention beyond the occasional derisive reference.

Almost by definition, they do not recognize the constraints of reality because the moral rightness of the battle ensures victory. Righteousness trumps resource limits and the world as it is. That formula spawned continuous claims of imminent victory in Iraq even when the facts compelled the opposite conclusion, and it is the formula used once again to lure the president into a military confrontation with Iran that can produce nothing but disaster.

There is little doubt that these chest-beating war advocates, detached from reality though they are, still exert the greatest influence on the thinking of the president, and the more decorated among them continue to command great respect from our nation's media stars. Their war-advocating rhetoric, dressed up in Manichean appeals to moral duty and accompanied by threats of losing one's manly courage if one shirks that duty, has not lost any of its persuasiveness for George Bush.

That the president faces intense and growing pressure to confront Iran militarily is simply beyond doubt. The American Enterprise Institute (AEI) has resolutely devoted itself to this goal, and the significance of that crusade is difficult to overstate.

The AEI sits in the innermost belly of the neoconservative beast, boasting a list of resident "Scholars and Fellows" that includes Richard Perle, David Frum, Michael Ledeen, John Yoo, and Laurie Mylorie (who, according to *The Washington Monthly*, "theorized that al Qaeda is an agency of Iraqi intelligence, that Saddam Hussein was behind the first bombing of the World Trade Center, and that Iraqi intelligence was linked to Oklahoma City bomber Terry Nichols"). Former Rumsfeld deputy and current World Bank president Paul Wolfowitz and Irving Kristol, among many other similar Middle East war–loving types, are former AEI resident scholars, and Lynne Cheney is still an active fellow.

Every top administration official, including the president, has appeared before the AEI several times. In 2006, the longtime editor of its magazine, Karl Zinsmeister, became the president's chief domestic policy adviser. The AEI played as significant a role as any other single entity in creating the justification for the invasion of Iraq. And one of its senior fellows, Frederick Kagan, is the architect of the president's surge strategy. The AEI is agitating—hard—for a military attack on Iran.

The Washington Monthly noted that of all the lobbying and special-interest groups, the AEI "is in a different league, because of the influence its scholars wield in Washington and their consequent power to turn research into government policy." The AEI is incredibly well funded, and its board of trustees is composed of numerous chairmen of the world's largest corporations along with some of America's wealthiest individuals. It is a very serious and influential organization and its positions typically reflect imminent government actions or cause those actions.

As with all topics, caricature should be avoided. The AEI does not run the world or act as some sort of shadow government. But it most assuredly does exert significant influence on the policies and actions of the Bush administration—the similarity between its advocacy and the administration's decisions is demonstrable fact—and its crusades ought to be taken seriously, for that reason.

One of the AEI's featured publications in September 2006 was by Richard Perle, one of the most influential neoconservative architects of the invasion of Iraq, lambasting the president for "dithering," "blinking," and "beat[ing] an ignominious retreat" in the face of the mortal Iranian threat. Still another, by Reuel Marc Gerecht, urges the Bush administration to stop being so "overwhelmed and deflated" by the war in Iraq and to get on with bombing Iranian facilities in "Natanz, Isfahan, Arak, Tehran, and Bushehr."

In September 2006, the *New York Sun* reported that Bill Kristol—fearful that Republicans would lose control of the Congress in November—began urging the administration to seek a Congressional resolution authorizing the use of military force against Iran, and even to make use of force against Iran the central issue in the election. The same month, Charles Krauthammer in his *Washington Post* column said of the president's statements regarding Iran, "The signal is unmistakable. An aerial attack on Iran's nuclear facilities lies just beyond the horizon of diplomacy." Krauthammer predicted: "The decision is no more than a year away."

In a *New York Post* column during the same time period, John Podhoretz said in reaction to one of the president's speeches regarding Iran, "barring a miraculous change of heart on the part of the Iranian regime, a military strike is all but inevitable. Bush himself will view his own presidency as a failure if he doesn't act. So act he will."

With a military depleted to the breaking point in Iraq and Afghanistan, the narrow, suffocating confines of the president's two-dimensional Manichean world renders the president's only option—chest-beating militarism—both impotent and entirely lacking in credibility. Yet the president knows no other way short of all-out militarism. And even if he were receptive to another course, the continuous manipulative appeals of his warmongering advisers about the Iranians, 1938, his warrior duties, his place in history, and his moral obligations would not allow him to pursue it.

The most striking evidence of the inability of both the president and his supporters to consider any course with Iran other than the war path was their extraordinary reaction to the report issued by the Iraq Study Group. Two of the report's most significant recommendations squarely contradicted the core premises of the president's disastrous Manichean Middle Eastern militarism—namely that (a) the Bush administration open direct negotiations with Iran (and Syria) as a means of averting further disaster in Iraq, and (b) the United States devote far more efforts to brokering a peace agreement between Israel and the Palestinians in order to diffuse much of the anti-American resentment in the Middle East fueled by that conflict and America's role in it.

The report—issued by a bipartisan commission of ten of America's most entrenched establishment figures—was widely seen to represent the views of Jim Baker, secretary of state under Bush 41 and a loyal

Republican ally to the Bush family. Baker's foreign policy approach has long been defined by placing American interests as the supreme value, and relatedly, by an aversion to moralistic wars against regimes considered "Evil" or crusades for "Good."

In Baker's view, the question for the U.S. government in formulating its relations with other nations is not whether those nations meet some moral test, but how to promote U.S. interests and enable the U.S. to maintain peaceful and constructive relations even with repressive regimes. Within this framework, Baker sees Iran not as a symbol of Evil on which the U.S. must wage war, but as a country with which the U.S. can re-establish constructive dialogue as a means of finding a way out of the catastrophe we have spawned in the Middle East and, beyond that, securing our interests further.

There is nothing exotic or novel about Baker's approach. Throughout history, nations have not typically sacrificed their resources and the lives of their citizens in order to wage moralistic wars against nations perceived to be "Evil," but rather nations have been guided by a calculation of what is in the interests of their citizens and what maximizes their security. Religions and charities are devoted to the aim of maximizing Good and combating Evil, but foreign policy is not missionary work. It has been viewed—almost universally—as a means of ensuring the national security of the country.

Throughout its history, the United States has negotiated and reached peace agreements with scores of nations that were previously anti-American at their core, including governments that were far more internally repressive than the Iranians. The U.S. has never perceived its role to be to wage war against any regimes that, in some abstract, moralistic sense, could be deemed "Evil."

The list of governments around the world that could qualify as Evil has always been extremely long. No nation that commits its resources and the lives of its citizens to waging war against Evil in the world will endure very long. Even the attempt is plainly unsustainable. The role of the U.S. government is and can only be to protect American citizens and preserve U.S. security, not to end Evil in the world through a series of hostile foreign policy declarations and wars.

Although Ronald Reagan is often held up by the president's war-loving supporters as the great Churchillian warrior—and his labeling of the Soviet Union as an "Evil Empire" is frequently compared to Bush's "axis of evil" speech—Reagan's emphasis in dealing with the Soviet Union was negotiation, not war. His objective was to achieve a sustainable peace with the Soviets as the result of negotiated agreements, at most to bring down that regime through economic pressures, not to wage war as a means of extinguishing Soviet Evil or even forcing regime change.

In fact, precisely because President Reagan emphasized the need to negotiate with rather than wage war on the Soviet Union, he himself was the target of the same "Chamberlain appeasement" denunciations now unleashed on those who want to avoid endless wars in the Middle East. For instance, a January 20, 1988, UPI article reported that Conservative Caucus chair Howard Phillips "scorned President Reagan as 'a useful idiot for Kremlin propaganda,'" and published ads that likened

> Reagan's signing of the INF Treaty to British Prime Minister Neville Chamberlain's signing of an accord with Nazi Germany's Adolf Hitler in 1938. The ad, with the headline, "Appeasement Is As Unwise In 1988 As In 1938," shows pictures of Chamberlain, Hitler, Reagan and Gorbachev overhung by an umbrella. Chamberlain carried an umbrella and it became a World War II symbol for appeasement.

According to the January 19, 1988, *St. Louis Post-Dispatch,* back when Pat Robertson was campaigning for president in Missouri, he "suggested that President Ronald Reagan could be compared to Neville Chamberlain . . . by agreeing to a medium-range nuclear arms agreement with Soviet leader Mikhail S. Gorbachev."

The *Orange County Register* editorialized in September 1988 that "Ronald Reagan has become the Neville Chamberlain of the 1980s. The apparent peace of 1988 may be followed by the new wars of 1989 or 1990." And Newt Gingrich, in 1985, denounced President Reagan's rapprochement with Gorbachev as potentially "the most dangerous summit for the West since Adolf Hitler met with Chamberlain in 1938 at Munich."

Donald Rumsfeld—who provoked controversy when he delivered a speech in mid-2006 equating the administration's foreign policy opponents to Neville Chamberlain appeasers—has been tossing around that same verbiage in order to promote his prowar views for almost thirty years. According to a November 26, 1979, Associated Press article regarding efforts to oppose ratification of the SALT treaty: " 'Our nation's situation is more dangerous today than it has been any time since Neville Chamberlain left Munich, setting the stage for World War II,' Rumsfeld said at a news conference."

Screaming "appeasement" and endlessly comparing political opponents to Neville Chamberlain is not a serious, thoughtful argument; nor is it the basis for any sort of foreign policy. At best, it is an empty, cheap platitude so overused by war seekers as to be impoverished of meaning. More often than not, though, it is worse than that; it is the disguised battle cry of those who want war for its own sake, and who want therefore to depict attempts to resolve conflicts without war as irresponsible and weak. Recall that the Cold War did not end via hot war on the Soviets but rather through engagement of them and treaties with them, signed by the "Neville Chamberlain of the 1980s," Ronald Reagan.

But once a president accepts and publicly declares that Nation X is not just hostile but Evil, and once he refuses even to negotiate with that country, all of the options typically available to a country in order to coexist peacefully are eliminated. But that is precisely the barren, suffocating corner in which the president's most fervent supporters want him to be with regard to Iran, and it is where the president has chosen to be.

The strength of a superpower resides in its ability to distinguish between serious and unserious threats. Leaders of militarily weak countries have long squeezed political advantage from symbolic gestures of independence from, even hostility toward, the United States. But such rhetoric coming from nations that lack the capability to threaten us is the equivalent of meaningless trash talking. Great powers do not feel compelled to descend to the level of playground taunts or to treat every provocative comment as a cause for war-threatening behavior. Yet like the empire that America's founders desperately warned us to avoid, the Bush administration has come to apply the term *Evil* to virtually any country that refuses to submit to the will of the current president and to America's dictates.

And worse, that mentality is accompanied by an insistence that Evil, by definition, can be dealt with only through maximum force, never with diplomacy or negotiations. The mind-set repeatedly expressed by Vice President Cheney, former Defense Secretary Rumsfeld, and even the president himself—namely, that the United States must constantly prove to the likes of Osama bin Laden and other petty Middle Eastern tyrants that we are tough and strong and will never back down—defines an insecure adolescent bully, not a responsible and secure superpower. Yet those are the premises that have placed the president on a collision course with Iran. To maintain that course, the first order of business for those seeking such a war is to attack viciously the possibility that other options short of war with Iran are feasible.

As always with the president's most steadfast supporters, that goal is achieved not by engaging the merits of others' substantive recommendations and options, but instead by demonizing those who advocate additional options. Most notable in that regard is the frothing intensity of the personal attacks on Jim Baker coming from the neoconservatives and assorted other warmongers as a result of the ISG's recommendations that Iran be engaged in negotiations and that more efforts be devoted to an Israel-Palestinian peace agreement.

Illustrative of these debate-stifling, deeply personal attacks on Baker is this December 2006 commentary from Marty Peretz, longtime editor of the allegedly sober and serious political and foreign policy magazine *The New Republic:*

> Yes, I can't get over James Baker being the chairman of a civil commission on war and statecraft. The first reason is that he is primarily responsible for American policy in the first Bush administration. That policy was a strategic disaster and a moral enormity. On Baker's head rests almost all of the responsibility for Saddam Hussein surviving in power after the first Gulf war.
>
> And, given that fact, also responsible for Saddam's atrocities against the Shia and Kurds for which the deposed tyrant is at last being tried in the very context of this war. James Baker is actually an accessory to war crimes of the Iraqi Baath Party in a war fought entirely against civilians. The truth is that he trusted Saddam . . . just as he seems to trust Bashar Assad and Mahmoud Ahmadinejad to be reasonable. If he truly trusts them on anything he is, well, as gullible as Chamberlain.

Beyond branding Baker as a war criminal, neoconservatives are also smearing him as an anti-Semite—again. Peretz, in a separate post on his blog, accused Baker of using the *ISG Report* to wage what Peretz calls "Baker's old war with the Israelis and with the Jews." *New York Post* columnist John Podhoretz accused Baker of having only one central objective: "Get Israel."

Rush Limbaugh accused Baker of leading the "Iraq Surrender Group," and at the right-wing blog site Pajamas Media, the AEI's Michael Ledeen described Limbaugh's glib formulation as "elegant" and himself pronounced the *ISG Report* "disgusting" because it recommended talks with Israel's enemies. Podhoretz said the commission was composed of "doddering old fools," while Charles Krauthammer mocked the report's "instant irrelevance" and called it a "farce," worthy only of "ridicule." *New York Post* columnist Ralph Peters said that the biblical figure Baker most resembles is Pontius Pilate, except the "difference is that Pilate just wanted to wash his hands of an annoyance, while Baker would wash his hands in the blood of our troops."

One source for the anti-Semitism smears hurled at Baker was the *ISG Report*'s acknowledgment of the obvious connection between the United States' blind and reflexive support for Israel regarding its conflict with the Palestinians on the one hand, and anti-U.S. resentment in the Middle East on the other. But the principal cause of these vicious accusations was Baker's attempt to introduce into America's public foreign policy debate the possibility that the U.S. may not need to wage war on Iran, but instead might be able to achieve constructive results, even rapprochement, by negotiating with Iran. That was plainly a top priority of the report—to expand and elevate the scope of the public debate that the U.S. is having over Iran specifically and its policies toward the Muslim world generally.

But such an expansion in the scope of the debate is precisely what the president and his followers fear most. The single-minded, cartoon depiction of Iran as pure Evil is their greatest asset, their most closely guarded weapon. That is what prevents any meaningful examination of the premises of our hostile Middle East policies and of our war posture to Iran—by both the American public and the president himself.

Plainly, the president is still firmly on board with this Manichean, war-driven view of the Middle East and of Iran. Before the ink was even dry on the Baker-Hamilton report, the White House made it unmistakably clear that the president would not even consider the report's recommendation that the U.S. negotiate with Iran. That recommendation was identified as one of two proposals—along with the report's attempt to set a target date for troop withdrawal from Iraq—which the president had, in advance, simply rejected out of hand.

An Alliance with "Pure Evil"

The cartoonish depiction of Iran embraced by Bush and his supporters is nothing more than pure fiction, completely removed from reality. The view of the Iranian government as irrational, intractable, single-minded evildoers bent on threatening the United States and wreaking world destruction stands in stark contrast to their actions over the last several years.

It is simply beyond dispute that Iran's behavior since the 9/11 attacks empirically disproves the president's assertions about what motivates them and how they behave. Indeed, the gap between reality and the president's rhetoric concerning Iran is almost impossible to overstate. It is true that Iran—like most countries—pursues its own interests and security, and that has placed it at times in opposition to the United States. It is also true that, like many governments around the world, including some of our closest and most important allies, the Iranian government is repressive in many ways toward its citizens and is far from a model democracy. It is absolutely the case that intense anti-American rhetoric is commonly expressed by Iranian leaders; and, in particular, Iran's president, Mahmoud Ahmadinejad, frequently issues ugly and threatening sentiments toward Israel.

But it is equally true that since 2001 the interests of the U.S. and Iran have on multiple occasions converged significantly, and at those times, the two countries—particularly during the early years of the Bush presidency—worked together toward common goals as virtual allies. During this same period, Iran has cultivated new and important allies around the world and developed substantial commercial relationships

with our own European allies. And it has maintained close and cooperative relations with many of its neighbors—including, most prominently,
the newly elected government of Iraq.

In short, the picture of Iran that emerges from its actions is one of a
rational state actor with which the United States can cooperate toward
common goals. Iran has invaded no other countries. While Iran's military
strength is greater than Saddam-led Iraq's, its military spending and military power are a tiny fraction of those of the U.S. Iranian armed forces
could not threaten the U.S. homeland in any meaningful way and the
calculating behavior of its leaders leaves little doubt that they realize that.

In the aftermath of the 9/11 attacks and the U.S. invasion of Afghanistan, Iran was one of the single greatest sources of assistance in helping
the United States to undermine the Taliban and stabilize the new Karzai
government. The U.S. and Iran worked together through numerous
channels and on numerous fronts in pursuit of the same goal in Afghanistan. To be sure, Iran's cooperation with the U.S.—like America's cooperation with Iran—was driven by self-interest. Iran viewed the Sunni
militants who controlled the Taliban as oppressive to Shiites and hostile
to Iran, and had long-standing tensions with the Taliban. The same
dynamic accounts for long-standing and intense Iranian hostility toward
the largely Sunni terrorists of Al Qaeda. And Iran perceived long-term
benefits from a more cooperative relationship with the U.S.

That Iran provided substantial assistance to the U.S. in Afghanistan is
beyond serious dispute. The fiercely nonpartisan Congressional Research
Service issued a June 2003 Report on Iran that noted, in its very first
paragraph, that President Bush declared Iran to be one of three members
of the "Axis of Evil . . . despite Iran's tacit cooperation with the United
States against the Taliban in the post–September 11, 2001, war in Afghanistan." Even the Bush State Department, in its December 2006 Report
on Afghanistan, expressly recognized Iran's active—and ongoing—
opposition to the Taliban, as well as its positive, stabilizing role in helping
the Karzai government. The State Department provided the historical
background that explains this cooperation:

Following the emergence of the Taliban and their harsh treatment of
Afghanistan's Shi'a minority, Iran stepped up assistance to the Northern

Alliance. Relations with the Taliban deteriorated further in 1998 after Taliban forces seized the Iranian consulate in Mazar-e-Sharif and executed Iranian diplomats. Since the fall of the Taliban, Afghanistan's relations with Iran have improved. Iran has been active in Afghan reconstruction efforts, particularly in the western portion of the country.

To facilitate this cooperation, Iran and the U.S., in late 2001 and 2002, engaged in direct, bilateral dialogue as part of the long-standing (pre-9/11) "6+2" Multinational Framework sponsored by the U.N. That group included both the United States and Iran. The U.S. used the cover of that framework to engage Iran directly in high-level contacts in the months following the 9/11 attacks, so as to maximize cooperation between the two countries.

The post-9/11 improvement in U.S.-Iran relations was actually a trend that began under the Clinton administration and was extended into the pre-9/11 Bush administration. Indeed, a more flexible posture toward Iran was one of the few significant Clinton policies that the Bush administration chose to continue.

At the beginning of Clinton's presidency, his administration took a hard line against Iran, implementing what it called a "dual containment" strategy of isolating both Iran and Iraq. In the mid-1990s, President Clinton imposed various new sanctions on Iran, including a 1995 ban on U.S. investment and trade and a 1996 law imposing sanctions on U.S. investment in Iran's energy sector.

But the 1997 democratic election of the moderate president Mohammad Khatami led Clinton officials to become more optimistic about positive relations with Iran. The remainder of the Clinton administration was marked by an incremental loosening of sanctions as a reward for conciliatory gestures by the Iranians, accompanied by an attempt, with the cooperation of the GOP-controlled Congress, to move toward further engagement with Iran. The last four years of the 1990s saw a steady improvement in U.S.-Iranian relations—a trend that continued, even accelerated, during the early stages of the Bush presidency.

Ever since a U.S. national emergency concerning Iran was declared during the 1979 hostage crisis—a declaration that vests the executive with broad powers for dealing with the emergency in question—each

American president has been legally required (in order to extend the emergency powers) to issue annual findings declaring that the emergency is ongoing. Under the Reagan, Bush 41, and Clinton administrations, it was typical to use very harsh language about the Iranians when renewing the national emergency. The March 16, 1998, Clinton declaration was typical, as it proclaimed Iran to "present an extraordinary and unusual threat to the national security, foreign policy, and economy of the United States."

But on November 13, 2001, the first time President Bush was required to issue such a statement, that language was softened considerably to reflect the improving relations between the two countries. In the place of the standard decades-old hostile language toward Iran, President Bush merely declared, rather meekly: "Relations with Iran have not yet returned to normal." That language was far more mild, and far less provocative, than any prior statement from any administration regarding Iran since 1979.

The cooperation in Afghanistan between the two countries unmistakably signaled an overall improvement in relations. In November 2001, Secretary of State Colin Powell shook hands with the Iranian foreign minister, Kamal Kharrazi, at the U.N. headquarters in New York City. PBS's *Frontline* described that event as "a simple yet historic gesture that seemed the most tantalizing hint of rapprochement between the U.S. and Iran since the Islamic revolution and the hostage crisis in 1979." Thereafter, Powell himself said "that we may be able to talk to Iran, that we may be able to have a reasonable conversation with Iranian leaders."

The opportunities for U.S.-Iranian rapprochement in the wake of the 9/11 attacks were real and substantial. In their December 28, 2001, op-ed in the *Washington Post,* Middle East experts John Newhouse and Thomas Pickering identified Iran as the first and most important of what they called the "big opportunities" resulting from 9/11. Citing the various forms of cooperation between the two countries, they predicted that "the turmoil that has long agitated U.S.-Iranian relations could begin to give way, if only gradually, to a balanced and productive relationship between two societies that have more in common than either cares to admit."

The benefits from such a rapprochement were self-evident and potentially region changing. According to Newhouse and Pickering:

> Iran could become a stabilizing influence in a congenitally unstable re-
> gion. It has attributes unique to the region: rudimentary but real politics
> based on free elections; a legitimate government; a history and culture all
> its own; and uncontested borders fixed by that experience, rather than
> imposed by other governments. Iran has had its revolution and never
> come close to imploding. Support for the hard-line Islamist clerics who
> came to power in that revolution has dwindled. Iran is a largely moderate
> and pro-American society.

They explained that "Iran wants to be treated by the United States as
a normal country and a respectable player within the international system" and identified multiple incentives the United States could offer
that would be critical to the Iranians and which could serve as the basis
for an overarching agreement. They concluded: "Friendly and productive relations between Iran and the United States can and should evolve."

The post-9/11 U.S.-Iranian rapprochement extended beyond Afghanistan. The 2003 Congressional Research Service Report also documented that "Iran was also quietly helpful in the U.S. effort to oust
Iraq's Saddam Hussein." Saddam, of course, had invaded Iran in 1980
and then prosecuted a brutal and merciless war, including the savage
use of chemical weapons, and he brutally repressed Iraqi Shiites in the
south who maintained close ethnic and religious ties to Iran. Few countries could have expected to benefit more from the removal of Saddam
than Iran, and with the planned U.S. invasion of Iraq, the Iranians and
the U.S. thus once again found themselves with aligned interests.

That Iran cooperated meaningfully and closely with the United
States in the wake of the 9/11 attacks is not in dispute. There are, however, differing views of Iran's motives for doing so. The Bush administration and its most vehement anti-Iranian supporters claim that Iran did
this only because Iran perceived the fanatical Sunni Taliban regime as a
threat and was motivated by its own interests to see that regime defeated. They make the same claim regarding Iran's tacit acceptance of the
American war to depose Saddam.

Others, including Flynt Leverett, a former CIA analyst who became a senior director for Middle East policy on the Bush National Security Council, disagree with that assessment, arguing instead that Iran's cooperation with the U.S. over Afghanistan was motivated by Iran's desire for a closer and more constructive overall relationship with the U.S. As Leverett wrote in a December 2006 op-ed in the *New York Times,*

> The argument that Iran helped America in Afghanistan because it was in Tehran's interest to get rid of the Taliban is misplaced. Iran could have let America remove the Taliban without getting its own hands dirty, as it remained neutral during the 1991 Gulf war. Tehran cooperated with United States efforts in Afghanistan primarily because it wanted a better relationship with Washington.

But one does not need to resolve this dispute over Iran's motives in order to draw the most important conclusion. Iran is a rational state actor, which, like most other countries in the world—including American allies—will eagerly cooperate with the United States when their interests converge with ours. It is empirically true that Iran and the U.S. are perfectly capable of working toward the same common goals, and it is empirically false that the Iranians are pursuing an agenda of pure anti-American Evil divorced from rational considerations of their own interests and/or driven by some sort of apocalyptic goal of destruction of the United States.

To know that a country and its leaders act rationally is to take a huge and critical step toward realizing that that country—no matter how internally repressive it might be—cannot and will not be a threat to the U.S. As "evil" as the U.S. government always maintained the Soviet Union was, we did not wage war on the Soviets but instead relied upon their rationality—i.e., their knowledge that they could not wage war on the U.S. without suffering full-scale (albeit mutual) annihilation.

The Iranians, with a military force that is a tiny fraction of the Soviet army, know this as well. That they are rational and that they act in their self-interest demonstrates by itself the absurdity of claiming that they are a threat to the security of the United States. Independently, to demonstrate a country's rationality is to demonstrate that it is susceptible to negotiations and agreements when it perceives such matters to be in its interest (which is, of course, the only time anyone, individual or nation, enters into an agreement).

Indeed, even *after* President Bush declared Iran to be a member of the "axis of evil" in January 2002, Iran continued to pursue a working relationship with the U.S. beyond the Afghanistan issue. The *Financial Times* reported that Iran's supreme leader, Ayatollah Khamenei, in April 2002, "has quietly authorised the Supreme National Security Council to assess the merits of starting talks with the U.S."

And in 2003, the Iranians made an extraordinary overture with the hope of achieving full-scale rapprochement with the U.S. In April of that year—almost immediately after the U.S. military had overrun Baghdad—the Iranian government made an unsolicited offer to the Bush administration with the hope of resolving all significant sources of conflict between the two countries, including the state of Iran's nuclear program. In mid-2006, the *Washington Post's* Glenn Kessler obtained the Iranian document and reported:

> Just after the lightning takeover of Baghdad by U.S. forces three years ago, an unusual two-page document spewed out of a fax machine at the Near East bureau of the State Department. It was a proposal from Iran for a broad dialogue with the United States, and the fax suggested every-thing was on the table—including full cooperation on nuclear programs, acceptance of Israel and the termination of Iranian support for Palestin-ian militant groups.

That offer was sent to the U.S. by the Swiss ambassador, who has been acting as the mediator for all U.S.-Iran communications ever since formal diplomatic relations ended during the 1979 seizure of the U.S. embassy in Tehran. When he conveyed the letter, the Swiss ambassador vouched that it "was an authoritative initiative that had the support of then-President Mohammad Khatami and supreme religious leader Ali Khamenei."

In the document, the Iranian government signaled a broad and flex-ible willingness to negotiate, and reach agreement on, the full panoply of issues to which the Bush administration had objected:

> The document lists a series of Iranian aims for the talks, such as ending sanctions, full access to peaceful nuclear technology and a recognition of its "legitimate security interests." Iran agreed to put a series of U.S. aims

on the agenda, including full cooperation on nuclear safeguards, "decisive action" against terrorists, coordination in Iraq, ending "material support" for Palestinian militias and accepting the Saudi initiative for a two-state solution in the Israeli-Palestinian conflict.

The document also laid out an agenda for negotiations, with possible steps to be achieved at a first meeting and the development of negotiating road maps on disarmament, terrorism and economic cooperation.

Trita Parsi, a Middle East expert at the Carnegie Endowment for International Peace, told Kessler that Iranian flexibility included even their posture toward Israel: "Iranians were ready to dramatically soften their stance on Israel, essentially taking the position of other Islamic countries such as Malaysia." (The official Malaysian policy toward Israel, shared by many Middle Eastern countries, is that it does not recognize Israel's right to exist but would consider relations with Israel once an Israeli-Palestinian peace agreement is reached.)

The Bush administration not only failed to respond to the Iranian overture but actually dismissed it out of hand. Worse, they went out of their way to belittle the offer and insult the Iranians for making it by formally complaining to the Swiss ambassador, telling him it was inappropriate even to convey such an offer on behalf of the Iranians.

In the midst of cooperating with the United States on critical matters, the Iranians came—hat in hand—to negotiate every issue generating U.S.-Iranian conflict, including Israel and the Iranian nuclear program, and the Bush administration refused even to come to the table. It is thus true that, at least over the last five years, one party to the U.S.-Iran conflict has been beyond reason and negotiation, but it is clearly not the Iranians.

The Bush administration's categorical refusal to speak with Iran back in 2003 is especially baffling given that prompting conciliatory gestures of this sort from hostile Middle Eastern governments was ostensibly one of the key objectives in invading Iraq. War advocates endlessly contended that once other Middle Eastern countries saw how strong and resolute the United States was in the post-9/11 world—once we overthrew the Iraqi tyrant and showed that we were willing to get our hands dirty in a real fight—other countries in that region would realize that they had no choice but to become more conciliatory and cooperative with the U.S., driven by the fear that they could be the next Iraq.

The 2003 accord between the United States and Libya was held up as the classic model for this theory. Repeatedly, the conciliations made by Libyan leader Muammar al-Gadhafi were pointed to by Bush officials as an illustrative, successful example of this "Show of Force" strategy. On December 19, 2003, President Bush convened the media at the White House to announce what he excitedly called "a development of great importance":

> Today in Tripoli, the leader of Libya, Colonel Moammar al-Ghadafi, publicly confirmed his commitment to disclose and dismantle all weapons-of-mass-destruction programs in his country. He has agreed immediately and unconditionally to allow inspectors from international organizations to enter Libya.

As the president himself explained, this agreement "came about through quiet diplomacy," specifically "nine months" of "talks" between the Libyan government and representatives of the United States and England. The commencement of the negotiations, then, was more or less simultaneous with the U.S. invasion of Iraq, exactly when Iran was making similar overtures. President Bush explicitly claimed a connection between the invasion of Iraq and the fear that, the president asserted, drove Libya to accept key concessions:

> We obtained an additional United Nations Security Council Resolution requiring Saddam Hussein to prove that he had disarmed, and when that resolution was defied, we led a coalition to enforce it. All of these actions by the United States and our allies have sent an unmistakable message to regimes that seek or possess weapons of mass destruction. Those weapons do not bring influence or prestige. They bring isolation and otherwise unwelcome consequences.

The president and his supporters repeatedly cited Libya as an example of the benefits of the fear-inducing aspects of using military force. During his September 30, 2004, debate with John Kerry, President Bush again explicitly touted this connection:

I would hope to never have to use force.

But by speaking clearly and sending messages that we mean what we say, we've affected the world in a positive way.

Look at Libya. Libya was a threat. Libya is now peacefully dismantling its weapons programs.

Libya understood that America and others will enforce doctrine [*sic*] and that the world is better for it.

This was precisely the dynamic that seemingly drove the Iranians to strike such a conciliatory pose with their April 2003 offer to negotiate with the United States. Parsi explained the Iranians' motivations this way: "The U.S. victory in Iraq frightened the Iranians because U.S. forces had routed in three weeks an army that Iran had failed to defeat during a bloody eight-year war."

Indeed, the Iranians sent the negotiation letter after the fall of Baghdad but before the beginning of any real insurgency against the American military—i.e., at the time when American power in Iraq was at its peak and before the Americans had any reason to believe that the Iranians were fueling an anti-American insurgency. Yet even with the Iranians in precisely the position of weakness and fear that Bush officials claimed they would have to be in before behavioral change would occur—and when the U.S. had its strongest hand in the Middle East—the administration categorically refused even to acknowledge the Iranian overture.

With the U.S. having conveyed to the Iranians that a cooperative framework was not even a possibility to be considered, what ensued was not difficult to predict: The Iranians had only one option, namely, to pursue a more hostile and aggressive course in order to be acknowledged, and perhaps to prepare for what seemed to be the Bush administration's affirmative desire for escalated conflict.

When the administration rejected the 2003 Iranian request to negotiate, the Iranians' nuclear program was close to dormant. At that time, Flynt Leverett was a senior director on the Bush National Security Council staff. He described the Iranian letter as "a serious effort, a respectable effort to lay out a comprehensive agenda for U.S.-Iranian rapprochement," and told the *Post*'s Kessler, "At the time, the Iranians were not spinning centrifuges, they were not enriching uranium."

By rejecting and outrightly scorning the Iranian offer, the Bush administration unmistakably signaled to the Iranians that offers of conciliation and compromise would not be respected. Carnegie's Parsi explained that in the wake of the humiliating U.S. rejection of their overture, "Iranian officials decided that the United States cared not about Iranian policies but about Iranian power." Worse, the incident "strengthened the hands of those in Iran who believe the only way to compel the United States to talk or deal with Iran is not by sending peace offers but by being a nuisance," Parsi said.

With the U.S. refusing meaningful diplomatic engagement with the Iranians, and with the president adopting increasingly bellicose and threatening rhetoric about them, U.S.-Iranian relations became more hostile than they had been since the 1979 revolution.

A CONFEDERATION OF WAR-SEEKING FACTIONS

Why would the president, in the midst of substantial and growing cooperation with the Iranians, suddenly decree Iran in 2002 to be part of an axis of evil, and all but declare Iran an enemy on whom war must inevitably be waged? Numerous and disparate factions surrounding the president each desired, albeit for different reasons and with different motives, hostility and conflict with Iran. Those factions perceive that belligerence toward Iran, rather than a negotiated peace, would promote their respective agendas. And each was able to depict Iran in the Manichean terms that would ensure that the president would see Iran as an implacable foe he was duty-bound to defeat.

Numerous ideologies and belief systems have played prominent roles in shaping the president's Manichean militarism toward Iran. Initially, the president surrounded himself with traditional, garden-variety hawks— those who are driven by a central belief in the virtue and justification of America's use of its superior military force to impose its will on other nations. Such hawkishness is embodied by both Vice President Cheney and former Defense Secretary Rumsfeld and exists independent of any specific geopolitical reasons for seeking Middle East hegemony. Hawks of this sort have cheered on every warmongering step taken by the president. A highly influential strain in the Bush administration seeks war because it believes in the use of war as a principal tool for securing America's interests and dealing with other nations that refuse to submit to America's will.

And then there is the related set of concerns: the emerging prospect that the world's demand for oil will outstrip supply, and that with Saudi oil production potentially peaking, the largest strategic reserves will be in Iran, where U.S. access can be ensured only with a pro-American government in place. Oil is a critical resource for a nation's strength, prosperity, and security. It is also finite and becoming scarce. Those who insist that such considerations are irrelevant to foreign policy decisions regarding the most oil-rich region on the planet, and the most oil-rich nations in that region, are advancing claims too frivolous to merit serious consideration. Access to and control over the Middle East's oil supply pervades, to one degree or another, virtually all power struggles within that region.

Such oil-related objectives would likely motivate most mainstream American political leaders, let alone ones such as George Bush and Dick Cheney, who share a background in the oil industry and who retain substantial ties of every type to that industry. There are multiple reasons why the United States continues to sacrifice so much of its resources, its attention, and many of its lives to continued influence and even domination of the Middle East (versus other regions of the world where we appear more or less indifferent). Those who seek to deny that ensuring our influence over the oil supply is a significant factor in why we have made the Middle East our predominant national priority are either incredibly naïve or indescribably dishonest.

Regarding the most important issues of the Bush presidency—the invasion of Iraq, the treatment of Iran, and enhanced and unprecedented domestic police powers—traditional hawkishness and concern over the Middle Eastern oil supply have worked in perfect tandem with one another. And that agenda has also converged with two other critically influential factions of the Bush presidency—namely, the president's base of Christian evangelicals who view political power as a means for promoting their theological objectives, and independently, the Israel-centric strain of neoconservatives. The agendas of all of those factions have been promoted by the same policies—the invasion of Iraq, expanded police powers at home, and the treatment of anti-American regimes in the Middle East as mortal enemies to be shunned, demonized, and attacked.

An influential faction of Christian evangelicals has loyally supported the Bush foreign policy in the Middle East (except to complain periodically that it is insufficiently aggressive). That faction is driven by the general theological belief that God's will is for Jews to occupy all of "Greater Israel," which will occur only once the enemies of Israel are defeated. There is no question—because many of their key leaders have said so themselves—that evangelicals, who compose a substantial part of President Bush's most loyal following, have become fanatically "pro-Israel" in their foreign policy views because they believe that strengthening Israel is a necessary prerequisite for Rapture to occur—for the world to be ruled by Christianity upon Jesus' apocalyptic return to Earth—and they believe that can occur only once "Greater Israel" is unified under Jewish control.

For obvious reasons, those theological yearnings have led evangelicals to be almost perfect allies of both the Israel-centric neoconservatives and the more traditional warmongers. All three groups—with different premises and different motives—have an interest in depicting multiple Middle East countries as Evil and urging the need to wage war on them.

Related to the specific evangelical drive to bring about Rapture by strengthening Israel is a more general belief among some evangelical Christians that wars against Muslims are justified and necessary because Muslims are an enemy of Christianity. The extent to which this belief is held is difficult to quantify, but various incidents have left no doubt that, at least in some discrete Bush-supporting circles, the "War on Terrorism"—and specifically more wars on more Islamic states such as Iran—is supported because they are seen as religious wars to be waged in defense of Christianity.

The president himself was forced to apologize after he described the U.S. War on Terrorism as a "new crusade," evoking the historic wars of invasion waged by Christians against Muslims. Further Muslim-Christian sectarian flames were fueled by the statements of U.S. General William G. Boykin, the Bush administration's deputy undersecretary of defense for intelligence, who specifically described the war against Islamic extremists as a war of righteousness against the forces of Satan and claimed Muslims are not protected by God because they worship a mere "idol."

In a November 2006 *New York Review of Books* article, Garry Wills detailed another incident involving General Boykin. After President Bush's 2000 election but before his 2004 re-election, General Boykin appeared in full military uniform before evangelical congregations and insisted that President Bush was installed in the White House by God:

> Ask yourself this: why is this man in the White House? The majority of Americans did not vote for him. Why is he there? . . . I tell you this morning he's in the White House because God put him there for such a time as this. God put him there to lead not only this nation but to lead the world, in such a time as this.

As Wills reports, Boykin, in part of his stump speech in churches, would typically present a slide show with photographs of individuals such as Osama bin Laden, Saddam Hussein, and various Taliban leaders while asking if each was "the enemy." He "gave a resounding no to each question," and then explained:

> The battle this nation is in is a spiritual battle, it's a battle for our soul. And the enemy is a guy called Satan. . . . Satan wants to destroy this nation. He wants to destroy us as a nation, and he wants to destroy us as a Christian army.

Though President Bush distanced himself from those remarks, claiming that they do not "reflect my point of view or the point of view of this administration," then-Secretary Rumsfeld defended General Boykin. And though a Pentagon review found that Boykin had violated several military regulations by failing to make clear that his comments were not made in his official capacity as a general, no action was taken against him and he continued to serve in critical Pentagon posts, involved at the highest levels of America's Middle Eastern wars.

Devout evangelicals are among the most steadfast supporters of his aggressive and militaristic policies toward the Islamic world, and many expressly defend those policies on theological and moral grounds. That the president finds some of his most loyal support for his War on Terrorism among such theologically driven groups lends further support to the connection between religious beliefs and President Bush's militaristic, Manichean foreign policy in the Middle East.

Of course, it has long been clear that Islamic extremists in the mold of Osama bin Laden also see the war they are waging as primarily religious in nature. Religious invocations to the Islamic duty to wage jihad against infidels are rhetorical staples for Muslim extremists. Most Muslim terrorists who engage in suicide missions or who devote their lives to violent attacks against the West are engaged in what they perceive as religious warfare on behalf of Islam. Beyond this Manichean fervor, some are motivated by more traditional political agendas, such as anti-imperialistic sentiments against U.S. influence in their region, the American alliance with Israel, or, in the case of Iraq and Afghanistan, garden-variety nationalistic opposition to an invading and occupying foreign military. But there is also clearly a similar theological component driving some of the support for increasingly warlike policies in the United States.

Evangelical leader James Dobson told Larry King in a November 2002 interview: "I feel very strongly about Israel. You know it is surrounded by its enemies. And it exists primarily because God has willed it to exist, I think, according to scripture." Dobson is an almost completely reliable supporter of the neoconservative line, condemning the Baker-Hamilton report's recommendation that the United States negotiate with Iran by predictably equating the recommendation to appeasement of the Nazis: "That has the same kind of feel to it as the British negotiating with Germany, Italy and Japan in the run-up to World War II."

And evangelical minister John Hagee of Texas addressed the first annual conference of his new group, Christians United for Israel, during the Israel-Hezbollah War in July-August 2006. He declared that war to be "a battle between good and evil" and insisted support for Israel was "God's foreign policy." The following day, Hagee went to the White House to meet with President Bush's top Middle East adviser, neoconservative Elliot Abrams, and he delivered the same message, adding that "appeasement has never helped the Jewish people." Hagee advised the *New York Times* that Abrams largely agreed with his views.

Evangelical leader Gary Bauer told the *Times* in November 2006 that as a result of his intensely anti-Israeli rhetoric, Iranian President Ahmadinejad has become one of the most despised foreign political figures among American Christians: "I am not sure there is a foreign leader who has made a bigger splash in American culture since Khrushchev, certainly among committed Christians."

U.S. senator James Inhofe, a Republican social conservative from Oklahoma, actually placed blame on the U.S. for the 9/11 attacks, by asserting that the U.S. had itself opened "the spiritual door" for those attacks by failing to support Israel steadfastly enough. Senator Inhofe declared in a March 2002 speech on the Senate floor:

> One of the reasons I believe the spiritual door was opened for an attack against the United States was that the policy of our government has been to ask the Israelis, and demand it with pressure, not to retaliate against the terrorist strikes that have been launched against them.

It is certainly true that this extremist, theological commitment to Israel as a means of facilitating Jesus' return is not shared by a majority of Christians. But these are hardly fringe views either. Christian evangelicals have played an important role in both of President Bush's election victories and in the general preservation of Republican power. Many of the evangelical leaders who spout these extremist "pro-Israeli" theological views exert substantial influence at high levels of the Bush administration and with the president himself. Their doctrinal convictions have played a substantial role in generating support for the president's militarism in the Middle East and his Manichean approach to Israel's enemies.

Those who seek to wage war on Iran typically cite the radical Islamic religious beliefs of President Ahmadinejad as evidence of Iran's irrational Evil. Specifically, Ahmadinejad subscribes to the view that, like Christians waiting for the return of Christ, Muslims are awaiting the return of the "twelfth imam," whose return will bring about the supremacy of Islam and the restoration of peace and the reign of the Good. The two doctrines are similar in their fundamentals, and both can generate demands for Manichean wars and conflagration.

General Boykin's view that the War on Terrorism is compelled by theological, pro-Christian objectives is shared by scores of evangelical leaders who are vital parts of the president's political base and who, in many cases, are close associates of the president himself. Thus, as Garry Wills put it, "Boykin was safe under the sheltering wings of a religious right that the White House did not dare to cross."

· · ·

A nd then there is America's alliance with Israel and the role it plays in our bellicose posture toward Iran. In examining the president's 2002 decision to include Iran in the axis of evil despite increasing U.S.-Iran cooperation—and to this day to insist that Iran is an enemy of the United States—the role played by Israeli interests (as perceived by its right-wing American supporters) simply cannot be ignored. But when it comes to discussions of Iran in the national media and by national political figures, that topic typically is ignored.

While Iran has repeatedly demonstrated a willingness to seek cooperative relations with the United States, relations between Iran and Israel have been genuinely, and mutually, hostile. The depiction of Iran as pure Evil being propagated by Bush-supporting, war-seeking Americans has been echoed by the Israelis with increasing fervor.

As is true for the rhetoric of the president's supporters and the president himself, 2006 saw a marked escalation in the Israelis' hostile rhetoric toward Iran. On October 27, 2006, Israel's prime minister Ehud Olmert invoked the standard neoconservative "historical analogy" by expressly comparing Iran to Nazi Germany. Referring to Iran, Prime Minister Olmert said: "We hear echoes of those very voices that started to spread across the world in the 1930s."

Ironically, Olmert, at the start of 2007, found himself the *target* of the same accusation invoking the specter of Neville Chamberlain. As UPI editor Arnaud de Borchgrave reported regarding Israeli debates over Iran: "In a New Year's Day message, superhawk and former Prime Minister Binyamin Netanyahu accused Prime Minister Ehud Olmert of the kind of appeasement that threatened Israel's very existence."

Israel's newest cabinet minister, Avigdor Lieberman, whose duties include strategic affairs with Iran, visited the United States in December 2006 and told the *New York Times:* "Our first task is to convince Western countries to adopt a tough approach to the Iranian problem," which he called "the biggest threat facing the Jewish people since the Second World War." Lieberman insisted that American efforts to negotiate with Iran were worthless and should not be attempted: "The dialogue with Iran will be a 100-percent failure, just like it was with North Korea."

In his 2007 New Year's speech, Netanyahu made clear that he shares the same goal—convincing the U.S. to consider Iran as an American problem, not just an Israeli one. He said that Israel

> must immediately launch an intense, international, public relations front first and foremost on the U.S., the goal being to encourage President Bush to live up to specific pledges he would not allow Iran to arm itself with nuclear weapons. We must make clear to the government, the Congress, and the American public that a nuclear Iran is a threat to the U.S. and the entire world, not only Israel.

UPI's de Borchgrave quoted from an article in *Ynet* by Oded Tira, chairman of the Israeli Manufacturers Association and former chief artillery officer in the IDF, in which he made clear that many Israelis are committed to finding a way to make an American attack on Iran a political necessity (emphasis added):

> Bush lacks the political power to attack Iran. *As an American air strike in Iran is essential for our existence,* we must help pave the way by lobbying the Democratic Party, which is conducting itself foolishly, and U.S. newspaper editors.
>
> *We need to turn the Iranian issue into a bipartisan one and unrelated to the Iraq failure.* Hillary Clinton and other potential presidential candidates in the Democratic Party (must) publicly support immediate action by Bush against Iran.

As the prewar "debate" over the invasion of Iraq demonstrated, the key to persuading Americans to support a new war is to convince them that the country targeted for attack is governed by terrorists and those who support international terrorism. Those terms, by design, evoke images of the 9/11 attacks, and the accusation is designed to tie the accused to those attacks even where the so-called terrorist supporters have nothing to do with 9/11.

Indeed, to claim that a country "supports international terrorism" is the most inflammatory accusation that can be made, as it will be understood by many Americans to designate specifically that the accused "participated in the 9/11 attacks," or more generally that they are close allies of Al Qaeda. Even with Americans' growing emotional distance from the 2001 attacks, many Americans will reflexively—one could even say understandably—support military action against not just anyone who directly participated in the 9/11 attacks but anyone who seems to have close proximity to those responsible.

Thus, even more than the alarming claims of Saddam's WMDs, the vague allegation that he supported "international terrorism" is what persuaded Americans of the wisdom and necessity of attacking Iraq. Although the specific allegation that Saddam participated in the 9/11 attacks was never explicitly made, the more general claim that he "supported terrorism" was sufficient to lead almost 70 percent of Americans to believe—even as late as September 2003, six months *after* the United States invaded Iraq—that Saddam personally participated in the planning of the 9/11 attacks.

This same manipulative tactic—accusing the Iranians of "supporting international terrorism" as a means of implicitly persuading Americans that Iran bears some responsibility for, or at least connection to, the 9/11 attacks, so therefore it, too, must be attacked—is the principal one on which the president and his supporters are relying to justify antagonism toward Iran. And the tactic is no less honest than it was when employed against Iraq. If anything, it is far more dishonest. The evidence that Iran sponsors or in any way abets terrorist attacks on the U.S. is nonexistent.

To document the ongoing threat posed to the United States by international terrorism, the Bush administration's 2006 *National Security Strategy* focuses on Al Qaeda and the type of terrorist attacks that have been directed at Americans or Westerners generally during the last decade—in London, Madrid, Bali, and New York during the first World Trade Center attack and on 9/11. But Iran had nothing to do with any of those. That country does not sponsor Al Qaeda or any groups affiliated with Al Qaeda, nor does it sponsor any other groups devoted to staging terrorist attacks on the United States.

Quite the contrary, Shiite Iran has long-standing animosities with Sunni-dominated Al Qaeda. That was one reason, among others, why Iran stalwartly opposed the Al Qaeda–sheltering Taliban and worked extensively with the U.S. in the aftermath of the 9/11 attacks in order to bring about an end to their rule.

To the extent that Iran can be said to have an association with "ter-rorist" groups, those groups are devoted to supporting the Palestinians against Israel as part of the conflict over the West Bank (Hamas) or de-voted to supporting the Lebanese against Israel (Hezbollah). Iran is *not* devoted to fighting along with Al Qaeda or any other group devoted to staging terrorist attacks on Americans or against the United States. Iran's support for what the Bush administration calls "international terrorist groups" is limited to those groups that are hostile to Israel, not those which pose a threat to the U.S.

The 2003 Congressional Research Service Report documented that "U.S. concerns about Iran's support for terrorism center on its assistance to *groups opposed to the Arab-Israeli peace process,* primarily Hamas, Pales-tinian Islamic Jihad, Hizbullah, and the Popular Front for the Libera-tion of Palestine-General Command" (emphasis added). The agendas of those groups are confined to anti-Israeli positions, and none stages attacks on the U.S.

Deliberately vague claims that Iran "supports international terrorism" are virtually always predicated on its support for anti-*Israeli*, not anti-U.S., groups. When Michael Gerson issued his call to war against Iran in the pages of *Newsweek* in August 2006, for instance, he accused Iran of sup-porting "terrorist groups like Hizbullah and Hamas." In Joe Lieberman's December 2006 op-ed in the *Washington Post,* which essentially declared the U.S. at war with Iran, he warned Americans of what he called "Iran's terrorist agents," whom he then identified as "Hezbollah and Hamas."

It is true that Hezbollah, a group created to defend Lebanon against military invasions from Israel, was responsible for the attack on U.S. troops in 1983 when American troops were inside that nation. Ronald Reagan then withdrew American troops from that country, and ever since, over the next twenty-four years, Hezbollah has staged no attacks of any kind on the United States.

Hezbollah was also quite possibly responsible for two bombings in Buenos Aires, Argentina, in the early 1990s—a 1992 car bomb attack at the Israeli embassy in Argentina and a similar 1994 bombing of a Jewish community center in Buenos Aires. But even assuming that those at-tacks were engineered by Hezbollah with Iranian backing—a precarious assumption for which, particularly with regard to Iranian involvement, there is no confirmation—the target of Hezbollah is plainly Israel, not the United States.

There are countless groups around the world engaged in what could be called terrorism, and the vast majority have nothing to do with attacks on the U.S. Some have domestic agendas and some have regional agendas. Only a tiny fraction have anything to do with Al Qaeda or are devoted in any way toward attacking America.

The groups that Iran supports—Hezbollah, Hamas, and the Palestine Islamic Jihad—are certainly hostile to Israel, and certainly include anti-American rhetoric as part of their speeches, but they pose no threat to the U.S. As Hezbollah's leader, Sheik Hassan Nasrallah, has himself pointed out repeatedly, "Outside this fight [against Israel], we have done nothing." Thus, claims that Iran "supports international terrorism"—even if true—do not translate into support for Al Qaeda or any group that poses a threat to the U.S., though the intent of the president and his war-seeking supporters is plainly to leave that false impression.

There may (or may not) be a compelling argument to make that the U.S. should view terrorist attacks on Israel as attacks on the U.S. There may (or may not) be a compelling argument to make that because Israel is an ally of the United States, America should be willing to wage war against countries that sponsor terrorist attacks on Israel, or that American commitment to spreading democracy requires the United States to come to the defense of Israel.

Or perhaps there is (or is not) a good case to be made that U.S. interests are so inextricably linked with Israel's that America cannot, or should not, attempt to distinguish between terrorist attacks directed at Israel and those directed at the U.S. If there are valid arguments for deeming Israel's enemies to be enemies of the U.S., then they should be made explicitly and clearly, without the type of misleading obfuscation that President Bush and his supporters clearly intend to create by implying that Iran supports anti-U.S. terrorist groups.

It may be true that Iran—as the Bush administration's *National Security Strategy* alleges—is involved in the state sponsorship of international terrorism, but, for Iran, that terrorism is directed against Israel, not against the U.S. That may or may not be a distinction that ultimately matters, but the factual lines should not be allowed to be blurred this way, because that is exactly what allows war advocates to mislead Americans into viewing Iran as an enemy of the U.S.

From its inception, the campaign to depict and treat Iran as pure, unadulterated Evil has been driven by this manipulative and dishonest attempt to conflate Iran's posture toward Israel with its posture toward the U.S. Whether the president himself was a victim of that manipulation or a knowing propagator of it is something one can debate, and the truth likely lies somewhere in between. But what is beyond dispute is the centrality of Israel and its right-wing American supporters in shaping the president's moralistic and absolutist view of Iran.

Indisputably, the Israelis perceive Iran as far and away their most formidable and serious enemy. And there is a strong argument to make that, from the Israeli perspective, this perception is justified. Iran provides critical support for anti-Israel groups based in two of Israeli's neighbors—Palestine and Lebanon—and Iran itself, like many Muslim countries around the world, formally opposes Israel's right to exist in the Middle East.

But it should go without saying that a country's opposition to Israel does not render it an enemy of the U.S., certainly not one on which *Americans* must wage war. Yet the president's view of Iran as Evil, and the collision course he has embarked upon with regard to Iran, critically depends upon the conflating of Israeli interests with American interests, as though the two are, by definition and in every instance, the same.

In the weeks before the president's 2002 State of the Union speech, relations between the U.S. and Iran were improving dramatically. But as a result of the January 2002 discovery by Israel that Iran was shipping relatively sophisticated weapons to the Palestinians, the Israelis were blaming Iran for what the Israelis perceived was an extremely significant threat to their security—specifically their ability to dominate the Palestinians militarily. These two visions of Iran—the American view of a country that was becoming increasingly cooperative, and the Israeli view of a country that was becoming increasingly threatening and hostile—were in direct and irreconcilable conflict.

President Bush—in a speech shaped by neoconservative speechwriter David Frum—resolved that conflict in favor of the Israeli view by pronouncing on January 30, 2002, that Iran was a member of the "axis of evil" and directing the most threatening language possible toward that country. In light of the actual state of U.S.-Iranian relations, the president's inclusion of Iran as an "axis of evil" member was both sudden and mystifying. The BBC in February 2002 drew the only rational conclusion:

> By taking such a hard line on Iran, Washington is once again falling in line with Israel's view of its most serious strategic long term threat.
>
> Israeli officials insist that Iran is less than three years from developing a nuclear weapon and is developing long range weapons that could deliver it.

Iranian journalist Haleh Anvari, writing in *Salon* in February 2002, made a similar observation:

> The Israeli seizure of the *Karine A,* a ship containing a cargo of arms that Israel and the United States claim Iran was shipping to Yasser Arafat's Palestinian Authority, and intense Israeli lobbying are seen as the decisive factors that led Bush to place Iran in the "evil" category.

All that mattered—and all that continues to matter—to the neoconservative supporters of George Bush is that a U.S.-Iranian rapprochement be avoided at all costs and that the United States wage war on Iran, spending American resources and risking American lives. It was in that deliberately generated climate that the Manichean and evangelical George Bush was persuaded to declare Iran Evil, and in which Bush thereafter sought to persuade Americans that we must consider Iran our Evil enemy. A February 2002 *Weekly Standard* article entitled "On to Iran," urged war with Iran less than six months after the 9/11 attacks. The article's author, AEI fellow Reuel Marc Gerecht, clearly understood how to persuade Bush to view Iran as the enemy:

> The president understands a basic truth about tyrannies that employ terrorism and seek weapons of mass destruction: They are systemically evil. Their leaders are amoral dictators, with an acute appreciation of power politics and their enemy's jugular. They inevitably corrupt and destroy their own civil societies. You negotiate with them at your peril.

As Gerecht recognized, the goal for those wishing to induce the president to act with entrenched belligerence toward another country is to persuade him that that country is "Evil." That is of far greater importance than persuading the president that the country is a threat to the U.S. And with those Manichean, moralistic premises the president embraced, Iran was decreed, in early 2002, to be our "evil" enemy, beyond reason and incapable of understanding anything other than brute force. And there it has immovably remained, for the next five years, while the Bush policy toward Iran has become ever more hostile and ineffective.

One can reasonably argue that the U.S. should have a policy of supporting its most important allies and/or other democracies, including Israel. The U.S. provides security guarantees for all sorts of countries. That's all fair game for open discussion. But few things are more threatening to *Israeli interests* than deceitfully securing American policies based on pretext, conflation, and contrivance whereby Americans are manipulated into supporting policies based on false pretenses. People can be fooled for only so long, and people who feel deceived generally backlash against the deceivers.

It is not the case that those who attempt to trigger U.S. military action against Israel's enemies are guilty of doing too much to help Israel. Though "helping Israel" might be their motive, they achieve the precise opposite result.

A strong argument can be made that Americans are likely to be supportive of a democratic, long-standing ally like Israel and to sympathize with the need for America to protect all of its allies—including Israel—from genuine existential threats. But if Americans are being induced to support wars not in American interests but rather Israel's, and if American lives and treasure are being squandered in wars justified by false pretenses, by a hidden agenda, they will realize that at some point—likely at the point when such a war has gone particularly awry and they begin to search for the real reasons we entered it in the first place.

When the realization begins to dawn that at least one substantial factor as to why America waged Middle Eastern war(s) is because influential individuals with an overarching devotion to Israel pushed for war against Israel's enemies, then an anti-Israeli backlash is highly likely to occur. And the backlash is likely to be far more severe and hostile than anything that would ever happen naturally, meaning in the absence of such manipulation.

Despite the fact that right-wing pro-Israeli advocates of the Iraq War have suffered significant losses of credibility over their prewar prognostications, the pressure on the president to view Iranian hostility toward Israel as a justification for American attacks on Iran has not waned any. To the contrary, in 2006, demands that the U.S. view Iran as the ultimate enemy have been increasing.

As Americans have soured on U.S. military intervention in the Middle East as a result of the Iraq disaster, neoconservatives have become more desperate and less risk-averse in the argumentation they use. They disguise their underlying beliefs far less and have become much more explicit about their demand that President Bush view Israel's enemies as Evil and wage war on them.

In July 2006, when war broke out between Israel and Hezbollah, Bill Kristol came right out and candidly put his views on the table. In a *Weekly Standard* article bluntly entitled "This Is Our War" (by "Our," he means the U.S.), Kristol argued explicitly what many have contended for some time is an unstated belief of neoconservatives: that the U.S. should view the threats to Israel as threats to the U.S., because the enemy is the same, and should join Israel in the destruction of those numerous enemies.

Kristol actually argued that President Bush should immediately abandon the G8 summit in Russia—where he was meeting with long-standing European allies of the U.S. whom Kristol disdains, largely because they are too evenhanded with regard to Israel's conflicts with its neighbors—and fly to Jerusalem in order to stand by Israel, in "our" new war, which should be waged against Iran, Syria, and Hezbollah, just for starters. With Israel in the midst of a brutal war it was widely perceived to be losing, Kristol all but demanded that the U.S. intervene and attack Iran, the country widely viewed as the ultimate supporter of Hezbollah (emphasis added):

> What's happening in the Middle East, then, isn't just another chapter in the Arab-Israeli conflict. What's happening is an Islamist-Israeli war. You might even say this is part of the Islamist war on the West—but is India part of the West? Better to say that what's under attack is liberal democratic civilization, whose leading representative right now happens to be the United States. . . .

The war against radical Islamism is likely to be a long one. Radical Islamism isn't going away anytime soon. But it will make a big difference how strong the state sponsors, harborers, and financiers of radical Islamism are. *Thus, our focus should be less on Hamas and Hezbollah, and more on their paymasters and real commanders—Syria and Iran. . . .*

For while Syria and Iran are enemies of Israel, they are also enemies of the United States. We have done a poor job of standing up to them and weakening them. They are now testing us more boldly than one would have thought possible a few years ago. Weakness is provocative. We have been too weak, and have allowed ourselves to be perceived as weak. . . .

The right response is renewed strength—in supporting the governments of Iraq and Afghanistan, in standing with Israel, and in pursuing regime change in Syria and Iran. For that matter, *we might consider countering this act of Iranian aggression with a military strike against Iranian nuclear facilities. Why wait? . . .*

But such a military strike would take a while to organize. In the meantime, perhaps President Bush can fly from the silly G8 summit in St. Petersburg—a summit that will most likely convey a message of moral confusion and political indecision—to Jerusalem, the capital of a nation that stands with us, *and is willing to fight with us, against our common enemies. This is our war, too.*

Kristol's demand that President Bush wage war against Iran in order to assist Israel was quickly echoed by some of the president's most influential Israeli-centric supporters. Writing the next day in *National Review*, John Podhoretz excitedly celebrated "Kristol's very arresting take," while Michael Ledeen, also in *National Review*, complained bitterly that President Bush hadn't yet thrown the U.S. militarily into this new war, and even unleashed the worst neoconservative insult there is by equating Bush with Chamberlain:

But we have not heard anything about "seizing the moment." We hear lawyer talk and diplotalk, surrender talk and appeasement talk, and there is no action whatsoever. Is this not the time to go after the terrorist training camps in Syria and Iran? What in the world are we waiting for?

And finally, if we dither through this one, the next one will be worse. Maybe much worse. It's not going away. Stability is a mirage. Chamberlain had a choice between dishonor and war. He chose war and got dishonor. You too, Mr. President. It's the way it works.

As the president's neoconservative supporters are now expressly arguing, Israel's enemies are America's enemies, and President Bush must wage war on all of them. If he refuses, he will be guilty of the dreaded sin of cowardly appeasement, of failing to confront pure Evil that threatens Western civilization.

All of these various influences and factions have fueled an approach to Iran by President Bush that is fraught with danger for the U.S. and is extremely difficult to derail. Yet the president is also without any credible military threat, with the burden being carried in Iraq, and is further burdened by an American public that plainly would not stand for a whole new war. Yet his depiction of Iran as Evil has left him with no real options. As intended, the wedge inserted between the U.S. and Iran seems impossible to remove during the Bush presidency.

THE NON-CARTOON IRAN

The caricature of Iran as pure Evil and the grave threat it poses to the U.S. are grounded in pure pretext. Much of the caricaturing of Iran has been enabled by the outlandish and malicious statements of Iran's elected president, Mahmoud Ahmadinejad, including his expressed desire for the elimination of Israel and doubts about whether the Holocaust really occurred. Though advocates of war with Iran have depicted Ahmadinejad as some sort of supreme leader of Iran, he is, in fact, nothing of the sort.

Iran's most powerful leaders are the unelected Ayatollahs and mullahs who control most of Iran's critical power centers; the power of the president in Iran is secondary and limited by multiple factors. Ironically, many of those who seek to inflate President Ahmadinejad into some sort of supreme dictator in order to capitalize on the outrageousness of his statements were the same ones who continuously belittled the power of the Iranian presidency when it was occupied from 1997 to 2005 by an Iranian moderate/reformist, Mohammad Khatami.

Indeed, Khatami openly rejected the notion that Iran was on the opposite side of a war of civilizations with the West, but instead aggressively advocated détente. During the Khatami presidency, those who sought to persuade the U.S. to continue to view Iran as an enemy repeatedly insisted that Khatami's moderation was irrelevant because it was the radical clerics who had the real power in Iran, and the position of president was a virtual sinecure, maintained to placate demands among Iranians for some type of democratic representation.

Writing in *National Review* in 2003, Amir Taheri, the neoconservatives' favorite Iran "expert," called Khatami "irrelevant" and a mere "figurehead." In 2002, *The New Republic* editors dismissed him as "timid and powerless." And the *Financial Times* warned that it is "doubtful he has the powers" to impede the agenda of Iranian radicals. But now that an easy-to-demonize hard-line figure, rather than a reformist, occupies the presidency, voices from the nation's war-hungry precincts focus almost exclusively on Iran's president as though he is its supreme leader (a title which is, revealingly, exactly that claimed by Iran's true leader, Ayatollah Ali Khamenei).

The notion that Ahmadinejad possesses absolute dictatorial power along the lines of Adolf Hitler, or even that he is the most powerful figure in Iran, is sheer fiction. Indeed, by the end of 2006, Ahmadinejad had suffered a series of significant defeats and public indignities, including the year-end loss of his supporters in local Iranian elections and the victory of one of his most powerful political rivals, Hashemi Rafsanjani.

Those elections installed moderate and reformist candidates who are opposed to Ahmadinejad in a whole spectrum of political positions. And the rebuke he suffered was personal in nature, as both his "spiritual adviser," Ayatollah Mohammed-Taghi Mesbah-Yazdi, and even his own sister, Parvine, suffered crushing electoral defeats.

One of the leading anti-Ahmadinejad parties, the reformist Islamic Iran Participation Front, issued a taunting victory statement after the election results were certified, which read in part:

> The initial results of elections throughout the country indicate that Mr. Ahmadinejad's list has experienced a decisive defeat nationwide. They

were tantamount to a big "no" to the government's authoritarian and inefficient methods.

Manifestly, the freedom of opposing political parties to mount serious challenges to Ahmadinejad's power, let alone to triumph over him and freely express such harsh criticism, negates the ludicrous attempt to depict him as some type of Hitler-like dictator with absolute power in Iran. He is nothing of the sort.

And while Ahmadinejad's rhetoric toward Israel and about the Holocaust is repugnant, there is nothing unique about Iran's position regarding Israel, particularly when compared to the broader Middle East. Scores of Middle Eastern countries share the Iranians' refusal to recognize Israel's right to exist, including countries cooperative with, even allies of, the United States.

President Bush, for instance, has long hailed the United Arab Emirates as a "good friend" of the U.S. He repeatedly praised that country and vouched for its reliability and Goodness during the controversy provoked by his administration's attempt to turn over operations of various American ports to a company controlled by the UAE government.

Yet the position of the UAE with respect to Israel is virtually indistinguishable from that held by Evil incarnate Iran. Both deny Israel's right to exist. Indeed, the UAE officially prohibits any Israeli citizen even from entering their country, to the point of refusing to allow Israeli athletes entrance in order to attend international sporting events, including an annual professional tennis tournament held in Dubai.

One can get a sense of just how extreme is the UAE's anti-Israeli position merely by reviewing its official website for tourists, which includes some information about the country's entrance and visa policies:

General Information

There are several types of visas for visitors to Dubai.
- Nationals of "Israel" may not enter the U.A.E.
- Citizens of the Arab Gulf Co-operation Council member states (Bahrain, Kuwait, Qatar, Oman, Saudi Arabia) do not need a visa.

It is not merely that Israeli citizens are barred from entering the country. Note the snide quotation marks around the word *Israel*—to the UAE (and Iran), that is a concept that is not real, that is nonexistent. By rather stark contrast, the UAE does not even require a visa before it welcomes citizens of Saudi Arabia—the country that gave us fifteen out of the nineteen 9/11 hijackers (with two sent courtesy of the UAE, and none from Iran).

There is nothing exceptional about Muslim states refusing to recognize Israel's right to exist and singling it out for hostility. Malaysia, for instance, is considered to be a perfectly moderate Muslim country and a reasonably friendly nation to the U.S., yet it expressly denies Israel's right to occupy the territory known as "Israel," and its formal policy pronouncements are replete with statements like this one:

> Bilateral relations with other Asian, African, Middle-Eastern, and Latin American countries would continue to be pursued without neglecting our traditional economic partners in Europe and America. Japan, the European Union, the US, and Australia and the Republic of Korea, would remain Malaysia's major trading partners as well as the source of investment and technology, particularly in connection with the establishment of Malaysia's multimedia super corridor. The only exception is Israel.

Iran's relations with other countries around the world by itself belies the claim that it is some sort of irrational, crazed personification of Evil, a reincarnation of Nazi Germany. Iran has developed cooperative relations and solid alliances with scores of countries in every region of the world, including countries that are also allies of the United States. To varying degrees, Iran has also developed close commercial and otherwise constructive ties with countries as diverse as China, Russia, France, Germany, and numerous others in the Middle East. As a world actor, Iran conducts itself in accordance with the basic principles of rational self-interest.

Moreover—and ironically—Iran has developed a particularly close relationship with the elected Shiite government of Iraq. Thus, the very Iraqi government which American troops are fighting to defend and stabilize has made clear that it intends to pursue a close alliance with its Iranian neighbors.

In September 2006, Iraqi Prime Minister Maliki visited Iran and met with President Ahmadinejad. The *New York Sun* documented the extremely friendly relations that both countries vowed to maintain with one another:

> Mr. Maliki, who lived in Iran during part of a long exile from Iraq during the rule of ousted leader Saddam Hussein, received a red-carpet reception at the presidential palace before talks with President Ahmadinejad.
>
> Asked at a joint press conference following their talks about allegations that Iran was interfering in Iraq, Mr. Maliki said, "There is no obstacle in the way of implementing agreements between Iran and Iraq."
>
> "All our assistance to the Iraqi people will be to establish complete security in this country," Mr. Ahmadinejad said, according to a state-run news agency report of the press conference. "Iran and Iraq enjoy historical relations. These relations go beyond neighborly ties. Our relations will remain excellent," Mr. Ahmadinejad said.

The Iranian president, on his own website, celebrated the "excellent bilateral ties between the Iranian and Iraqi governments and nations." And Iran's official news agency made clear on the day following Prime Minister Maliki's visit that the event evidenced a true lovefest between the two countries:

> Nuri al-Maliki described Iran as the good and great neighbor of Iraq and reiterated that there resides no impediment in the way of the implementation of the agreements signed with Iran.
>
> "We have witnessed Iran's tolerance and preparedness and the agreements we have concluded in the different political, security and economic areas prove fruitfulness of our visit to Tehran," he stressed.

It is certainly true that Iran is internally oppressive and a severe violator of human rights. International human rights groups across the spectrum agree that Iran violates basic precepts of liberty. But even in that regard, it is hardly the worst regime around. Quite the contrary, there are close and important allies of the U.S. that are at least as repressive and brutal, in some cases more so. The *Washington Post* reported on Dick Cheney's activities during one week in January 2006 as follows:

Vice President Dick Cheney met with Egyptian President Hosni Mubarak Tuesday for talks on the political process in Iraq and the West's standoffs with Syria and Iran.

After meeting with Mubarak, Cheney was expected to travel to Saudi Arabia later Tuesday for talks with King Abdullah. . . .

Saudi Arabia and Egypt—both key U.S. allies—are the two Arab powers behind an Iraqi national reconciliation conference that is expected to convene next month in Iraq to clear the way for a larger Sunni participation in the political process.

Both of those close U.S. allies regularly commit human rights abuses equally as egregious as those of the Iranians. Neither country has established anything close to the democratic processes that allow Iranians to elect many of their leaders. Criticisms of leaders of the type voiced regularly about President Ahmadinejad are strictly prohibited in both Egypt and Saudi Arabia, where citizens sit in prison for years for far more mild dissent.

Yet George Bush has entertained both tyrants—the one ruling Egypt and the one ruling Saudi Arabia—at his Texas ranch, a distinction which, as we are so often told, is reserved only for Bush's closest and most important friends in the world. If internal repression is the metric for determining the new Hitlers in the Middle East, there are several countries (at least) ahead of Iran on that list, including some of the closest friends the Bush administration has in that region.

Indeed, a centerpiece of U.S. foreign policy in the Middle East is a dependence upon our alliances with some of that region's most repressive dictators. Former Bush speechwriter David Frum, who helped craft the president's speeches touting the need to promote democracy in the Middle East, complained on his *National Review* blog in January 2007 about the fact that the president has failed to adhere to his own claimed doctrine:

Having declared war on tyranny, it hardly makes sense to expect the help and cooperation of the tyrants in question. Right? And yet, the foreign policy of the Bush administration has been founded on the assumption that the military regime in Pakistan wishes the US to succeed in Afghanistan and that the authoritarian regimes of the Persian Gulf wish the US to succeed in Iraq.

President Bush's ostensible veneration of democracy as a measuring stick for the morality of other countries suggests that Iran is far from the top of the list of repressive tyrannies. While the mullahs who exercise true power are beyond the reach of the democratic processes, President Ahmadinejad himself was voted for by Iranians in an election widely considered imperfect though generally legitimate. Lower political officeholders in Iran are routinely chosen via the democratic process, and an independent and spirited opposition movement has flourished in that country.

In addition to the partial democratic rights, Iranian society is far more pluralistic than most other Middle Eastern nations. With some minor exceptions (such as a prohibition on becoming army officers), Jewish Iranians have full rights of citizenship and even have an elected representative in the Iranian Parliament. Many Iranian Jews have relatives in Israel and travel freely between the two countries. Tehran hosts a Jewish charity hospital, one of only four such worldwide. If there is a threat against any synagogue, Iranian security forces protect them. Unees Hammami, a Jewish community leader in Iran, told the BBC in 2006, "Because of our long history here, we are tolerated."

Additionally, multiple other non-Islamic religions are practiced openly and freely in Iran. The country is home to several Armenian Orthodox churches, where congregants worship openly and without restriction.

In addition to diverse religionists, Iranian women enjoy far greater civic rights than their peers in most Middle Eastern and/or Muslim countries. In 2005, 60 percent of university students and 38 percent of government administrators were female. According to Julie Hill of the School of International Relations and Pacific Studies, a third of all Iranian physicians are female, and literacy among women improved from 5 percent at the time of the Islamic Revolution to 55 percent today. Fertility rates have decreased to near-Western levels. And women are elected to Parliament and serve in important appointed positions.

None of this is to suggest that Iran is some sort of beacon of egalitarianism and pluralism or a haven for human rights. As noted, the human rights abuses by its repressive theocratic government are pervasive and severe, and should neither be minimized nor excused. Women are denied numerous, fundamental rights by law. And much of the rhetoric emanating from some Iranian leaders is reprehensible.

But, particularly when compared to other countries in that region, including many with whom the U.S. maintains extremely friendly relations, Iran is far from the bastion of pure Nazi-like Evil it has been depicted to be. Just as those who wished to invade Iraq persuaded Americans to support that war by portraying Saddam as a unique threat and pure Evil, the demonization of Iran is being perpetrated in order to mislead Americans into accepting war against that nation. Put simply, the cartoon picture of Iran painted by those—including the president—who seek belligerence against Iran is simply misleading.

Iran's alleged pursuit of nuclear weapons highlights a substantial incoherence with the claim of pure Evil. Iran chose to be a signatory to the Nuclear Non-Proliferation Treaty (NPT), the framework used to prevent additional countries from acquiring nuclear capabilities, and nobody has claimed that Iran has violated its treaty obligations in any way.

By rather stark contrast, several of the United States' most critical allies—India, Pakistan, and Israel—not only refused to sign the NPT but have built nuclear weapons, and in Israel's case developed one of the world's largest stockpiles, estimated somewhere between three hundred and five hundred nuclear bombs. Several of Iran's neighbors—who are close allies of the United States—refused to take part in the world's efforts to stem the tide of proliferation of nuclear weapons, and instead have secretly acquired those weapons and continue to expand their capabilities.

None of the foregoing is to deny that it is preferable for Iran not to acquire nuclear weapons. And particularly since the U.S. president publicly declared Iran to be one of three Evil countries in the world which would henceforth be treated as America's enemy, it is certainly the case that Iran's pursuit of its interests has frequently been at odds with America's pursuit of its own interests. But none of that amounts to anything resembling a picture of pure fanatical Evil.

PROHIBITED DEBATES

Just as the cartoonish demonization of the evil Saddam precluded a meaningful national debate about the consequences of invading Iraq, so, too, is the president's embrace of the same caricature of the Iranians precluding meaningful debate about our policy toward Iran, as well as concerning the Middle East generally. Complex questions that the United States must resolve regarding our overall Middle East policy are urgent and pressing. Yet, in a virtual repeat of the debate-stifling war march into Iraq, arguments that treat these matters as nothing more complex than League of Justice cartoons—in which the Good heroes must and will defeat the Evil villains—dominate discourse, ensuring that no meaningful debate occurs.

The president and his supporters have spent the last several years insisting that the reason it is too dangerous to leave Iraq prior to the "completion of the mission"—whatever that might mean—is because premature withdrawal would create a "vacuum" that would enable Al Qaeda to use Iraq as a base for training and other activities. And it is possibly true that that could happen. But that (according to the U.S. military) is exactly what we *already* created in a substantial portion of Iraq, the Anbar province, where Sunni insurgents who at least claim the "Al Qaeda" name have all but exerted full dominion.

Worse still, the power vacuum we are told is so dangerous already exists not only in Iraq *but also in Afghanistan*. Remember Afghanistan—the one great success of the Bush administration—the country we rid of the evil Taliban and where we denied Al Qaeda free rein? . . . Except we have not done any of that. Quite the opposite, as the *Washington Post* documented in November 2006:

> Al-Qaeda's influence and numbers are rapidly growing in Afghanistan, with fighters operating from new havens and mimicking techniques learned on the Iraqi battlefield for use against U.S. and allied troops, the directors of the CIA and defense intelligence told Congress yesterday.
>
> Five years after the United States drove al-Qaeda and the Taliban from Afghanistan, Gen. Michael V. Hayden, director of the CIA, told the Senate Armed Services Committee that both groups are back, waging a "bloody insurgency" in the south and east of the country. U.S. support for the Kabul government of Hamid Karzai will be needed for "at least a decade" to ensure that the country does not fall again, he said.

Americans have been inundated with endless happy talk about how the U.S. shattered Al Qaeda's infrastructure and has them on the run, impotently hiding in caves with no leadership. Excluded from that depiction are the rather striking exceptions of Osama bin Laden and Ayman al-Zawahiri, the group's two top leaders for the last decade. Yet all of that rosy rhetoric about how much the U.S. has crippled Al Qaeda is greatly exaggerated, as even the president's handpicked CIA director acknowledged according to the same *Post* article:

> Hayden told the Senate panel that the Taliban, aided by al-Qaeda, "has built momentum this year" in Afghanistan and that "the level of violence associated with the insurgency has increased significantly." He also noted that Karzai's government "is nowhere to be seen" in many rural areas where a lack of security is affecting millions of Afghans for whom the quality of life has not advanced since the U.S. military arrived in October 2001. . . .
>
> Hayden said yesterday that "the group's cadre of seasoned, committed leaders" remains fairly cohesive and focused on strategic objectives, "despite having lost a number of veterans over the years." Bin Laden himself, and his deputy Ayman al-Zawahiri, continue to play a crucial role while hiding out somewhere along the Afghan-Pakistani border.
>
> Hayden said the organization had lost a series of leaders since the Sept. 11, 2001, attacks. But the losses have been "mitigated by what is, frankly, a pretty deep bench of low-ranking personnel capable of stepping up to assume leadership positions." Hayden said the lower ranks are dominated by men in their early 40s with two decades of experience fighting.

Shortly before the November 2006 midterm elections, a CIA assessment was leaked to David Rohde and Jim Risen, who wrote an article in the *New York Times* describing the CIA's concerns about the inability of the "Afghan Government" to "exert authority beyond Kabul," as well as the corruption of the Afghani police force and army that is so pervasive that they likely must be rebuilt from scratch. Even Bush officials, on the record, are voicing extremely grim assessments of Afghanistan:

> Ronald E. Neumann, the American ambassador in Kabul, said in an interview recently that the United States faced "stark choices" in Afghanistan. Averting failure, he said, would take "multiple years" and "multiple billions." "We're going to have to stay at it," he said. "Or we're going to fail and the country will fall apart again."

What is the United States going to do about all of this? The remaining hard line, pro-Bush war advocates insist that all we need in Iraq are just some more troops and some more time. Except we do not have many more troops (according to the military itself), and the ones we do have are spread thin and are exhausted from multiple tours of duty. Even if we did have some magic troops materialize for Iraq, what would the U.S. do about Afghanistan, which—according to Bush's own ambassador—requires a commitment of enormous additional resources over many years just to prevent the country from "fall[ing] apart again"?

And even if these severe and dangerous problems could be solved with a massive increase in resources (money and troops)—an extremely dubious premise—how would we pay for such an increase? The Bush propaganda machine has made even the mere mention of tax increases politically toxic, and the U.S. is swamped by massive federal deficits and dangerous levels of debt to foreign countries, particularly China. "Imperial overstretch" does not begin to describe the untenability of our predicament, and yet Bush and his movement endlessly call for still more and more military expansion and adventure.

The fundamental problem is that as a nation we do not actually debate the real issues because they are too politically radioactive, and because the simplistic appeals to victory over Evil obscure, by design, the genuine limits on American power and the drain these conflicts are placing on finite American resources. The real issue is whether the U.S. wants to maintain its presence and controlling influence in the Middle East and, if so, (a) why the U.S. wants to do that, and (b) what Americans are willing to sacrifice to preserve its dominance.

But Americans during the Bush presidency have had no significant, constructive discussion of whether the U.S. has any real interests in continuing to exert dominance in the Middle East, primarily because doing so requires a debate about the role of oil and our commitment to Israel, both of which are strictly off-limits, as the president himself told us in a January 2006 speech:

> The American people know the difference between responsible and irresponsible debate when they see it. They know the difference between honest critics who question the way the war is being prosecuted and partisan

critics who claim that we acted in Iraq *because of oil, or because of Israel, or because we misled the American people*. And they know the difference between a loyal opposition that points out what is wrong, and defeatists who refuse to see that anything is right [emphasis added].

It may be the case that the United States should seek to preserve its influence in the Middle East. Perhaps we want to control oil resources or assume primary responsibility for ensuring a steady and orderly world oil market. Or perhaps we want to commit ourselves to defending Israel as the only real outpost of Middle Eastern democracy and/or an ally of one degree or another in protecting our vital strategic interests, if any, in that region.

There are coherent (if not persuasive) arguments, pro and con, for all of those positions, but these issues have been embargoed by social and political orthodoxy, and no examination of them is allowed (if one wants to continue to be heard in the mainstream). So we dance around the real questions and are stuck with superficial and contrived "debates" about what we are actually doing—about all the new Hitlers and the "Evil" we must confront and our need to be Churchill instead of Chamberlain— all of which obscures our choices, our limits, and basic reality.

If preserving our dominance of the Middle East is a goal we want to prioritize, then we need to decide what sacrifices we are willing to bear in order to reach it. We must determine whether and how we will massively expand our military, the increase in indiscriminate force we are willing to accept, and how we are going to pay for our imperial missions. Because as long as we are committed to dominating that region, we are going to be engaged in a long and likely endless series of brutal wars against religious fanatics and various nationalists who simply do not want us there and are willing to fight to the death—making all sorts of sacrifices themselves—to prevent us from dominating their countries.

If we, the American people, want to fight the wars necessary to maintain our dominance in the Middle East, then we should do so. And if we do not, then we should not. But this middle course—where we plod along aimlessly, starting wars and constantly threatening new ones that we are not really committed to winning—is not only the most incoherent course but also the most destructive one.

Indisputably, the course charted by President Bush is totally unsustainable. That is just reality. It is not merely that things have progressed too slowly in Afghanistan and Iraq. It is that the situation has deteriorated in both countries to the point where Al Qaeda now has not one but two countries (not counting a nuclear-armed Pakistan) in which it can operate.

And the stronger they get, the more of our resources are needed to keep up. Yet we lack the willingness—and perhaps the ability—to make the sacrifices necessary to sustain imperial domination in that region. The president has literally pretended that this is not the case by insisting on our divine entitlement to magical victory over Evil, and depicting those who claim otherwise as people who hate the troops and do not want to win.

The damage done to the United States by the Bush administration over the last six years is truly severe. It is fundamental damage, and it requires much, much more than some tinkering around the edges. America urgently needs to debate and re-examine the core premises of our foreign policy and our role in the world. That, in turn, requires a willingness to transcend the taboos and most sacred orthodoxies and to dispense with the Manichean delusions that have substituted for rational debate.

"Evil" Iran: A Self-fulfilling Prophecy

The president's rhetoric of threats and demonization severely exacerbates almost every Iran-related problem. By refusing even to negotiate with Iran and directing unambiguous threats to it, the president is (a) emboldening the very Iranian extremists whom the administration claims pose the real threat, (b) forcing the Iranians into an increasing militaristic posture, and (c) moving the U.S. ever closer to a military confrontation which—whether commenced deliberately or accidentally—could not possibly be in America's interests under any conceivable scenario.

Since the mid-1990s, Iran has been torn by internal divisiveness between its ruling fundamentalist mullahs and its more reform-minded moderates. It is not an exaggeration to say that few things have solidified the power of Iran's religious extremists more than President Bush's treatment of that country. Such a result is tragic in its own right, but particularly so considering that the president himself has identified the promotion of Islamic moderates as one of the centerpieces to defeating the terrorist threat.

Writing in *Salon* in February 2002, Iranian journalist Haleh Anvari described the almost immediate sociopolitical changes in Iran resulting from the president's inclusion of Iran in the "axis of evil," beginning with a newfound unity between previously warring moderate and extremist political factions:

> Bush's speech dismayed Iranians of all political stripes. Reformers and conservatives have been locked in a bitter power struggle, but they suspended their infighting to make common cause against a speech widely regarded here as bullying, ignorant, and counterproductive.

As Anvari noted, Iranian leaders who were previously considered moderate and who had been spearheading cooperation with the U.S. had little choice but to return the rhetorical fire:

> Iran's leaders fired back fiercely. The country's supreme leader, Ayatollah Khamenei, called the tone of the U.S. president's speech "bloodthirsty." President Khatami, leader of the reformers, was equally blunt.
>
> During his five years in office, Khatami has made a concerted effort to tone down hostile rhetoric toward the U.S. as part of a more pragmatic foreign policy, but he condemned Bush's demonizing of Iran as "meddling, warmongering, insulting and a repetition of old propaganda."
>
> It was perhaps the strongest language Khatami has yet used against the U.S., and belied his dismay at the abrupt change in the U.S. position towards Iran, which most observers believe has been softening in the past four years. . . .
>
> The spokesman of the powerful Guardian Council, which oversees all legislation to make sure it adheres to the values of the Islamic Revolution, called for unity among Iran's internal camps—an appeal that would have little chance of being heard before Bush's speech.

These results were hardly surprising. The dynamic whereby warring political factions in a country become united in opposition to hostility from an outside force is hardly unique to Iran. Quite the contrary, it is as close to a universal political phenomenon as one can find. The 9/11 attacks on New York and Washington elevated an American president who was elected with fewer votes than his opponent to one whose job approval rating skyrocketed near 90 percent.

Bush's hostile rhetorical attack on Iran in 2002 vindicated the world-view of the extremists there that the U.S. was Iran's enemy (just as an ever-new hostile pronouncement from Ahmadinejad emboldens hard-liners in the U.S.). Conversely, it severely undercut the worldview of the moderates that Iran could establish a mutually beneficial and peaceful relationship with the U.S. Anvari noted the "irony in the fact that what is good for a right-wing American president is also good for the right-wing Iranian administration." As journalist Saiid Layaz put it: "For some bizarre reason, whenever the USA decides to talk about Iran, it accidentally ends up benefiting the hard-liners."

The president's bellicose denunciations of Iran as an Evil enemy of the U.S.—which embolden Iranian extremists, and even provide justification for the Iranian nuclear program—are only intensifying. In April 2006, the Council on Foreign Relations' Ray Takeyh lamented: "To properly address the complexities of the Iranian challenge, Washington should appreciate that its policy of relentlessly threatening Iran with economic coercion and even military reprisals only empowers reactionaries and validates their pro-nuclear argument."

In his 2005 State of the Union address, President Bush proclaimed: "Iran remains the world's primary state sponsor of terror, pursuing nuclear weapons while depriving its people of the freedom they seek and deserve." That declaration led the Iranians to announce that they were strengthening their military and preparing to defend against an attack from the United States. As the *San Francisco Chronicle* reported in the aftermath of that speech, in February 2005:

> Iran has begun publicly preparing for a possible U.S. attack, as tensions mount between the Bush administration and this country's hard-line leaders over Tehran's purported nuclear weapons program. . . .
>
> The Tehran government has announced efforts to bolster and mobilize recruits in its citizens' militia and is making plans to engage in the type of "asymmetrical" warfare that has bogged down U.S. troops in neighboring Iraq, officials and analysts say.

The Pentagon recently revealed that, as a matter of routine prepared-ness, it had upgraded its Iranian war plans, and the *Washington Post* has reported that unmanned U.S. drones have been flying over suspected nuclear sites in Iran.

Iranian authorities, too, say they have been getting ready for a pos-sible attack. Newspapers have announced efforts to increase the number of the country's 7 million-strong "Basiji" volunteer militia, which was deployed in human-wave attacks during the Iran-Iraq war in the 1980s. Iranian military authorities have paraded long-range North Korean–designed Shahab missiles before television cameras.

In October 2006, defense hawk and former Georgia senator Sam Nunn attributed Iran's pursuit of nuclear weapons to this dynamic: "We started with Iraq in the 'axis of evil' side, when we thought they did not yet have nuclear weapons, and that sent the signal to others that they better get them quick." Charles Wolfson, former Tel Aviv bureau chief for CBS News, similarly observed that "leaders in both capitals [Tehran and Pyongyang] saw what the Bush administration did to Saddam Hus-sein, their fellow axis of evil club member, and concluded, 'Maybe we will not be invaded by the Americans if we have the bomb.'"

For multiple reasons, led by American vulnerability from the occu-pation of Iraq, there has arisen a virtual consensus, across the ideological spectrum, that there is no such thing as a good—or even viable—military option for the U.S. to use against Iran. Republican senator Chuck Hagel said in April 2006, "A military strike against Iran, a military option, is not a viable, feasible, responsible option." James Carafano of the right-wing Heritage Foundation acknowledged in 2005, "There are no good military options."

After retired Air Force Lt. Col. Sam Gardner, a simulations expert at the U.S. Army War College, oversaw various "war games" on Iran in late 2004, he warned, "After all this effort, I am left with two simple sen-tences for policymakers. *You have no military solution for the issues of Iran. And you have to make diplomacy work*" (emphasis added).

In 2006, David Albright, a former U.N. weapons inspector and current president of the Institute for Science and International Security, was interviewed by the *Mercury News* concerning Iran, and the article summed up the dilemma that President Bush has created for himself:

Iran "could cause all kinds of disruption clandestinely in Iraq." For that reason, and several others, [Albright] said there are no good military options on the table for confronting Iran. He also said loud external threats, especially from the United States, tend to backfire by sending Iranian moderates and reformers running under the banners of the clerical regime that Washington opposes.

Most disturbing, a military confrontation between Iran and the United States is becoming increasingly likely even if the president does not actively choose to attack. The proximity of Iran to Iraq, and the nature of the president's rhetoric make an unintentional war—one that is sparked by miscalculation or misperception—increasingly likely.

In December 2006, media reports of increasing U.S. military activity in the Persian Gulf aimed at Iran began to emerge. On December 21, the *New York Times* confirmed that "the United States and Britain will begin moving additional warships and strike aircraft into the Persian Gulf region in a display of military resolve toward Iran." The buildup includes "a second aircraft carrier and its supporting ships to be stationed within quick sailing distance of Iran by early next year."

There is no doubt that these moves were intended to signal to the Iranians (as well as to what the *Times* describes as "Washington's allies in the region who are concerned about Iran's intentions") that we are capable of an offensive military strike against Iran:

> Senior American officers said the increase in naval power should not be viewed as preparations for any offensive strike against Iran. But they acknowledged that the ability to hit Iran would be increased and that Iranian leaders might well call the growing presence provocative.
>
> One purpose of the deployment, they said, is to make clear that the focus on ground troops in Iraq has not made it impossible for the United States and its allies to maintain a military watch on Iran.

Bush officials cited two "justifications" for these maneuvers: (1) to enforce any sanctions imposed by the U.N. Security Council as a result of Iran's refusal to comply with its resolutions, and (2) to deter Iran from a military blockade of oil shipments in retaliation for U.N. sanctions.

According to the *Times*, Bush officials "view recent bold moves by Iran—and by North Korea as well—as at least partly explained by assessments in Tehran and North Korea that the American military is bogged down in Iraq and incapable of fully projecting power elsewhere." There is undoubtedly truth in that.

The same week the *Times* article reported on the planned military buildup in the Persian Gulf, U.S. soldiers in Iraq engaged in their most provocative action yet against Iran when they detained five senior Iranian military officials in Iraq, who were then detained for months.

In light of the close ties the Iraq government is establishing with Iran, the detentions "deeply upset Iraqi government officials," according to the *Times* account, because they "have been making strenuous efforts to engage Iran on matters of security." The Iraqis, not the Iranians, took the lead in "appeal[ing] to the American military, including to Gen. George W. Casey Jr., the senior American ground commander in Iraq, to release the Iranians." A spokesman for Iraqi President Talabani said flatly, "The president is unhappy with the arrests."

National Security Council spokesman Gordon Johndroe not only justified the detentions but claimed that they bolster the case that the U.S. has been making against Iran: "We suspect this event validates our claims about Iranian meddling."

The very idea that the Bush administration—which invaded Iraq, shattered its infrastructure, removed its government, and then settled in for a four-year (and counting) occupation—would accuse another country of "meddling" in Iraq achieves an entirely new level of irony. But the goal here plainly is to escalate tensions with the Iranians through a series of provocative acts, and thereby undermine the recommendation of the ISG that Iran be engaged in order to solve American problems in Iraq.

Bush officials all but admitted that the objective of the detentions was to compel confrontation with Iran—either through the Iraqi government or directly—regarding its role in Iraq. One Bush official told the *Times*, "This is going to be a tense but clarifying moment." Another claimed:

> It's our position that the Iraqis have to seize this opportunity to sort out with the Iranians just what kind of behavior they are going to tolerate. . . . They are going to have to confront the evidence that the Iranians are deeply involved in some of the acts of violence.

In early January 2007, on the same day President Bush delivered his Iraq surge speech to the country, an even more serious act of hostility toward the Iranians took place: The U.S. military stormed an Iranian consulate in the Kurdish town of Arbīl in Northern Iraq. As the BBC reported,

> One Iranian news agency with a correspondent in Irbil says five US helicopters were used to land troops on the roof of the Iranian consulate.
>
> It reports that a number of vehicles cordoned off the streets around the building, while US soldiers warned the occupants in three different languages that they should surrender or be killed.

It all but amounts to a definitive act of war for one country to storm the consulate of another, threaten to kill them if they do not surrender, and then detain six consulate officers. Several days later, the Bush administration acknowledged that all of these offensives against the Iranians in Iraq were undertaken pursuant to an order signed by President Bush himself. The *New York Times* reported on January 13:

> A recent series of American raids against Iranians in Iraq was authorized under an order that President Bush decided to issue several months ago to undertake a broad military offensive against Iranian operatives in the country, Secretary of State Condoleezza Rice said Friday.
>
> "There has been a decision to go after these networks," Ms. Rice said in an interview with *The New York Times* in her office on Friday afternoon, before leaving on a trip to the Middle East.

Any action that brings us even a small step closer to military confrontation with Iran should be, by definition, the most attention-generating news story. Any military conflict with Iran would be so disastrous for the United States that it cannot be adequately described. In contrast to the weakened, isolated, universally reviled Saddam regime, the Iranians are smart, resourceful, shrewd, and supported by scores of vitally important allies around the world. And that is to say nothing of the resources that are being drained away and the ever-increasing U.S. isolation that occurs every day we continue to occupy Iraq.

The war advocates who unquestionably still have the president's ear sought to transform the debate (prompted by the *ISG Report*) over whether we should negotiate with Iran into an argument that Iran is our real enemy. And they believe that Iran is our enemy not only in Iraq, but generally, and that Iran should therefore be attacked, not negotiated with. Dismissing out of hand these wild-eyed, war-loving elements who are wholly detached from reality is tempting, but they continue to occupy places of high influence with the president (both inside and outside of the White House).

Worse, there are convincing signs that the president is *one of them,* i.e., that he now irreversibly shares their worldview that war with Islamic extremism requires a progressive series of wars with various states, the next of which is Iran. Beyond doubt, if the president is convinced that some sort of military action is necessary or even warranted, nothing—not public opinion nor his supposed lame-duck status nor the sheer insanity of the proposal—is going to stop him.

Few things have been as disturbing as the president's now implacable belief—which he has been decreeing with increased frequency—that he is the modern-day Harry Truman, fighting a necessary war even in the face of widespread opposition from weak and blind people in his own country and around the world, but that he is destined to be vindicated by history. And, as he sees it, the more he fights against antiwar headwinds and the bolder he is in the risks he takes, the greater his vindication will be.

By 2007, it was alarmingly clear that geopolitical considerations do not determine what the United States will do vis-a-vis Iran. The president's personality does.

And even if the president and/or his top advisers are less than clear about their intent with regard to Iran, it may not matter. Military buildups of this sort, plainly aimed at one country in particular, can easily produce miscalculations or lead to unintended provocations. That danger is heightened incalculably when one of the parties to the increasing tensions has 150,000 troops occupying a country that borders the other.

In response to U.S. provocations, Iran's leaders may be incentivized, or feel pressure, to act against what they perceive is an inevitable attack. Independently, they may perceive that a restless antimullah movement can be quieted by uniting the country behind conflict with the U.S. It is an incomparably dangerous game and the consequences are almost certainly beyond the Bush administration's capacity to predict, let alone manage.

There are also myriad constitutional questions about the type of Congressional authorization that would be required in order for the president to act militarily against Iran. But those would almost certainly be swept aside—as most constitutional dilemmas have been—by an administration that would claim that it already has such authorization either "inherently" or as a result of Iran's involvement in our war in Iraq. If the president were really intent on war with Iran, it is very difficult to envision Congressional Democrats, or really anything else, stopping him.

The president is boxed into a corner. Having decreed Iran Evil, he cannot negotiate with that country. Having decreed the threat Iran poses to be tantamount to that posed by Adolf Hitler and the Nazis, he cannot ignore it or simply allow it to fester. Having committed virtually all U.S. military power to Iraq and Afghanistan—where still more, not less, resources are needed, and where the U.S. is highly vulnerable—the threat of military force is neither credible nor plausible. As disastrous as the next two years in Iraq are certain to be, the situation with respect to Iran appears even grimmer.

When the president declared in early 2002 that Iran was "Evil," it all but sealed the fate of U.S.-Iranian relations for the duration of his presidency. The president's Manichean prison precludes him from following any course other than unmitigated belligerence once he embraces that moralistic premise, and indeed, nothing—not a deeply unpopular war in Iraq, nor the stinging repudiation of his policies by the American voters nor the ISG—has convinced him to change course even slightly with regard to Iran. He placed himself, or allowed himself to be placed, inside the suffocating confines of this Manichean box, and despite the grave dangers and great harm it has engendered, he appears to have no ability, and worse, no incentive, to find an alternative for the last two years of his presidency.

CHAPTER FIVE

The Manichean Paradox:
Moral Certitude Tramples Moral Constraints

We all remember how many religious wars were fought for a religion of love and gentleness; how many bodies were burned alive with the genuinely kind intention of saving souls from the eternal fire of hell.

—SIR KARL POPPER, twentieth-century British philosopher of science

O ne of the principal dangers of vesting power in a leader who is convinced of his own righteousness—who believes that, by virtue of his ascension to political power, he has been called to a crusade against Evil—is that the moral imperative driving the mission will justify any and all means used to achieve it. Those who have become convinced that they are waging an epic and all-consuming existential war against Evil cannot, by the very premises of their belief system, accept any limitations— moral, pragmatic, or otherwise—on the methods adopted to triumph in this battle.

Efforts to impose limits on waging war against Evil will themselves be seen as impediments to Good, if not as an attempt to aid and abet Evil. In a Manichean worldview, there is no imperative that can compete with the mission of defeating Evil. The primacy of that mandate is un-challengeable. Hence, there are no valid reasons for declaring off-limits any weapons that can be deployed in service of the war against Evil.

Equally operative in the Manichean worldview is the principle that those who are warriors for a universal Good cannot recognize that the particular means they employ in service of their mission may be im-moral or even misguided. The very fact that the instruments they em-brace are employed in service of their Manichean mission renders any such objections incoherent. How can an act undertaken in order to strengthen the side of Good, and to weaken the forces of Evil, ever be anything other than Good in itself? Thus, any act undertaken by a war-rior of Good in service of the war against Evil is inherently moral for that reason alone.

It is from these premises that the most amoral or even most repre-hensible outcomes can be—and often are—produced by political move-ments and political leaders grounded in universal moral certainties. Intoxicated by his own righteousness and therefore immune from doubt, the Manichean warrior becomes capable of acts of moral monstrousness that would be unthinkable in the absence of such unquestionable moral conviction. One who believes himself to be leading a supreme war against Evil on behalf of Good will be incapable of understanding any claims that he himself is acting immorally.

These principles illuminate a central, and tragic, paradox at the heart of the Bush presidency. The president who vowed to lead America in a moral crusade to win hearts and minds around the world has so in-flamed anti-American sentiment that America's moral standing in the world is at an all-time low. The president who vowed to defend the Good in the world from the forces of Evil has caused the United States to be held in deep contempt by large segments of virtually every country on every continent of the world, including large portions of nations with which the U.S. has historically been allied. The president who vowed to undertake a war in defense of American values and freedoms has presided over such radical departures from the defining values and liberties of this country that many Americans find their country and its government unrecognizable. And the president who vowed to lead the war for freedom and democracy has made torture, rendition, abductions, lawless detentions of even our own citizens, secret "black site" prisons, Abu Ghraib dog leashes, and orange Guantánamo jumpsuits the strange, new symbols of America around the world.

In sum, the great and tragic irony of the Bush presidency is that its morally convicted foundations have yielded some of the most morally grotesque acts and radical departures from American values in our country's history. The president who insists that he is driven by a clear and compelling moral framework, in which the forces of Good and Evil battle toward a decisive resolution, has done more than almost any American in history to make the world question on which side of that battle this country is fighting. The more convinced President Bush and his followers become of the unchallengeable righteousness of their cause, the fewer limits they recognize. And America's moral standing in the world, and our national character, continue to erode to previously unthinkable depths.

The Tools of the "Good"

In November 2006, the U.S. Congress enacted legislation, the Military Commissions Act of 2006, that vested in the president the power to order individuals (including legal residents of the United States) to be detained and imprisoned *indefinitely* without having been charged with any crimes or provided with a forum to prove their innocence. In reality, all of the powers granted by the Congress with that legislation were already being exercised by the Bush administration in the absence of legal authority. Ever since 9/11, and without any Congressional authorization, the president has asserted the power to imprison anyone without being charged with a crime and even with no ability to contact the outside world. And he has so imprisoned *even U.S. citizens,* including José Padilla and Yaser Esam Hamdi.

The power to order people detained and imprisoned based solely on accusation is one of the most extraordinary and tyrannical powers any political leader can hold. One of the core rights established against the British king by the Magna Carta in the thirteenth century was that the king could not order subjects imprisoned except upon a finding of guilt arrived at in accordance with legal process. The Military Commissions Act thus literally vested in President Bush—and in subsequent

U.S. presidents—a power no British king has possessed since 1244. The founders of the United States thoroughly objected to such tyrannical power. Thomas Jefferson wrote in a 1789 letter to Thomas Paine, "I consider trial by jury as the only anchor ever yet imagined by man, by which a government can be held to the principles of its constitution."

Beyond indefinite detentions, the Bush presidency has ushered in a host of practices that Americans have generally found to be unconscionable and that violate virtually every principle America has long endorsed. From admitted presidential lawbreaking, to the use of torture (or "rendering" our detainees to other countries for torture, including detainees we later *admit* were wholly innocent), to enlisting the resources of our foreign intelligence agencies (the NSA and CIA) to spy inside the U.S. and collect and maintain all sorts of personal data about American citizens, the Bush administration has seized and exercised powers that have long been anathema to what "America" has meant at its core.

The president has been able to engage in this conduct because the country collectively accepted the dualistic framework with which *he* views the world, whereby the goal of "protecting" ourselves from the "forces of Evil" outweighs every other consideration and justifies every means employed in service of this battle. When President Bush acts in the name of fighting The Terrorists, with the goal of battling Evil, what he does is *by definition* justifiable and Good *because he is doing it.*

This absolutist Manichean mind-set venerates physical safety above all else. When President Bush signed the Military Commissions Act into law in October 2006, he dismissed objections to its Draconian and tyrannical provisions with one very simple and straightforward argument (emphasis added):

> Over the past few months the debate over this bill has been heated, and the questions raised can seem complex. *Yet, with the distance of history, the questions will be narrowed and few: Did this generation of Americans take the threat seriously, and did we do what it takes to defeat that threat?* Every member of Congress who voted for this bill has helped our nation rise to the task that history has given us.

That paragraph summarizes the Bush movement. Because the threat posed by The Evil Terrorists is so grave, maximizing protections against it is the paramount, overriding goal. No other value competes with that objective, nor can any other value limit our efforts to protect ourselves against The Terrorists.

That is the essence of virtually every argument Bush supporters make regarding terrorism. No matter what objection is raised to the never-ending expansions of executive power, no matter what competing values are touted (due process, the rule of law, the principles our country embodies, how we are perceived around the world), the response will always be that The Terrorists are waging war against us and our overarching priority—one that overrides all others—is to protect ourselves, to triumph over Evil. By definition, then, there can never be any good reason to oppose vesting powers in the government to protect us from The Terrorists because that goal outweighs all others.

But our entire system of government, from its inception, has been based upon a very different calculus—that is, that many things matter besides merely protecting ourselves against threats, and consequently, we are willing to accept risks, even potentially fatal ones, in order to secure those other values. From its founding, America has rejected the worldview of prioritizing physical safety above all else, as such a mentality leads to an impoverished and empty civic life. The premise of America is and always has been that imposing limitations on government power is necessary to secure liberty and avoid tryanny *even if it means accepting an increased risk of death as a result. That* is the foundational American value.

It is *this* courageous demand for core liberties *even if such liberties provide less than maximum protection from physical risks* that has made America bold, brave, and free. Societies driven exclusively or primarily by a fear of avoiding Evil, minimizing risks, and seeking above all else that our government "protects" us are not free. That is a path that inevitably leads to authoritarianism—an increasingly strong and empowered leader in whom the citizens vest ever-increasing faith and power in exchange for promises of safety. That is most assuredly *not* the historical ethos of the United States.

The Bill of Rights contains numerous limitations on government power, and many of them render us *more vulnerable to threats.* If there is a serial killer on the loose in a community, the police would be able to find and apprehend him much more easily if they could simply invade and search everyone's homes at will and without warning. Nonetheless, the Fourth Amendment expressly prohibits the police from undertaking such searches. It requires both probable cause and a judicial warrant before police may do so, even though such limitations on state power will enable dangerous killers to elude capture.

Imagine George Bush present during pre-founding debates over the Constitution. Is there any doubt that he or Dick Cheney or Alberto Gonzales would have argued in opposition to proposed Fourth Amendment restrictions on police powers by stressing that violent criminals can kill our children, that we must do everything to protect ourselves against Evil, and that those who favor search warrant requirements for the police are "pro-murderer"? And surely the Constitutional Convention would have been subjected to this argument: "If you're not doing anything wrong in your home, what do you have to hide from the police?"

Our country is centrally based upon the principle that we are willing to assume risks in order to limit government power. Numerous other amendments in the Bill of Rights are grounded in that same principle. And, of course, that is the central belief that drove the founders to risk death by waging war against the most powerful empire on earth. Objectives other than physical protection matter greatly. We have never been a country that ignores other objectives and asks *only*, as the president put it, did "Americans take the threat seriously, and did we do what it takes to defeat that threat?"

The president's mind-set is utterly contrary to core American principles. Historically, the worst mistakes America has made—those instances in which it has departed most radically from its ideals—happened *not* when Americans failed to take seriously enough some Evil lurking in the world, but, to the contrary, they occurred when our government leaders *exaggerated* the threat of Evil and accordingly induced overreactions among citizens.

Historians will almost certainly ask about the Bush presidency: Did America adhere to its values and principles when defending itself against the threat posed by terrorism, or did it succumb to fear, overreaction, and violate its core beliefs in pursuit of illusions of maximum protection? As history professor Joseph Ellis wrote in 2006 in the *New York Times*:

My second question is this: What does history tell us about our earlier responses to traumatic events?

My list of precedents for the Patriot Act and government wiretapping of American citizens would include the Alien and Sedition Acts in 1798, which allowed the federal government to close newspapers and deport foreigners during the "quasi-war" with France; the denial of habeas corpus during the Civil War, which permitted the pre-emptive arrest of suspected Southern sympathizers; the Red Scare of 1919, which emboldened the attorney general to round up leftist critics in the wake of the Russian Revolution; the internment of Japanese-Americans during World War II, which was justified on the grounds that their ancestry made them potential threats to national security; the McCarthy scare of the early 1950's, which used cold war anxieties to pursue a witch hunt against putative Communists in government, universities and the film industry.

In retrospect, none of these domestic responses to perceived national security threats looks justifiable. Every history textbook I know describes them as lamentable, excessive, even embarrassing. . . .

But it defies reason and experience to make Sept. 11 the defining influence on our foreign and domestic policy. History suggests that we have faced greater challenges and triumphed, and *that overreaction is a greater danger than complacency* [emphasis added].

The scare tactic of telling Americans that every desired expansion of government power is justified by the Evil Terrorist Threat—and that there is no need to worry because the president is Good and will use these powers only to protect us—is effective because it has immediate rhetorical appeal. Most people, especially when placed in fear of potentially fatal threats, are receptive to the argument that maximizing protection is the only thing that matters, and that no abstract concept (such as liberty, or freedom, or due process, or adhering to civilized norms) is worth risking one's life by accepting heightened levels of vulnerability.

But nothing in life is perfectly safe. Perfect safety is an illusion. When pursued by an individual to the exclusion of all else, it creates a tragically worthless, paralyzed way of life. On the political level, safety as the paramount goal produces tyranny, causing people to vest as much power as possible in the government, without limits, in exchange for the promise of maximum protection.

All of this is independent of the fact that vesting ever-increasing and unchecked power in a political leader most assuredly does not make a country "safer." Though it is beyond the ken of the discussion here, it is well-established that open governments with substantial checks and oversight operate far more efficiently than highly secretive, unchecked governments run by unaccountable political leaders. As the American founders well understood, transparent government is critical for detecting errors, uncovering corruption, and ensuring accountability, while political leaders who operate in the dark, wielding vast powers with little oversight, virtually always conceal their mistakes and act to maximize their own interests rather than the country's.

For that reason, the most radical and controversial Bush policies—from warrantless eavesdropping to detentions, torture and rendition carried out in secret and with no oversight—have not made us remotely "safer." But even if one assumes that they had, our core political values are profoundly betrayed by the notion that we should vest blind faith and tyrannical powers in the president in exchange for promises of "protection." The central rhetorical premise of the Bush presidency, however, has been that eliminating all risk of the Evil Terrorist Threat is paramount. Hence, the whole array of authoritarian powers seized by this administration is justified because none of the principles and values that are destroyed in the process really matter when set next to the scary prospect that The Terrorists will kill us. In his 2004 acceptance speech at the Republican National Convention, the president described his all-consuming mission this way:

> **THE PRESIDENT:** This election will also determine how America responds to the continuing danger of terrorism—and you know where I stand. (*Applause.*) . . . Since that day [9/11], I wake up every morning thinking about how to better protect our country. I will never relent in defending America, whatever it takes.
> **AUDIENCE:** U-S-A! U-S-A! U-S-A!

This approach has radically transformed America's national character and has led us to engage systematically and openly in behavior we previously scorned when engaged in by other nations. *That* is why the Bush legacy has left the U.S. with the burden and danger of rising anti-American sentiment. A superpower—especially the world's only superpower—can be either respected and admired or despised and feared. Since the end of World War II, America—albeit with numerous exceptions—has largely chosen the former. America's leadership in advocating and defending universally applicable principles did not weaken it, nor did our efforts to avoid war make us appear "weak." Quite the contrary. America's strength has been grounded in the legitimacy and moral credibility of its power.

But with his monomaniacal obsession with annihilating perceived Evil, the president has squandered virtually all of the goodwill and respect that the United States built up in the last century. Accurately or not, large numbers of people around the world, on virtually every continent, now perceive the United States as a threat to peace. As they watched us invade and relentlessly bomb Iraq, a country that had not attacked us, and as we threaten still more countries with invasion, citizens around the world—including many of our own allies whose citizens had previously admired America—have come to view our country as a source of instability and aggression. Eight years is a long time, and millions and millions of young adults around the world have formed their perceptions of "America" based on its actions during the Bush presidency.

What is "Good" and what is "Evil" are not determined by some preordained or intrinsic distinction. Those are designations determined only by one's conduct. America has always touted its principles as the source of its moral credibility in the world. But once those principles are relinquished and violated, America's moral credibility and its legitimate claim to "Good" cease to exist.

THE ABYSS LOOKS BACK

That anti-Americanism around the world has reached an all-time high is not, standing alone, conclusive evidence that America has veered off course from its ideals. Just as domestic majorities may be wrong in the views they hold, so, too, can international majorities. Like all other countries, America cannot, and should not, determine its actions solely by what makes it most popular in the world. All countries act in their own interests, and the U.S. has every right to do the same.

Nonetheless, in light of America's need for international cooperation on virtually every front, the U.S. cannot be indifferent to surging anti-Americanism. U.S. interests generally, and national security specifically, can only suffer if the world turns against the U.S., or worse still, unites in opposition. There are reasons why America's moral credibility in the world has declined so precipitously during the Bush presidency, and it is indisputable that many of those reasons lie in the decisions and policies of George Bush.

Perhaps the most potent example of the Bush presidency's evisceration of American values is the administration's May 2002 lawless detention of U.S. *citizen* José Padilla. The administration arrested Padilla on U.S. soil and declared him an "enemy combatant," threw him in a military prison, and refused to charge him with any crime or allow him access *even to a lawyer.* He stayed in a black hole, kept there by his own government, for the next *three and a half years* with no charges brought against him, while the administration insisted on the right to detain him (and any other American citizen) *indefinitely*—all based solely on the secret, unchallengeable say-so of the president that Padilla was an "enemy combatant."

To this day, one has trouble believing that we have a government that claims this power against American citizens, exercises that power, and aggressively defends it—and even more trouble believing that there are so many blindly loyal followers of that government who defend this conduct. The outrage that such conduct provokes when thinking about it has not diminished and prevails no matter how many times one reads, writes, or speaks about it. It is as profound a betrayal of the most core American political principles as one can fathom.

In late 2005, the Bush administration finally charged Padilla with a crime only because the U.S. Supreme Court was set to rule on the legality of its treatment of Padilla. Indicting Padilla enabled the administration to argue that his constitutional challenge was now "moot." The government's indictment made no mention of the flamboyant allegation they originally trumpeted to justify his lawless incarceration—namely, that he was a "Dirty Bomber" attempting to detonate a radiological bomb in an American city. That accusation was not asserted against Padilla in court because the "evidence" for that accusation was itself procured by torture and was therefore unreliable and unusable. Instead, the indictment contained only the vaguest and most generic terrorism allegations.

In September 2006, Padilla's lawyers filed an extraordinary Motion to Dismiss the Indictment against him on the grounds that the government has engaged in outrageous conduct—specifically, that they tortured him for the three and a half years he remained in captivity, particularly for the almost two full years that they denied him access even to a lawyer. All of the treatment Padilla describes has been cited by numerous other detainees, and much of that treatment is now part of the "interrogation and detention techniques" which the president has the legal authority to inflict pursuant to the Military Commissions Act. Thus, much of what Padilla describes is now perfectly legal in the United States—even when applied against individuals charged with no crimes of any kind.

The argument section of Padilla's brief begins:

> "Whoever fights monsters should see to it that in the process he does not become a monster. And when you look long into an abyss, the abyss also looks into you."
>
> Friedrich Nietzsche, Beyond Good and Evil 89 (Walter Kaufmann trans., Vintage Books 1966) (1886).

Padilla's brief then details the treatment to which he was subjected, a small portion of which follows. One should bear in mind that José Padilla is a U.S. citizen, born in New York, and had never been charged with, let alone convicted of, any terrorism-related crime:

> In an effort to gain Mr. Padilla's "dependency and trust," he was tortured for nearly the entire three years and eight months of his unlawful detention. The torture took myriad forms, each designed to cause pain, anguish, depression and, ultimately, the loss of will to live. The base ingredient in Mr. Padilla's torture was stark isolation for a substantial portion of his captivity.
>
> For nearly two years—from June 9, 2002 until March 2, 2004, when the Department of Defense permitted Mr. Padilla to have contact with his lawyers—Mr. Padilla was in complete isolation. Even after he was

permitted contact with counsel, his conditions of confinement remained essentially the same.

He was kept in a unit comprising sixteen individual cells, eight on the upper level and eight on the lower level, where Mr. Padilla's cell was located. No other cells in the unit were occupied. His cell was electronically monitored twenty-four hours a day, eliminating the need for a guard to patrol his unit. His only contact with another person was when a guard would deliver and retrieve trays of food and when the government desired to interrogate him.

His isolation, furthermore, was aggravated by the efforts of his captors to maintain complete sensory deprivation. His tiny cell—nine feet by seven feet—had no view to the outside world. The door to his cell had a window, however, it was covered by a magnetic sticker, depriving Mr. Padilla of even a view into the hallway and adjacent common areas of his unit. He was not given a clock or a watch and for most of the time of his captivity, he was unaware whether it was day or night, or what time of year or day it was.

In addition to his extreme isolation, Mr. Padilla was also viciously deprived of sleep. This sleep deprivation was achieved in a variety of ways. For a substantial period of his captivity, Mr. Padilla's cell contained only a steel bunk with no mattress. The pain and discomfort of sleeping on a cold, steel bunk made it impossible for him to sleep. Mr. Padilla was not given a mattress until the tail end of his captivity. . . .

Other times, his captors would bang the walls and cell bars creating loud startling noises. These disruptions would occur throughout the night and cease only in the morning, when Mr. Padilla's interrogations would begin. Efforts to manipulate Mr. Padilla and break his will also took the form of the denial of the few benefits he possessed in his cell. . . .

Mr. Padilla's dehumanization at the hands of his captors also took more sinister forms. Mr. Padilla was often put in stress positions for hours at a time. He would be shackled and manacled, with a belly chain, for hours in his cell. Noxious fumes would be introduced to his room causing his eyes and nose to run. The temperature of his cell would be manipulated, making his cell extremely cold for long stretches of time. Mr. Padilla was denied even the smallest, and most personal shreds of human dignity by being deprived of showering for weeks at a time, yet having to endure forced grooming at the whim of his captors. . . .

He was threatened with being cut with a knife and having alcohol poured on the wounds. He was also threatened with imminent execution. He was hooded and forced to stand in stress positions for long durations of time. He was forced to endure exceedingly long interrogation sessions, without adequate sleep, wherein he would be confronted with false information, scenarios, and documents to further disorient him. Often he had to endure multiple interrogators who would scream, shake, and otherwise assault Mr. Padilla.

Additionally, Mr. Padilla was given drugs against his will, believed to be some form of lysergic acid diethylamide (LSD) or phencyclidine (PCP), to act as a sort of truth serum during his interrogations.

Throughout most of the time Mr. Padilla was held captive in the Naval Brig he had no contact with the outside world. In March 2004, one year and eight months after arriving in the Naval Brig, Mr. Padilla was permitted his first contact with his attorneys. Even thereafter, although Mr. Padilla had access to counsel, and thereby some contact with the outside world, those visits were extremely limited and restricted. . . .

The deprivations, physical abuse, and other forms of inhumane treatment visited upon Mr. Padilla caused serious medical problems that were not adequately addressed. Apart from the psychological damage done to Mr. Padilla, there were numerous health problems brought on by the conditions of his captivity. Mr. Padilla frequently experienced cardiothoracic difficulties while sleeping, or attempting to fall asleep, including a heavy pressure on his chest and an inability to breathe or move his body.

It is worth noting that throughout his captivity, none of the restrictive and inhumane conditions visited upon Mr. Padilla were brought on by his behavior or by any actions on his part. There were no incidents of Mr. Padilla violating any regulation of the Naval Brig or taking any aggressive action towards any of his captors. Mr. Padilla has always been peaceful and compliant with his captors. He was, and remains to the time of this filing, docile and resigned—a model detainee. . . .

In sum, many of the conditions Mr. Padilla experienced were inhumane and caused him great physical and psychological pain and anguish. Other deprivations experienced by Mr. Padilla, taken in isolation, are merely cruel and some, merely petty. However, it is important to recognize that all of the deprivations and assaults recounted above were employed in concert in a calculated manner to cause him maximum anguish.

It is also extremely important to note that the torturous acts visited upon Mr. Padilla were done over the course of almost the entire three years and seven months of his captivity in the Naval Brig. For most of one thousand three hundred and seven days, Mr. Padilla was tortured by the United States government without cause or justification. Mr. Padilla's treatment at the hands of the United States government is shocking to even the most hardened conscience, and such outrageous conduct on the part of the government divests it of jurisdiction, under the Due Process clause of the Fifth Amendment, to prosecute Mr. Padilla in the instant matter.

The case of José Padilla is one of the most despicable and outright un-American travesties the U.S. government has perpetrated for a long time. It is impossible to defend that behavior, let alone engage in it, while claiming with any legitimacy that one believes in the principles that have defined and guided this country since its founding. But there has been no retreat from this conduct. Quite the contrary, the legislative atrocity known as the Military Commissions Act of 2006 is a huge leap toward elevating the Padilla treatment from the lawless shadows into full-fledged, officially sanctioned, and legally authorized policy of the U.S. government. The case of José Padilla is no longer a vile aberration, but is instead emblematic of the kind of government we have chosen to have under the Bush presidency, justified by our war for Good.

These abuses are hardly confined to the case of Padilla. The Bush administration's treatment of Ali Saleh Kahlah al-Marri also ought to be shocking and horrifying. Instead, it is now not only depressingly familiar but also formally sanctioned by the U.S. Congress.

In 2001, al-Marri, a citizen of Qatar, was in the United States legally on a student visa. He was a computer science graduate student at Bradley University in Peoria, Illinois, where he had earned an undergraduate degree a decade earlier. In Peoria, he lived with his wife and five children.

In December 2001, he was detained as a "material witness" to suspected acts of terrorism and ultimately charged with various terrorism-related offenses, mostly relating to false statements the FBI claimed he had made as part of its 9/11 investigation. Al-Marri vehemently denied the charges, and after lengthy pretrial proceedings, his criminal trial on those charges was scheduled to begin on July 21, 2003.

But his trial never took place, because in June 2003—immediately before the trial was to start—President Bush declared al-Marri to be an "enemy combatant." As a result, the Justice Department told the court it wanted to turn him over to the U.S. military, and thus asked the court to dismiss the criminal charges against him. The court did so. Thus, right before his trial, the Bush administration simply removed al-Marri from the jurisdiction of the judicial system—based solely on the unilateral order of the president—and thus prevented him from contesting the charges against him.

Instead, the administration transferred al-Marri to a military prison in South Carolina (where the administration brings its "enemy combatants" in order to ensure that the executive-power-friendly Fourth Circuit Court of Appeals has jurisdiction over all such cases). Al-Marri was given the "Padilla Treatment"—kept in solitary confinement and denied all contact with the outside world, even including his attorneys. He was not charged with any further crimes and was given no opportunity to prove his innocence. Instead, the Bush administration simply asserted the right to imprison him indefinitely.

In November 2006, Congress ratified this executive behavior when it enacted the Military Commissions Act (MCA). And the Bush administration wasted no time relying on that statutory authority to justify the exercise of this extreme detention power. From the Associated Press report in December regarding al-Marri's case:

> In court documents filed with the 4th U.S. Circuit Court of Appeals in Richmond, Va., the Justice Department said a new anti-terrorism law being used to hold detainees in Guantánamo Bay also applies to foreigners captured and held in the United States.
>
> Immigrants arrested in the United States may be held indefinitely on suspicion of terrorism and may not challenge their imprisonment in civilian courts, the Bush administration said Monday, opening a new legal front in the fight over the rights of detainees.

The MCA authorizes the president to detain any noncitizen as an enemy combatant and does not require that detainees be charged with any crime. That includes resident aliens and foreigners who have legally entered the United States:

"It's pretty stunning that any alien living in the United States can be denied this right," said Jonathan Hafetz, an attorney for Al-Marri. "It means any non-citizen, and there are millions of them, can be whisked off at night and be put in detention."

These are precisely the practices the U.S., for decades, has vocally condemned when employed by other countries. As Amnesty International has said with respect to this case:

> The practice of detaining people incommunicado has been condemned by human rights bodies, including the UN Special Rapporteur on Torture, as a human rights violation which can lead to other violations such as torture or ill-treatment or interrogation without due process safeguards.
>
> Access to a lawyer is an important safeguard to ensure that detainees' rights are protected, not only with regard to criminal or other proceedings, but also with regard to conditions of detention and a detainee's physical and mental health. Prolonged incommunicado detention or solitary confinement can in itself be a form of cruel, inhuman or degrading treatment.

Sermons like that about the value of basic individual rights and the imperatives of due process were previously delivered *by* the United States. Now, they need to be delivered *to* us, because we seem to have rejected them. By submitting to the president's Manichean imperatives, we have become a country that vests in the president the power to order people imprisoned indefinitely with no meaningful review of the charges against them, even when the detainees are not detained on any battlefield, and even when they are detained on U.S. soil.

There is no greater betrayal of the core principles of American political values than to have the federal government sweep people off the streets, throw them into a black hole incommunicado, with no charges asserted of any kind, for as long as the president desires—in the case of al-Marri's detention, now five years and counting. Principles once beyond debate, constituting the bedrock of our political system, are now openly violated by our own government.

Defending America by Abandoning Its Values

The treatment of Padilla and al-Marri, and the new executive powers routinely exercised by the president, would provoke outrage if engaged in by any other country. But the fact that it is the U.S. that has empowered the president to take such steps reveals what a radical legacy George Bush will leave. The U.S. has spent decades condemning precisely this kind of behavior when engaged in by other countries, even calling it Evil.

As for one highly illustrative example showing we do not tolerate such conduct from other nations, Florida senator Mel Martinez, who in 2007 also became the Republican Party chairman, sent around an e-mail in the fall of 2006 praising himself for his intervention in the case of Cuc Foshee, a U.S. citizen who had just been released from a Vietnamese prison. The month prior, Foshee had been convicted after a trial of a plot to overthrow the Vietnamese government (deemed to be "terrorism" under Vietnamese law), which included planned bombings as well as radio devices "to jam the airwaves of pro-government radio stations and broadcast their own message of uprising."

Martinez made Foshee's release a personal crusade, single-handedly obstructing U.S. normalization of trade relations with Vietnam unless Foshee was released. To justify and celebrate his intervention in this case, Senator Martinez claimed in his e-mail that Foshee was subjected to oppressive and unjust treatment by the Vietnamese government. His e-mail proclaimed:

> This week, Senator Martinez praised the return to the United States of Thuong Nguyen "Cuc" Foshee, a U.S. citizen residing in Orlando, Florida. Mrs. Foshee was arrested and imprisoned in Vietnam and for the first 14 months of her imprisonment, she was not formally charged nor allowed to seek legal counsel. . . .
>
> Senator Martinez, U.S. Representative Ric Keller and State Department officials worked together to encourage the Vietnam government cooperated [*sic*] and Mrs. Foshee was allowed to return to the United States last Monday.

The United States is currently holding at least fourteen thousand detainees in its custody around the world (former Clinton official Sidney Blumenthal has reported, based on interviews with Colin Powell's former chief of staff, Colonel Lawrence Wilkerson, that the number is closer to thirty-five thousand, only an extremely small percentage of which have any connection to terrorism). Virtually none of those detainees is given a trial of any kind, and some—such as Padilla—are held in those circumstances not for fourteen months like Foshee, but for many years.

On his Senate website, Martinez trumpets his heroic efforts to save Foshee from Communist tyranny in Vietnam by securing her release from prison even in the wake of her terrorism conviction. Yet also on Senator Martinez's website is an October 17, 2006, press release, issued on the day the president signed into law the Military Commissions Act of 2006, authorizing the U.S. president to detain "terrorist suspects" forever with no access to courts of any kind:

> U.S. Senator Mel Martinez (R-FL) today applauded President Bush's signing of S. 3930, the Military Commissions Act of 2006. . . .
> Senator Martinez said: "We must remember the detainees this law affects are terrorists engaged in an ongoing war against the United States."

Martinez, like every senator (other than Lincoln Chafee) in the Republican Party that he now chairs, voted in favor of the MCA. Martinez also voted against a proposed amendment to that bill which would have allowed terrorist *suspects* the right to challenge the accusations against them in court—the very right given to Foshee by the Communist regime in Vietnam. Additionally, throughout her incarceration, Foshee "had regular contact with the U.S. consul in Vietnam." As was true for José Padilla, most terrorist *suspects* in U.S. custody are held for lengthy periods without any contact with the outside world at all. Some have been even held in *secret prisons* to ensure that not even international human rights groups such as the Red Cross would know of their existence. While Martinez voted to legalize such conduct in the U.S., he vigorously protested far less egregious abuses in the Foshee case.

Similarly, whereas the U.S. was once a worldwide leader in protecting the rights of journalists, we have now become, in pursuit of George Bush's battle against Evil, a systematic violator of such rights. Indeed, in the eyes of many international journalists, the U.S. is a genuine threat to their freedom to report on the conduct of our country.

Bilal Hussein is a Pulitzer Prize–winning Associated Press photographer who was detained by the U.S. military in Iraq in April 2006. The U.S. continued to hold him through the remainder of the year without charging him with a single crime. The U.S. military has vaguely claimed that he has close ties with Iraqi insurgents, but steadfastly refuses to specify what he is alleged to have done, refuses to provide any hearing or process of any kind for him to learn of the charges or contest them, and refuses to respond to AP's requests for information about why their photographer is imprisoned.

Hussein's detention was preceded by months of vicious complaints from Bush followers in the blogosphere and elsewhere that Hussein's photojournalism was anti-American and suggestive of support for the insurgents. Before there were even any news reports anywhere about Hussein's detention, right-wing blogger and Fox News contributor Michelle Malkin learned of Hussein's arrest—she claims "from an anonymous military source in Iraq"—and blogged about it. She asserted that "Hussein was captured earlier today by American forces in a building in Ramadi, Iraq, with a cache of weapons."

What is notable and encouraging in the Hussein case is that the Associated Press has become increasingly aggressive about defending press freedoms and objecting to the U.S. government's lawless detention of one of its journalists. After first attempting unsuccessfully to negotiate with the U.S. military to obtain *either* formal charges against Hussein *or* his release, AP, with increasing passion, has been publicly complaining about the treatment of its photographer. Toward the end of 2006, they escalated their campaign by reporting aggressively on this incident, as exemplified by this article:

> The U.S. military's indefinite detention of an Associated Press photographer in Iraq without charges is an outrage and should be seen as such by the journalistic community, AP editors said Friday.

"We are angry, and we hope you are, too," AP International Editor John Daniszewski told a gathering of the Associated Press Managing Editors.

Given the irreplaceable function of journalists to expose and convey truth, especially in war zones, such lawless detentions pose extreme and obvious dangers that require safeguards. But the Bush administration has simply arrogated unto itself the power to detain whichever journalists it wants, while accounting to nobody. In the Hussein case, there are, at the very least, compelling grounds to believe that the Hussein detention was motivated by his legitimate work as a journalist, as noted in the AP article:

Daniszewski said that when the news cooperative pressed for further details, the best it could learn was that Hussein was allegedly involved in the kidnapping of two journalists by insurgents in Ramadi.

However, Daniszewski said the two journalists were asked by AP about the incident and that they recalled Hussein as a "hero," who helped evacuate them from harm's way.

[AP director of photography Santiago] Lyon said he reviewed Hussein's images and interviewed his colleagues and found nothing to suggest he was doing more than his job in a war zone. The vast majority of images depicts the realities of war, Lyon said, and "may be an inconvenient truth, but a truth nonetheless."

David Zeeck, president of ASNE and executive editor of *The News Tribune*, of Tacoma, Wash., called Hussein's detention without charges "contrary to American values."

"This is how Saddam Hussein dealt with reporters; he would hold them incommunicado," Zeeck said.

This overt assault on press freedoms abroad is consistent with the administration's incremental attacks on the American media domestically, including explicit threats to commence criminal prosecutions against reporters who reveal administration actions of dubious legality, such as James Risen and Eric Lichtblau of the *New York Times* (who disclosed the president's warrantless eavesdropping activities in violation of the law) and the *Washington Post*'s Dana Priest (who disclosed the existence of secret CIA prisons in Eastern Europe). Strikingly, attacks of this sort have been met with virtual silence from most of the national media. In that regard, perhaps this exchange is the most revealing part of the AP's article regarding Bilal Hussein:

> Rosemary Goudreau, editorial page editor of *The Tampa Tribune,* asked AP Executive Editor Kathleen Carroll what papers like hers could do.
> "You run an editorial page, as I recall," Carroll said.

Just as astonishing as the Bush administration's attack on the work of journalists is the almost total acquiescence of the American media to those attacks—so much so that AP is forced to beg their fellow journalists to editorialize against the administration's lawless and dangerous detention of one of its journalists. If, as has been the case to an astonishing extent, American journalists are unwilling to defend their press freedoms, who is going to? The American media, like much of the country, seems willing to continue accepting the premise that in his battle with Evil, the president must be permitted to engage in behavior which the U.S. as a nation has previously condemned.

In 2006, the international journalist group Reporters Without Borders conducted its annual rankings of countries as determined by their respect for press freedoms. As one representative international news report described:

> The press is freer in Mozambique than it is in the United States, according to the latest Worldwide Press Freedom Index, published by the Paris-based press freedom body, Reporters sans Frontières (RSF—Reporters without Borders).
>
> The RSF index gives each country a score, based on the degree of freedom for journalists and media organisations. . . . But the United States has been falling steadily. In the first year the index was published it was in 17th position. Last year the US was in 44th position, and this year it is ranked as number 53 alongside Botswana, Croatia and Tonga.
>
> RSF explains that this decline arises from the deterioration in relations between the Bush administration and the media "after the President used the pretext of 'national security' to regard as suspicious any journalist who questioned his 'war on terrorism.'" RSF also points out that US federal courts refuse to recognise journalists' cherished right not

to reveal their sources. This practice "even threatens journalists whose investigations have no connection at all with terrorism."

RSF notes, in particular, the cases of freelance journalist Josh Wolf, imprisoned by the US authorities when he refused to hand over his video archive; of Sudanese cameraman Sami al-Haj, held without trial at the US military base of Guantánamo since June 2002; and of an Associated Press photographer, Bilal Hussein, held by the US in Iraq since April this year.

The RSF annual survey is widely respected and free of any serious bias. It cannot be dismissed as the work of some sort of left-wing, tyranny-blind internationalist group, since the bottom of the list—well below the U.S.—is filled with exactly the countries one would expect to find there, such as North Korea, Cuba, Iran, Saudi Arabia, Pakistan, Russia, and Iraq. And the United States has traditionally sat at or near the top of those rankings. In 2002, for instance, it was ranked 17. After six years of the Bush presidency, the U.S. falls below countries such as Ghana, El Salvador, Namibia, Chile, Israel, and virtually every European country.

And it is always worth underscoring the fact that these observations are compelled by *what we know*. The Bush administration has been one of the most secretive in history, aided by a Congress controlled by loyal allies engaged in virtually no oversight of the executive branch. Those facts leave no doubt that there is a whole universe of Bush administration actions that remain concealed.

Journalist Ron Suskind was interviewed in November 2006 by *Der Spiegel*, and was asked: "You quote former CIA director George Tenet in your book as saying after Sept. 11: 'There is nothing we won't do, nothing we won't try.' Are there any other dirty stories?":

> Logically, I would have to say yes. You're dealing with an oddity here, a secret war. Wars tend to be very public things, they are visible. There are correspondents traveling with the troops and you get daily dispatches. This is a new conflict, fought largely in secret. *The public is only informed on a kind of "need to know basis."* Based on that, I would assume that there remains something of an undiscovered country of activity in terms of what we have done over the past five years* [emphasis added].

Beyond our assault on journalists, since the 9/11 attacks, the U.S. has been (and still is) a country that kidnaps other countries' *innocent* citizens (including those of its own allies); brings them to Jordan, Syria, and Egypt to be tortured (sometimes for as long as a year); and lies to its allies about what it is doing with their citizens. Thereafter, when the innocent citizens are finally released and they seek redress in an American court for their disappearance and torture, the Bush administration tells the presiding federal judge that the case must be summarily dismissed because national security would be harmed if the administration were held accountable in a court (and the courts then comply).

The case of Maher Arar—a Canadian citizen abducted by the U.S. and sent to Jordan for a year to be tortured despite having no terrorist ties of any kind—received moderate attention in 2006 because a Canadian government commission issued a report that "say[s] categorically that there is no evidence to indicate that Mr. Arar has committed any offense or that his activities constituted a threat to the security of Canada." The report also blasts the Bush administration, which abducted Arar during a layover at JFK Airport when he was flying home to Canada from a vacation in Tunisia:

On Oct. 8 [2002], he was flown to Jordan in an American government plane and taken overland to Syria, where he says he was held for 10 months in a tiny cell and beaten repeatedly with a metal cable. He was freed in October 2003, after Syrian officials concluded that he had no connection to terrorism and returned him to Canada. . . .

Evidence presented to the commission, said Paul J. J. Cavalluzzo, its lead counsel, showed that the F.B.I. continued to keep its Canadian counterparts in the dark even while an American jet was carrying Mr. Arar to Jordan. The panel found that American officials "believed—quite correctly—that, if informed, the Canadians would have serious concerns about the plan to remove Mr. Arar to Syria."

Mr. Arar arrived in Syria on Oct. 9, 2002, and was imprisoned there until Oct. 5, 2003. It took Canadian officials, however, until Oct. 21 to locate him in Syria. The commission concludes that Syrian officials at first denied knowing Mr. Arar's whereabouts to hide the fact that he was being tortured. It says that, among other things, he was beaten with a shredded electrical cable until he was disoriented.

Though extreme, there was nothing new about our government's treatment of Arar. Khalid El-Masri is a German citizen who alleges—with the support of German prosecutors—that the U.S. government abducted him, drugged him, flew him to multiple torture-using countries (and shuttled him at least to Kabul, Baghdad, and Skopje, Macedonia) as part of the administration's "rendition" program, only to then release him after five months when the U.S. realized it had abducted the wrong person (El-Masri has a name similar to a suspected terrorist's). There is no dispute about El-Masri's complete innocence, as a *Washington Post* article detailed:

> This year [2006], German investigators confirmed most of Masri's allegations, which have received extensive publicity in Europe. In December, during a joint news conference with Secretary of State Condoleezza Rice, German Chancellor Angela Merkel said Rice had admitted the mistake.

Of course, complaints about all of this behavior are met with the accusation that one is "proterrorist" or concerned with "terrorist rights," and that the imperatives of America's battle against Evil justifies and even compels the most radical actions. Yet cases such as Arar's and El-Masri's demonstrate the core corruption that shapes that reasoning.

It is impossible to imagine a more potent case than Arar's to underscore the point that *being detained by the Bush administration, or being accused by them of being a terrorist, does not mean that someone is, in fact, a terrorist.* For years, Bush followers have deliberately ignored the principle that is central to our political system: the government's accusation is not tantamount to guilt. That everyone apprehended and detained by the Bush administration is, by definition, "a terrorist" is a patent falsehood. Yet that myth is repeated endlessly.

Senate Republican Minority Leader Mitch McConnell demonstrated this tactic when he explained why he expected Democrats as well as Republicans to vote in favor of a provision in the Military Commissions Act allowing *accused terrorists* at Guantánamo to be convicted on the basis of evidence that they are *prohibited from examining:* "For example, I imagine it would be awkward for many of my Democrat colleagues to go home and explain a vote to provide sensitive, classified information *to terrorists*" (emphasis added).

Senator Mel Martinez said this about why he voted to deny habeas corpus to detainees in U.S. custody: "We must remember the detainees this law affects are terrorists. . . ."

The deceit here is manifest—and uniquely dangerous. The fact that someone is accused by the Bush administration of being a terrorist or suspected by the administration of working with terrorists does not, in fact, mean that they are a "terrorist."

Advocating minimal due process protections for military commissions before people are executed for being "terrorists" *cannot* honestly be described as "giving rights to terrorists" because they are not terrorists solely by being accused—and anyone who describes it as such is engaged in outright dishonesty, not merely "framing" techniques or political spin. The same is true of opposition to torture, warrantless eavesdropping, and every other related debate. Those who are subjected to such behavior are not "terrorists," but rather merely those who the government accuses, with no proof required, of terrorist connections. That is not a petty, legalistic distinction. It lies at the heart of our political system, and it is what distinguishes free societies from tyrannical ones.

There are only two choices recognized by advocates of these radical policies: (1) support the War on Terrorism by endorsing the administration's lawless imprisonment and treatment of detainees, or (2) side with the terrorists. To them, there is no third option (such as charge detainees with terrorism and then determine in a hearing, with due process, if the Bush administration's accusation is true) because, to those inhabiting Bush's Manichean world, the president's accusation of terrorism is tantamount to proof. Anyone who objects to the Bush administration's detention of any detainees is, by definition, objecting to the "detention of a terrorist." Why wait to figure out if the detainee really is a terrorist? The Leader, who is Good and seeks to protect us, has said it is so. Thus it is so.

This mindless belief in presidential infallibility repeats itself in almost every debate we have had over the Bush administration's expansion of presidential power. The American founders viewed checks and limits on government power as vital for avoiding tyranny. The Bush movement sees such limits as "terrorist rights," unnecessary interference with the Good Leaders' efforts to protect us.

Highly disturbing behavior by our government during the Bush presidency has become far too common to be considered an aberration. MSNBC's Bill Dedman published an investigative report in late 2006 regarding the Guantánamo interrogation of Mohammed al-Qahtani, the currently alleged twentieth hijacker. Dedman described the treatment to which al-Qahtani was subjected in U.S. custody:

> Mohammed al-Qahtani, detainee No. 063, was forced to wear a bra. He had a thong placed on his head. He was massaged by a female interrogator who straddled him like a lap dancer. He was told that his mother and sisters were whores. He was told that other detainees knew he was gay. He was forced to dance with a male interrogator. He was strip-searched in front of women. He was led on a leash and forced to perform dog tricks. He was doused with water. He was prevented from praying. He was forced to watch as an interrogator squatted over his Koran.

These are not merely al-Qahtani's allegations and they are not in dispute. Rather, they are "among the findings of the U.S. Army's investigation of al-Qahtani's aggressive interrogation at Guantánamo Bay, Cuba."

The way in which Abu Ghraib and similar abuses were all dismissed as the isolated, rogue acts of a few deranged low-level soldiers is one of the administration's worst deceits. Most of the abusive techniques were expressly approved at the highest levels of the administration, even *after* numerous intelligence officials and FBI agents vigorously complained about them. As Dedman reported:

> In interviews with MSNBC.com—the first time they have spoken publicly—former senior law enforcement agents described their attempts to stop the abusive interrogations. The agents of the Pentagon's Criminal Investigation Task Force, working to build legal cases against suspected terrorists, said they objected to coercive tactics used by a separate team of intelligence interrogators soon after Guantánamo's prison camp opened in early 2002. They ultimately carried their battle up to the office of Secretary of Defense Donald H. Rumsfeld, who approved the more aggressive techniques to be used on al-Qahtani and others.

It was widely recognized even back then that these tactics were illegal, but nobody—not even those objecting to these tactics—was bothered by *that*. In the Bush administration, even knowing illegality has never been viewed as anything more than a petty inconvenience to be managed. Dedman continued:

> Although they believed the abusive techniques were probably illegal, the Pentagon cops said their objection was practical. They argued that abusive interrogations were not likely to produce truthful information, either for preventing more al-Qaida attacks or prosecuting terrorists.

The officer in charge of Guantánamo during these abuses was General Geoffrey Miller, who was thereafter sent in 2004 to Iraq to import these interrogation techniques there. It was several weeks after his arrival in Iraq when the Abu Ghraib abuses were revealed. On his very first visit to Abu Ghraib, General Miller demanded that "interrogators adopt 'emerging strategic interrogation strategies and techniques' being used at Guantánamo." Most revealing of all is the source the U.S. military used to develop these abusive techniques:

> The al-Qahtani plan went much further. The law enforcement agents began to hear a new term, SERE, an acronym for Survival, Evasion, Resistance and Escape. SERE training is provided to U.S. Special Forces and other military personnel to prepare them to withstand torture if they become prisoners of war. It includes mocking of their religious beliefs, sexual taunting, and a technique called water-boarding, which induces water through the nose to make a prisoner feel like he's drowning.
>
> Intelligence interrogators had the idea to "reverse-engineer" SERE, to use its techniques to pry information out of the suspected al-Qaida and Taliban terrorists. Pentagon e-mails seen by MSNBC.com show that at least a half dozen military intelligence personnel from Guantánamo, including at least one medical adviser, went to Fort Bragg, N.C., on Sept. 16–20, 2002, for SERE training. It was an experiment, apparently not unlike what the CIA had been trying on the few high-value detainees kept at secret locations.

In other words, by studying the torture methods used by America's enemies—those uncivilized, extremist regimes and groups which embody pure Evil—we learned how to torture people and then decided to copy their torture techniques. As always, the "rationale" of the Bush administration is that in order to defend our values and culture from the Evil forces seeking to destroy us, we have to emulate their behavior as much as possible.

It seems virtually certain that the entire top level of the Bush administration was fully aware of the techniques being used at Guantánamo. Many key Bush officials took frequent trips to Guantánamo and met with General Miller. One particular trip that MSNBC learned about took place in October 2002, when various top Bush administration lawyers—including Alberto Gonzales, David Addington, and John Yoo—visited Guantánamo. It was this same group that, just a couple of months prior to that trip, churned out the now infamous "torture memo" authored by Yoo in August 2002, which sought to both redefine and justify the administration's use of torture.

Without defending those methods, one should not be entirely unsympathetic to the defense that in the immediate aftermath of the 9/11 attacks, military and intelligence officials would be tempted to use unusually aggressive, even extreme, interrogation methods on the person who was likely intended to be the twentieth hijacker. But these extreme and vile techniques became standard operating procedure for interrogating detainees. Far worse, five years after September 11, the U.S. Congress voted expressly to authorize the use of most if not all of these techniques and empower the president to use them at will. Put another way, our country, after five years of distance from 9/11 and after much debate and deliberation, decided to enshrine this behavior as legally authorized and reflective of our new national values.

BORED BY GOVERNING

When assessing the Bush presidency and the way it has transformed America's national character, one of the most striking features is the administration's almost complete neglect of any issues that could not fit within the president's Manichean mission. Whereas domestic issues dominated America's political debates throughout the 1990s, they disappeared almost completely during Bush's tenure. Other than a single-minded devotion to reducing taxes—something he pursued relentlessly even in the face of record deficits—the president displayed almost no interest in domestic matters. In fact, the president has demonstrated almost no real interest in anything other than his perceived battle against Evil.

For that reason, many of the most significant and damaging failures that afflicted his presidency have been the result of his complete inability to remove himself from the Manichean framework and actually *govern*. While the Good vs. Evil mentality fueled the president's political success for a couple of years in the wake of 9/11, his inability to operate within any other framework has doomed the rest of his tenure. The rhetoric and worldview of this president and his allies remain the same, but the public's reaction has changed fundamentally.

The issues that the president has been forced to confront from 2004 into 2007—the years his presidency gradually collapsed—have been wholly insusceptible to being depicted as a pure battle of Good vs. Evil. One of the most enduring blows to the president's political strength occurred almost immediately after his re-election. In January 2005, the president announced what was to be the crown jewel of his domestic program, the initiative that would establish his domestic legacy: namely, his sweeping program to reform Social Security. But from the beginning, this initiative was an abject political failure, and that failure had a potent impact in stripping away the aura of political omnipotence the administration had previously enjoyed. With no enemy to demonize and no war to declare, the president's Social Security rhetoric seemed empty and listless.

President Bush's concerted nationwide campaign to advocate his program actually intensified rather than diminished opposition. For the first time in the four years of his presidency, even Congressional Republicans ran away from and publicly opposed the president's plan, and it died a quick and ignominious death as a result of widespread rejection.

From almost the beginning of President Bush's second term, issues began to dominate the political agenda that did not turn on Manichean moral dichotomies, but instead were shaped by more pedestrian—more complex, murkier, and enemyless—matters of competence and balanced solutions. In a severely weakened state, the president who had relied almost exclusively on a straightforward and elegantly simple Good-Evil paradigm lacked any framework for thinking about, and even talking about, these issues. And as these more complex issues predominated, he appeared increasingly aimless, inept, and even confused.

The disaster wrought by Hurricane Katrina, an event that entirely lacked an identifiable Enemy to attack, was precisely the type of issue that was wholly incompatible with the president's binary moralistic framework. To respond appropriately, competence and management skills were required. The administration's appallingly slow, inept, and virtually indifferent reaction to this disaster highlighted a long-lurking and obscured deficiency—a president who was deeply passionate about railing against the forces of Evil but who was entirely lost when it came to dealing with issues that could not be reduced to moralistic equations.

The politically damaging controversy of the United Arab Emirates/ Dubai deal further highlighted this inadequacy. When the controversy over the port deal emerged, the president sought to assuage widespread concerns by insisting that the UAE was an "ally in the war on terror" and that he had personally concluded that the deal posed no threat to American security.

But—as opponents of the deal were quick and eager to emphasize— the UAE is a country from which two of the 9/11 hijackers originated. It does not recognize Israel or even allow Israeli citizens to enter its country. And it maintains close alliances with some of the most extremist countries in the Middle East, including Iran, the country that the administration by then was already depicting as the new Nazi Germany. Ironically, opponents of Bush's deal relied primarily upon an invocation of *his* relentlessly advocated worldview—that every country is either firmly on our side, the side of Good, or on the other side, the side of Evil—and opponents advocated within that paradigm to sow serious doubts about the allegiances of the UAE.

Even Congressional Republicans, frightened by the deal and by the president's political weakness, invoked Bush's trademarked dichotomized rhetoric against him, piously insisting that we should not turn over our ports to countries associated with terrorism. And with that attack launched at him, the president suffered another humiliating defeat. After having vowed to use his veto power for the first time in his presidency in order to compel approval of the port deal, the administration was forced to abandon it. Far worse for the president, this controversy even raised doubts about whether he was tough on terrorism, the sole political asset he had left; one March 2006 poll from Rasmussen Reports even showed that by then the public trusted Democrats more than Republicans to manage the terrorist threat.

And in Iraq, the president's "successes" came early on, when Manichean precepts were applicable, and his failures came once they were not. The initial stage of the invasion of Iraq was widely deemed a success. Under the president's command, the U.S. military invaded Iraq, marched to Baghdad, shattered the Hussein government, removed it from power, and then apprehended Saddam. There, the Good vs. Evil framework applied neatly; the goal was to defeat the Evil dictator and his army, and the president achieved that goal.

But once Saddam was gone, Manichean imperatives were worthless. There was no longer a clearly identifiable "Evil." There were complex sectarian tensions, both among the various sects and within them. Military assaults could not achieve our objectives. To the extent they could be achieved at all, skillful diplomatic and political solutions were required— ones that focused not on the destruction of some identifiable Evil but on the building of coalitions, the engagement of potential though convertible enemies, and helping that nation to rebuild the civic institutions and infrastructure that our invasion had shattered. And as was true with all challenges faced by the president that did not enliven his Manichean evangelical mission, he was incapable of even minimal success and displayed virtually no interest in such matters.

Long after it was applicable, the president continued to speak of Iraq as though the country required nothing more than a determined, resolute commitment to waging powerful war on Evil. We were in Iraq fighting the terrorists. We could not leave because they would follow us back. Yet, to the extent the war in Iraq was ever accurately described in such simplistic Manichean terms, it had ceased to resemble the president's basic black-and-white descriptions almost immediately following the occupation. But since the president knows no other approach, to this day his "policy" in Iraq amounts to nothing more than the view that the terrorists will win if we leave, which means we can never leave.

The president's Manichean mind-set justifies every decision he makes and requires no limits and no reexamination. Like all other major policy initiatives of his tenure, like his presidency itself, the president's signature mission, the war in Iraq, lay in ruins. And because the president's core, defining convictions engendered that failure, he is without the ability to change course at all, even if he believed he should. Repudiated, disliked, rejected, and virtually alone, the president remains in power, seemingly unwilling and unable to do anything other than cling tenaciously to the same failed path.

Bush Manicheanism Reshapes the Political Spectrum

And thus we end where we began—with the observation that, whatever one might think of the president, it is impossible to contest the sweeping significance of his presidency. The president has not only altered the United States in long-lasting and fundamental ways, but he has altered the political landscape of the country to such an extent that there has been a significant political realignment as a result of his presidency.

American political conflicts have long been described in terms of "liberal versus conservative," but that is really no longer the division which drives our most important debates. The predominant political conflicts over the last six years have been driven by a different dichotomy: those who believe in the radical, militaristic, and Manichean Bush approach to the world—an approach that can roughly be described as neoconservatism—versus those who do not.

Neoconservatism is but one term for the Bush Manichean framework, with neoconservatives having cloaked themselves and their underlying war-making agenda in the language of the president's Good vs. Evil framework. These Manichean justifications are what fuel and justify the neoconservative agenda, and it is that political ideology which is responsible for virtually every significant political controversy during the Bush administration—from the invasion of Iraq to the threatened conflict with Iran to the array of constitutional abuses perpetrated in the name of fighting terrorism.

Although *neoconservatism* is rarely defined, its central tenets are, by now, quite clear. At its core, neoconservatism—just like the president's Manichean approach that grew out of it—maintains a fervent, borderline-religious belief in American exceptionalism, the view that America is destined to enforce its will on the rest of the world through an application of superior military force.

In essence, it believes in America as an empire, an imperial power maintaining dominion over the rest of the world. Neoconservatives have come specifically to believe, or at least claim, that the greatest threat to America is hostile Muslims in the Middle East, and that this poses not merely a threat to be managed but an actual existential threat to freedom and civilization itself. In this worldview, the only real solution is increased militarism and belligerence, usually with war as the necessary course of action.

Adherents of neoconservatism typically argue that to the extent Bush has erred, his flaw has been *excessive restraint*, a lack of courage, and a naïve and cowardly belief that measures short of war and all-out aggression will be effective in dealing with this problem. In this worldview, the Islamic threat is not just uniquely dangerous but also unprecedentedly so, such that Islamic extremists render prior American ideals and principles—both foreign and domestic—obsolete, and only radically militaristic approaches on our part have any chance of saving us from destruction at their hands.

This is the neoconservative mentality: the Manichean, bloodthirsty, militaristic, largely authoritarian worldview that has been driving not only our foreign policy since the September 11 attacks but also the bulk of our most controversial domestic policies undertaken in the name of fighting terrorists. In the Bush era, right-wing neoconservatism has been the central force of American political life, and it has resulted in a fundamental ideological realignment. Far more important than one's views on traditional matters of political controversy is the extent to which one supports or opposes neoconservative theories.

Throughout the 1990s, one's political orientation was determined by a finite set of primarily domestic issues—social spending, affirmative action, government regulation, gun control, welfare reform, abortion, gay rights. One's position on those issues determined whether one was conservative, liberal, moderate, etc. But those issues have become entirely secondary, at most, in our political debates. Instead, what predominates are terrorism-related issues—Iraq, U.S. treatment of detainees, domestic surveillance, attacks on press freedoms, executive power abuses, Iran, the equating of dissent with treason.

It is one's positions on *those* issues—and, more specifically, whether one agrees with the neoconservative approach which has dominated the Bush administration's approach to those issues—that now determines one's political orientation. That is why so many traditional conservatives who reject neoconservatism—the Pat Buchanans, Bob Barrs, Andrew Sullivans, George Wills, even Chuck Hagels and a long roster of military generals—have broken with the Bush administration. And it is also why certain so-called traditional liberals—embodied by Joe Lieberman— were among the most vocal and reliable supporters of the president's most militaristic and extremist policies. Indeed, many individuals who held traditionally conservative views on 1990s issues are now considered "liberals" solely by virtue of their opposition to the radical neoconservative agenda of the Bush presidency.

More than anything else, this ideological realignment was what accounted for the intense passions ignited by the Joe Lieberman Senate race in mid-2006. Despite his history as a life-long Democrat and a liberal on the predominant 1990s issues, Joe Lieberman is a pure neoconservative, which now matters much more. On the predominant issues of the day, his political comrades—and his most enthusiastic supporters— are Bill Kristol, Sean Hannity, Rush Limbaugh, the editors of *National Review* and the *New York Sun*, and Dick Cheney.

Why would hard-core Republican neoconservatives be so emotionally attached to defending then-Democrat Joe Lieberman? Why were so many pro-Bush, highly conservative Republicans pronouncing themselves to be "huge fans" of Lieberman? And, for that matter, why did liberal activists devote so much of their time and energy to his defeat rather than to the defeat of standard Republican officeholders?

Far more than being a Democrat, a liberal, a moderate, or anything else, Joe Lieberman is a neoconservative and therefore—on the issues that matter most—has become the ideological and political compatriot of Bush supporters. In the 1990s, Joe Lieberman's positions on the dominant issues of the day may have rendered him "liberal" or "moderate," but on the issues that matter most now—in light of the ideological realignment we have had in the wake of the Bush presidency—he is nothing of the sort.

George Bush's presidency has been so radical and so consequential that it has fundamentally shifted the ideological and political landscape in America. That is because the Manichean worldview he has embraced is unprecedented. Though related in key ways to how both Nixon and Reagan governed, the unrestrained absolutism of Bush's worldview exists well outside the standard ideological spectrum that has shaped and defined American political debates for decades. Far more than a political agenda, President Bush has pursued a grand and overarching moralistic mission, and he enlisted and severely expanded the powers of the American federal government—both preexisting powers and newly created ones—in service of that mission. All of this was justified, and continues to be justified, by the premise that the mission President Bush is pursuing was not only of the highest moral Good but also literally necessary for the preservation of our civilization. As a result, no limits on the president's powers in pursuing these ends could be accepted.

The now infamous January 2002 memorandum from Bush's then–White House counsel Alberto Gonzales, addressed to President Bush, vividly illustrates this mind-set. It was there that Gonzales helped lay the foundation for the array of the most extremist Bush policies:

> As you have said, the war against terrorism is a new kind of war. . . . In my judgment, this new paradigm renders obsolete Geneva's strict limitations on questioning of enemy prisoners and renders quaint some of its provisions.

The political values and precepts of civilization long embraced and advocated by America—not only for itself but for the world—became obsolete and were dismissed as quaint relics of the past. The overarching moral imperative of George Bush's mission ushered in a "new paradigm" in America, and it outweighed all other considerations and subordinated all other values. George Bush was fighting to preserve our civilization, our very existence, and no limitations on his powers could be tolerated. And whether one embraces those premises and the resulting Bush Doctrine—the Bush mission and Manichean worldview—is now, more than anything else, what determines where one falls on the American political spectrum. *That* is the fundamental political realignment which George Bush's presidency has spawned.

Beyond the Bush presidency, whether the United States will continue to follow the increasingly militaristic and authoritarian approach advocated by President Bush and his right-wing supporters is the predominant political question we face. In 2008, the overarching political choice facing our country will be whether it will seek to contain and then reverse the profound damage of the Bush legacy, or whether we will choose to replace the president with someone eager to continue on his path, or even one who believes that Bush has been insufficiently aggressive and intends to pursue an even *more* militaristic and extremist course. Just as the U.S. established its moral credibility and defining principles through its actions over the course of decades, that credibility and those principles can be restored by returning to the nation we were prior to its extreme transformation under the Bush presidency. What is really at stake as we decide whether to repudiate or embrace the Bush legacy is the national character of our nation.

CHAPTER SIX

The Tragic Legacy of George W. Bush

Following President Bush's 2004 re-election victory, Karl Rove widely boasted that the president's second term would be composed of a series of large domestic policy victories, which would create what Rove called a "permanent Republican majority." The president's spokesmen and most ardent supporters, and even President Bush himself, began boldly comparing his "war presidency" and legacy to those of George Washington, Abraham Lincoln, and Harry S. Truman.

In February of 2007, Bush spoke at an event commemorating Presidents' Day and he invoked George Washington's prosecution of the Revolutionary War in order to defend his own conduct:

> On the field of battle, Washington's forces were facing a mighty empire, and the odds against them were overwhelming. The ragged Continental Army lost more battles than it won, suffered waves of desertions, and stood on the brink of disaster many times. Yet George Washington's calm hand and determination kept the cause of independence and the principles of our Declaration alive. . . .
>
> In the end, General Washington understood that the Revolutionary War was a test of wills, and his will was unbreakable. After winning the

war, Washington did what victorious leaders rarely did at the time. He voluntarily gave up power.

At a 2005 ceremony marking the sixtieth anniversary of America's victory over Japan in World War II, President Bush repeatedly compared the triumphant legacy of Franklin Roosevelt to his own. Speaking at the naval base that is the home to the USS *Ronald Reagan,* Bush emphasized that Iraqi insurgents are just as "ruthless" an enemy as were the Germans and the Japanese, and then he extended the Bush-Roosevelt equivalence further:

> Now, as then, they are trying to intimidate free people and break our will, and now, as then, they will fail. They will fail, because the terrorists of our century are making the same mistake that the followers of other totalitarian ideologies made in the last century. They believe that democracies are inherently weak and corrupt and can be brought to their knees. America will not run in defeat, and we will not forget our responsibilities. . . .
>
> [Roosevelt] knew that it was the lack of democracy in Japan that allowed an unelected group of militarists to take control of the state, threaten our neighbors, attack America, and plunge an entire region into war. And he knew that the best way to bring peace and stability to the region was by bringing freedom to Japan.

In January 2007, when Rudy Giuliani spoke to a Republican gathering in New Hampshire, he, according to an account from *The Politico,* chose Abraham Lincoln as the president to whom Bush should be compared:

> "I don't imagine that they had those favorable/unfavorable things back during the Civil War," but Lincoln would not have fared well, Giuliani said.
>
> Seeming to draw present-day comparisons, Giuliani noted that Lincoln even faced riots in New York City because people were unhappy with the war. "They wanted to quit because it was getting too tough."

And the same month, Bush's spokesman, Tony Snow, attempted to defend Bush's 2003 declaration that Iraq was a "Mission Accomplished," and Cheney's 2005 assurance that the Iraqi insurgency was in its "last throes." Snow's defense:

If you had asked any other president in American history during a time of war whether they had a credibility problem because they had not foreseen changes on the battlefield, you probably would have had plenty of cause. I mean, Abraham Lincoln constantly guessed from Manassas straight through until the final months of the war.

During a December 2006 meeting with leading Congressional Democrats convened in order to discuss how the new Democratic majority would work with Bush on issues relating to the war in Iraq, Bush astonished—and angered—Senator Dick Durbin by expressly comparing himself to Harry Truman. According to Durbin:

> Bush said that "in years to come they realized [Truman] was right and then his doctrine became the standard for America." He's trying to position himself in history and to justify those who continue to stand by him, saying sometimes if you're right you're unpopular, and be prepared for criticism.

Clearly, the president who had previously dismissed the judgment of history as irrelevant has changed his mind, and his legacy has become one of his central concerns. Bush told Fred Barnes during interviews for the latter's Bush-glorifying book, *Rebel in Chief*, that he had just finished reading three consecutive books on George Washington's legacy and, according to Barnes, Bush said: "Even after two hundred years, they're still reassessing George Washington. What will they say about me?"

As documented in the first chapter, few, if any, presidents can match the sheer duration and intensity of Bush's unpopularity with the American people. And regardless of one's views on the Bush presidency, there is virtually universal agreement that Bush's legacy will be shaped and dominated by one decision: his decision to invade Iraq.

In March 2006, Mark McKinnon, a senior Bush campaign adviser, acknowledged to *USA Today*: "There's no question the president's legacy will be dominated by Iraq. The war is really driving almost everything in government." Political scientist Steven Schier added that Iraq has virtually eliminated the Bush administration's ability to focus on any other issue: "They were expecting to move on to a bunch of other things in the second term like Social Security reform and the 'ownership society,' but all that has been pushed aside because of Iraq. It's the whale in the bathtub for the administration." The *USA Today* article was accompanied by a poll demonstrating that Americans generally also concur that history's judgment of Bush will be shaped by one issue—Iraq:

> Nearly two-thirds of Americans say the Iraq war will be what Bush is most remembered for, according to a USA TODAY/CNN/Gallup Poll taken Friday through Sunday. Just 18% cite the president's efforts against terrorism, 10% his response to Hurricane Katrina, 5% his Supreme Court appointments. Tax cuts, the hallmark of his first year in office, were chosen by 2%.

Historians have frequently noted that wars, especially long ones, virtually always end up dominating a president's legacy and rendering almost irrelevant every other issue. Lincoln is remembered for the Civil War, Woodrow Wilson for World War I, Franklin Roosevelt for World War II, and Lyndon Johnson for the Vietnam War. The legacy of those presidents is shaped overwhelmingly by those wars, and the success of their war management is what, in turn, drives the judgment of them by history. As Robert Dallek, a biographer of Lyndon Johnson, put it: "War kills reform. It consumes the energy of the administration, the public, the press. This is what the focus is on."

The most obvious comparison is between the Bush legacy and that of Lyndon Johnson, whose presidency was so crippled by the intense unpopularity of the Vietnam War that he was all but precluded from seeking a second term. In one sense, however, a fatal flaw with that comparison is that President Johnson achieved a string of extraordinary domestic policy successes—from the enactment of the groundbreaking Civil Rights Act of 1964 to the various domestic safety net programs and reforms that created The Great Society. As PBS's *American Experience Online* put it:

> If the record of Lyndon Johnson's presidency were to end in 1965, his would surely be ranked among our nation's finest.
>
> Thrust into the role of Chief Executive on that tragic day in Dallas in November 1963, Johnson reassured an emotionally devastated public by pledging to honor, and build upon, the legacy of his slain predecessor: "John Kennedy's death commands what his life conveyed—that America

must move forward." Johnson did indeed move forward, presenting a program of domestic reforms originally crafted in the mold of the New Deal and imbued with the vigor of the New Frontier. By 1965, Johnson had devised and signed into law more than two hundred pieces of major legislation, including a sizable tax cut, a billion dollar anti-poverty program, and a groundbreaking civil rights bill.

By stark and obvious contrast, not even President Bush's most fervent supporters would claim that the Bush administration has achieved anything close to Johnson's record of epic successes on the domestic front. Indeed, to the extent that Bush's domestic record will be remembered for anything positive in the eyes of his supporters, that achievement is confined almost exclusively to one item—his relentless commitment to cut taxes. And even there, such enthusiasm would likely be tempered even in the most fervent antitax precincts by the fact that such cuts occurred in the face of massive and growing budget deficits and redounded to the benefit of only a small portion of Americans.

Beyond single-mindedly cutting taxes, there are few, if any, discernible Bush accomplishments on the domestic front. Beginning with the 9/11 attacks, domestic policy was almost completely overshadowed by matters of foreign policy, particularly Iraq. And during those fleeting and isolated instances in which domestic issues took center stage, sheer failure pervades Bush's record on virtually every front—from the resounding rejection of the president's Social Security reform plan to his administration's tragically inept and indifferent handling of the Hurricane Katrina disaster, to the spectacle of converting the Schiavo drama literally into a federal case, to increasingly dangerous dependence on Chinese credit and loans, to Bush's conversion of the multi-hundred-billion-dollar budget surplus he inherited into a multi-hundred-billion-dollar budget deficit.

While discretionary spending has skyrocketed under the Bush presidency, there is no Great Society or New Deal for his supporters to tout, nor is there any shrinking of government spending or federal power. As a result, even some Bush supporters have been aggressively critical of the utter disarray and failure that characterizes the Bush domestic record, and many have specifically argued that domestic policy has been treated by the Bush White House as nothing more than a means for consolidating political support. John DiIulio, a former top domestic policy adviser in the Bush White House, famously complained during an interview with Ron Suskind:

> Everything [is] run by the political arm. It's the reign of the Mayberry Machiavellis. . . . The lack of even basic policy knowledge and the only casual interest in knowing more, was somewhat breathtaking: discussions by fairly senior people who meant *Medicaid* but were talking *Medicare;* near instant shifts from discussing any actual policy pros and cons to discussing political communications, media strategy, et cetera.

Former Bush treasury secretary Paul O'Neill echoed those sentiments when he contrasted his time in government in the mid-1970s to his tenure under the Bush administration by pointing out that the primary difference "is that our [mid-'70s] group was mostly about evidence and analysis, and Karl, Dick [Cheney], [Bush communications strategist] Karen [Hughes] and the gang seemed to be mostly about politics."

Conservative economist Bruce Bartlett became a leading Bush critic based upon his central complaint that the Bush administration simply never had any coherent domestic governance at all, but instead viewed domestic policy solely as a tool for gaining political power. Bartlett told the *Washington Post* that whereas domestic policy has traditionally been developed by policy experts in federal government agencies, the process was turned upside down in the Bush administration: "Ideas are hatched in the White House, for political or ideological reasons, then are thrust on the bureaucracy, 'not for analysis, but for sale.'" Republican economist Richard Rahn similarly complained in a 2004 *Washington Times* column that "from the beginning of the Bush administration, sympathetic, experienced economists have warned its officials about the need to avoid some obvious mistakes. Unfortunately, these warnings have gone unheeded." In sum, domestic policy was almost completely ignored under the Bush presidency, except when it was hopelessly botched.

The temptation to compare the Bush legacy to that of Lyndon Johnson must thus be tempered by this critical difference. Whereas Johnson's domestic record was highly successful, even extraordinary in some respects, Bush's is almost entirely bereft of any notable achievement, and is

instead characterized by a series of clear, often embarrassing, and sometimes tragic failures.

Ultimately, though, even the Johnson legacy could not be saved by
domestic achievements. Johnson's domestic successes are rendered minor
in the judgment of history as a result of the seemingly unbending axiom
that wartime presidents are remembered by their wars. As PBS's *American Experience* described it, "the promises of [Johnson's] Great Society
were swallowed up in the quagmire of Vietnam." In that regard, there
is a compelling parallel between the Bush and Johnson legacies. From
American Experience:

> The presidency of Lyndon Johnson is described as having all the charac-
> teristics of a classic tragedy. Johnson aspired to be "the greatest of them
> all," and for a moment greatness seemed within his grasp. But his fall was
> as swift and as sure as that of any tragic literary figure.

As documented in the first chapter of this book, this Johnson narrative also perfectly describes the tragic rise and fall of the Bush presidency. Both presidents had the opportunity for successes on a historic
scale, and for a time, both seemed poised to seize that opportunity. Yet
in both cases, those opportunities were squandered by a deeply unpopular and unsuccessful foreign war of choice that seemed to get bloodier
and more consuming by the day, yet with fewer and fewer prospects for
anything that could be deemed a success, let alone a justification of the
war itself.

That the legacies of Johnson and Bush seem almost identical, at
least with regard to their wars, is unsurprising given the overwhelming
similarities, on multiple levels, between the war in Vietnam and the war
in Iraq. The divisions spawned among Americans by the Vietnam War,
and the intense unpopularity of that war, are reflected by Johnson's
March 31, 1968, speech to the nation, in which he announced that he
would not seek re-election to a second term:

> Tonight I want to speak to you of peace in Vietnam and Southeast Asia.
>   No other question so preoccupies our people. No other dream so
> absorbs the 250 million human beings who live in that part of the
> world. No other goal motivates American policy in Southeast Asia. . . .

For thirty-seven years in the service of our Nation, first as a Congressman, as a Senator, and as Vice President, and now as your President, I have put the unity of the people first. I have put it ahead of any divisive partisanship.

And in these times as in times before, it is true that a house divided against itself by the spirit of faction, of party, of region, of religion, of race, is a house that cannot stand.

There is division in the American house now. There is divisiveness among us all tonight. And holding the trust that is mine, as President of all the people, I cannot disregard the peril to the progress of the American people and the hope and the prospect of peace for all peoples. . . .

With America's sons in the fields far away, with America's future under challenge right here at home, with our hopes and the world's hopes for peace in the balance every day, I do not believe that I should devote an hour or a day of my time to any personal partisan causes or to any duties other than the awesome duties of this office—the Presidency of your country.

Accordingly, I shall not seek, and I will not accept, the nomination of my party for another term as your President.

Johnson's decision was compelled by his pervasive unpopularity as a result of the war. A 1968 Gallup poll conducted shortly before his announcement revealed that only 26 percent of the American people approved of Johnson's handling of the war, and the belief that Johnson had misled the nation regarding the war's progress was so widespread that he had virtually no credibility with the country.

A poll commissioned by the *New York Times* and CBS News in late February 2007 found that Americans disapproved of President Bush's handling of Iraq by an even *greater* margin: a mere 23 percent approved; 71 percent disapproved. Similarly, a solid majority of Americans have long believed that they were misled into supporting the war in Iraq in the first place and have consequently ceased trusting the president.

Beyond public opinion, there are striking similarities between the rhetoric deployed by Johnson to justify the Vietnam War and that used by Bush with regard to Iraq. The Bush administration and its supporters constantly claim that the threat posed by Al Qaeda and terrorists is unique and unprecedented. As but one of countless examples, the president in October 2005 delivered a speech on international terrorism and argued that "our time in history will be remembered for new challenges and unprecedented dangers." And the president and his supporters have sought to justify a whole array of radical policies—from lawless detentions of American citizens to the abuses of Guantánamo to "coercive" interrogation techniques (i.e., torture)—by claiming that terrorists are an enemy whose barbarism and disregard for civilized norms make them unlike any enemies we have ever faced in the past.

President Johnson and Vietnam War supporters made virtually identical claims about the North Vietnamese. Demonizing the enemy as a unique, unprecedented threat is routine. It is a tool used by every government to justify every war. In his 1965 speech at Johns Hopkins University, President Johnson spoke of what he claimed was the unique Evil of the North Vietnamese (emphases added):

> And it is a war of *unparalleled brutality*. Simple farmers are the targets of assassination and kidnapping. Women and children are strangled in the night because their men are loyal to their government. And helpless villages are ravaged by sneak attacks. Large-scale raids are conducted on towns, and *terror strikes in the heart of cities*.

And in his State of the Union speech of 1967, President Johnson railed against what he called the terrorist tactics used by the North Vietnamese:

> This war—like the war in Vietnam—is not a simple one. There is no single battleline which you can plot each day on a chart. The enemy is not easy to perceive, or to isolate, or to destroy. There are mistakes and there are setbacks. But we are moving, and our direction is forward. . . .
>
> I think I reveal no secret when I tell you that we are dealing with a stubborn adversary who is committed to the use of force and terror to settle political questions. . . .
>
> Our South Vietnamese allies are also being tested tonight. Because they must provide real security to the people living in the countryside. And this means reducing the terrorism and the armed attacks which kidnapped and killed 26,900 civilians in the last 32 months, to levels where they can be successfully controlled by the regular South Vietnamese security forces. . . .

And beyond the rhetorical attempt to demonize the enemy as a pure and unique Evil, if one reads virtually any of the speeches by Lyndon Johnson or his top aides regarding Vietnam, it is utterly striking how identical their reasoning is—both in terms of why we must not abandon the war and why we are winning—to the speeches President Bush has been giving for five straight years about Iraq. As just one example, this is an excerpt from Johnson's 1965 speech at Johns Hopkins University:

> We are also there because there are great stakes in the balance. Let no one think for a moment that retreat from Viet-Nam would bring an end to conflict. The battle would be renewed in one country and then another. The central lesson of our time is that the appetite of aggression is never satisfied. To withdraw from one battlefield means only to prepare for the next. We must say in southeast Asia—as we did in Europe—in the words of the Bible: "Hitherto shalt thou come, but no further."

And in his State of the Union speech in 1966, President Johnson argued that the establishment of a fledgling democracy in Southeast Asia would foster greater peace: "Support of national independence—the right of each people to govern themselves—and to shape their own institutions. For a peaceful world order will be possible only when each country walks the way that it has chosen to walk for itself."

Claims that the enemy we face poses an unprecedented, mortal threat—and that it operates beyond all bounds of decency, humanity, and civilized norms—is something that Americans have heard (sometimes accurately, sometimes manipulatively) about all sorts of enemies over the last hundred years. There is plainly nothing new or unprecedented about the magnitude of the threat we have faced under the Bush presidency. Quite the contrary, the language and substantive arguments invoked by President Johnson to justify the continuation and escalation of the Vietnam War are virtually indistinguishable from those upon which President Bush has relentlessly relied in defending the equally unpopular ongoing occupation of Iraq.

Even the origins of the Vietnam War contain glaring similarities to the president's commencement and early prosecution of the war in Iraq. As early as 1962, the military was assuring Americans that progress was being made in Vietnam and victory was at hand. In a 1962 interview with U.S. Army Major Robert Ryan, the following exchange occurred:

Q: Major, how would you say the war was going in your sector?

A: Well, I think here, lately, the . . . it's going a lot better; I think we're beginning to win the people over; our operations are going better. We're actually getting VC.

Q: What evidence do you have that the . . . you're winning the people over?

A: Well, we've got the "strategic hamlet" program going on. And when we go out on these operations, it seems like the people are more friendly. Several times recently we've had people warn the Vietnamese troops that there was an ambush ahead, or something like that. This means the people are getting on our side.

And in a December 1962 press conference, President Kennedy gave similar assurances:

There is great difficulty, however, in fighting a guerrilla war; you need ten to one, or eleven to one, especially in terrain as difficult as South Vietnam. But I'm, uh . . . so we're not, uh . . . we don't see the end of the tunnel; but, I must say, I don't think it's darker than it was a year ago—in some ways, lighter.

During a visit to South Vietnam in 1964, Johnson's defense secretary Robert McNamara sought to assure the South Vietnamese of America's willingness to wage war for as long as it takes to achieve victory against the "insurgents":

We are here to emphasize that the United States will maintain its interest and its presence in your country. There is no question whatsoever of our abandoning that interest. We'll stay for as long as it takes. We shall provide whatever help is required to win the battle against the Communist insurgents.

The same year, the U.S. military misleadingly depicted the Gulf of Tonkin incident as an unprovoked torpedo attack on the USS *Maddox* by North Vietnam in international waters, a claim which heightened war fever among Americans. Those deceitful claims also led Congress to enact, almost unanimously, the 1964 war-enabling Gulf of Tonkin Resolution.

Thereafter, President Johnson ceaselessly defended the righteousness of the war and America's unending resolve to wage it. In 1965, he vowed: "We will not surrender. And we will not retreat. We intend to convince the Communists that we cannot be defeated by force of arms or by superior power." And during a 1967 press conference, U.S. General William Westmoreland provided this sunny assessment when asked how he viewed U.S. progress in the war, one which he had repeated many times before and which he was to repeat many times thereafter: "Very very encouraged. I've never been more encouraged during my entire, almost four years in this country. I think we're making real progress. Everybody is very optimistic that I know of, who is intimately associated with our effort there."

Yet Americans began, gradually though inexorably, to realize that assurances by President Johnson of great progress in the war were misleading, even false. More and more Americans came to question the veracity of the claims made at the outset of the war to justify its commencement and escalation. And as it became increasingly apparent that the war was both unnecessary from the start and the by-product of less-than-candid assertions by the president, the country turned against both the war and the president who had become its principal advocate. A president who is burdened with a failed and unpopular war, and who has lost the trust of the country, simply can no longer govern. He is destined to become as much a failure as his war.

While this dynamic compelled President Johnson to leave office, President Bush has remained in this depleted and discredited state for virtually his entire second term. And in the midst of his lame-duck tenure, Bush's situation has only worsened, to a point of isolation, abandonment, weakness, and loss of national trust that even Lyndon Johnson did not encounter.

Yet unlike Johnson—whose standing among Americans was improved by his decision not to seek re-election and his accompanying call for peace in Vietnam—George Bush has become more, not less, committed to the Iraq War as its unpopularity increases. And far from calling for peace, he announced his decision to *escalate* the conflict almost immediately after Americans turned his party out of office, in November 2006, due primarily to their desire for an end to the war. As a result of his unyielding conviction that he was right about Iraq all along, and his increasingly resolute commitment to the war, Bush's approval ratings and support have continued to tumble toward the depths to which Richard Nixon sunk immediately prior to resigning the presidency.

The president's bizarrely misguided efforts to shape his own legacy will fail. And his and his supporters' glorifying comparisons of the Bush presidency and those of other wartime presidents, such as Lincoln, Roosevelt, and Truman, are simply frivolous.

The Civil War, which propelled Lincoln's presidency, was a true existential threat to the nation, one that was fought on American soil and resulted in the deaths of 600,000 Americans (a full 5 percent of the national population) and another 1 million wounded. In today's population terms, that would translate into the deaths of 15 million Americans. Some weekend battles standing alone resulted in as many as 50,000 casualties. The scope of carnage and national endangerment—again, all carried out on American soil—finds no remote comparison in anything George Bush has faced.

Similarly, World War II entailed warfare against the most formidable military force in the world, in the form of Hitler's Germany, which in turn was fueled by the incomparable strength of German industry. That enormous capacity enabled Germany to invade and successfully occupy some of the most powerful countries in the world. And the United States was attacked by a Japanese nation united behind its emperor in an all-out commitment to winning the war against the U.S.

During World War II, Americans were mobilized behind their president because they believed in the necessity and justice of the battle. Even prior to the Pearl Harbor attacks, President Roosevelt demonstrated the sincerity of his belief that that war was of urgent necessity for the security of the U.S. by arguing for American involvement despite there being very little prowar sentiment. More significant, President Roosevelt repeatedly demanded that Americans genuinely sacrifice for their country. All of America was galvanized into supporting the war by word and deed by President Roosevelt, and he ran for re-election in 1940 expressly on a platform of reinstating the draft in order to enable America to defend itself. In his acceptance speech at the Democratic National Convention, President Roosevelt said (emphasis added):

> Because of the millions of citizens involved in the conduct of defense, most right thinking persons are agreed that some form of selection by draft is as necessary and fair today as it was in 1917 and 1918.
>
> Nearly every American is willing to do his share or her share to defend the United States. It is neither just nor efficient to permit that task to fall upon any one section or any one group. For every section and every group depend for their existence upon the survival of the nation as a whole.
>
> Lying awake, as I have, on many nights, I have asked myself whether I have the right, as Commander-in-Chief of the Army and Navy, to call on men and women to serve their country or to train themselves to serve and, at the same time, decline to serve my country in my own personal capacity, if I am called upon to do so by the people of my country. . . .
>
> It is the continuance of civilization as we know it versus the ultimate destruction of all that we have held dear—religion against godlessness; the ideal of justice against the practice of force; moral decency versus the firing squad; courage to speak out, and to act, versus the false lullaby of appeasement.
>
> But it has been well said that a selfish and greedy people cannot be free.
>
> *The American people must decide whether these things are worth making sacrifices of money, of energy, and of self.*

The greatness of President Roosevelt is attested to by the fact that Americans believed in the cause he touted and answered his call to sacrifice. American men willingly accepted the draft and American women entered the workforce and undertook enormous burdens in order to support the country's war efforts. President Roosevelt did not merely play-act as a "War President" (as George Bush once labeled himself), nor did he use wartime rhetoric for political gain while failing to follow his premises to their logical conclusions. Instead, he led the nation in a cause that he was able to persuade his fellow citizens was so just and so compelling that the nation was willing to devote itself at great cost to its success.

The contrast between the greatness of Roosevelt's war leadership and the barren and disingenuous exploitation of War and Enemy rhetoric by

President Bush could not be more glaring. And Americans have come to see those stark differences on their own. While President Bush has endlessly exploited the rhetoric of war and America's alleged struggles to defend freedom, he has lacked the political courage to follow those claims through to their logical conclusions—by demanding, or even requesting, that Americans sacrifice for this claimed overarching struggle against Evil.

In 2007, when President Bush announced to the nation that he intended to escalate the Iraq War by deploying still more troops, he was implementing the so-called surge plan formulated by Frederick Kagan of the American Enterprise Institute. Yet Kagan had warned that the success of that specific mission, as well as the general ability of the U.S. to succeed in its overall War on Terrorism strategy, was severely jeopardized by a shortage of American volunteers to fight in those wars. As a result, when Kagan, along with retired General Jack Keane, published a defense of the "surge" plan, he warned of the urgent need for President Bush to call for more Americans to volunteer for military service (emphases added):

> Victory in Iraq is still possible at an acceptable level of effort. We must adopt a new approach to the war and implement it quickly and decisively. . . . This approach requires a *national commitment to victory* in Iraq: . . .
>
> The president must request a substantial increase in ground forces end strength. This increase is vital to sustaining the morale of the combat forces by ensuring that relief is on the way. *The president must issue a personal call for young Americans to volunteer to fight in the decisive conflict of this generation.*

The reason for Kagan's plea for more Americans to enlist is self-evident. The country simply does not have the available troops to sustain the president's glorious Churchillian ambitions, nor to satisfy the endless warmongering of those who want to take a belligerent and militaristic stance against "Islamofascism" by waging war against more Middle Eastern countries. In fact, according to the U.S. military itself, we do not have enough troops to sustain Kagan's "surge" plan, let alone the broader regional war toward which the president, fueled by the faux warriors who compose his political base, is headed. Indeed, a consensus of military and intelligence conclusions have warned that even our mission to banish the Taliban and Al Qaeda from Afghanistan—the one previous success trumpeted by the Bush administration—is in danger of failing due to insufficient troop strength in that country.

Regardless of disputes over specific numbers, Kagan has insisted that "Victory" in Iraq requires that more Americans volunteer to fight. According to Kagan and Keane's *Washington Post* op-ed advocating their surge plan:

> We need to cut through the confusion. Bringing security to Baghdad— the essential precondition for political compromise, national reconciliation and economic development—is possible only with a surge of at least 30,000 combat troops lasting 18 months or so. Any other option is likely to fail.

Yet President Bush, despite all of his soaring speeches about the unparalleled importance of this War of Civilizations we are allegedly fighting, has never once called for Americans to sacrifice in any way for this war, because doing so would entail political risks. Not only has the president been adamantly opposed even to the idea of a draft to support his seemingly endless quest for war, he has never once *suggested* that more Americans consider volunteering for military service.

Moreover, the president has threatened to veto legislation designed to make America safer from real terrorism threats, such as bills to require more thorough inspections of cargo entering the country, on the grounds that such measures are too costly. Yet in between his attempts to depict the threat of terrorism as an "unprecedented" danger—the same threat that measures such as port inspections are intended to address— he never once entertained the idea that even a delay, let alone a cancellation, of his scheduled tax cuts may be necessary to pay for measures designed to protect the American homeland. The president endlessly proclaims terrorism as a towering, paramount threat to freedom and American security, yet he has been completely unwilling to undertake even the most minimal political risks, or ask the American voter to sacrifice in any way, in order to battle that threat.

To the contrary, in November 2001, when the nation was most galvanized and eager to act in support of their country against terrorism, President Bush famously instructed that Americans need do nothing other than "go about their daily lives, working and shopping and playing, worshipping at churches and synagogues and mosques, going to movies and to baseball games." While such reassurances may have been necessary to calm the nation immediately after 9/11, the president never once requested, let alone inspired, any sacrifices by Americans as a whole. The contrast between the war leadership of President Roosevelt and the "war" exploitation of George W. Bush could not be greater.

The president's soaring war rhetoric and invocation of Franklin Roosevelt and Abraham Lincoln simply can no longer obscure the self-evident reality that Americans now see for themselves. The threat of terrorism and the continuous reliance upon the need to battle against America's enemies has taken center stage during the Bush presidency only when those concepts served the president's political agenda.

Those threats have been endlessly milked and exploited to justify a war which, as Americans realized belatedly though conclusively, never had any connection to that terrorism threat other than to exacerbate it. Unlike Presidents Lincoln, Roosevelt, and Truman—who led the country in wars of necessity and who faced down genuinely formidable threats to the security and/or very existence of the United States—President Bush has exploited the rhetoric of Enemy and Evil to promote an agenda that has little real connection to either. His eagerness to claim the mantle of the greatness of past American War Presidents is grounded in pure delusion and myth.

The president's inability to view the world as anything other than a paramount battle between the forces of Good and Evil—along with his unshakable conviction that not only he, but every decision he makes, is in service of that Manichean crusade—has kept him wedded to a war and to a method of governance long past the time when both have been revealed to be utter failures. And his core belief in both his own righteousness and the moral imperative of his mission have led him to engage in behavior that has all but destroyed America's credibility and moral standing in the world. That credibility and standing have been

built by American presidents, Democratic and Republican alike, throughout the twentieth century, and will take extraordinary efforts, and years
if not decades, to restore.

There is a reason why, pursuant to the Constitution, wars in the
United States cannot be declared by the president, but instead require
the consent of the American people through their Congress. As John Jay
warned in Federalist 4, requiring that the American people approve of
wars is essential for avoiding unnecessary wars, because presidents will
start them unnecessarily, i.e., for their own benefit, but the people are
much less likely to do so:

> It is too true, however disgraceful it may be to human nature, that na-
> tions in general will make war whenever they have a prospect of getting
> anything by it; nay, absolute monarchs will often make war when their
> nations are to get nothing by it, but for the purposes and objects merely
> personal, such as thirst for military glory, revenge for personal affronts,
> ambition, or private compacts to aggrandize or support their particular
> families or partisans. These and a variety of other motives, which affect
> only the mind of the sovereign, often lead him to engage in wars not
> sanctified by justice or the voice and interests of his people.

Americans have come to recognize that George Bush's Iraq War is
described almost perfectly, with eerie prescience, by this passage. And
just as was true for President Johnson, this realization has almost single-
handedly destroyed the presidency of George W. Bush.

America's overarching choice in 2008—whether to reaffirm the values
for which America has long stood, whether to work toward restoration
of our credibility and moral standing in the world—has unparalleled
urgency in light of the fundamental changes to our national character
wrought by the Bush presidency. George Bush repeatedly vowed to
demonstrate that the United States is the world's leader in individual liberty, human rights, and commitment to peace, yet the world, over the
last six years, has reached precisely the opposite conclusion concerning
the values this country embodies. And it pains one to acknowledge that
the conclusion has been reached with good reason; the moralistic certainty that fueled Bush's actions enabled, justified, and ensured an end-

less string of policies that violated our most basic values and led us to engage in the very behavior we have long vocally condemned.

On March 29, 2007, Harold Hongju Koh, dean of Yale Law School, testified before the House Committee on Foreign Affairs and observed:

> We now fail to tell the full truth about our human rights conduct, or that of our allies in the War on Terror. Increasingly, we avoid application of universal standards: whether the rules against torture and cruel, inhuman or degrading treatment or Common Article Three of the Geneva Conventions. But the United States cannot lead the world with moral authority unless we hold ourselves to the same high standards that we demand from others.
>
> The U.S. has put its own human rights practices center stage by promoting double standards for our allies, and arguing in favor of "law-free zones" (like Guantánamo), "law-free practices" (like extraordinary rendition), "law-free persons" (who are dubbed "enemy combatants"), and "law-free" courts (like the system of military commissions, which have failed to deliver credible justice and are currently being challenged in our courts for the recent stripping of the writ of habeas corpus). Through these misguided policies, the Administration has shifted the world's focus from the grotesque human rights abuses of the terrorists to America's own human rights misconduct, leaving other, equally pressing issues elsewhere ignored or unaddressed.

The president who insisted that the key to American security was our moral credibility in the world single-handedly destroyed that credibility. The president who vowed to defend Good from the forces of Evil relied in that battle upon the very practices the United States has long insisted were the hallmarks of Evil—from an unprovoked, offensive invasion of a sovereign country that was not threatening us; to the creation of a secret and lawless worldwide prison network stocked with detainees who, in many cases, were abducted, tortured, and given no process of any kind to demonstrate their innocence; to the assertion of a limitless entitlement to act outside of any international conventions of law and ethics; to bellicose threats toward still other sovereign countries of more invasions, bombing campaigns, regime changes, and wars. The very values that the president insisted demonstrated America's moral righteousness and political exceptionalism have been precisely those he has most vigorously repudiated and, indeed, betrayed.

The Bush legacy is one whereby not only our moral standing but also our strength and security as a nation have been dangerously eroded. The president who venerated values of "strength" and subordinated all other goals to "security" has done more to diminish both than any modern American president. Our military force has been severely depleted by countless imperial commitments around the world and the endless occupation of Iraq specifically; the strength of our deterrent power has been severely weakened by the visible failures in Iraq and the accompanying resource constraints on our country and our military force; and we have suffered a virtually complete loss of our "soft power" tools of diplomacy and deterrence as a result of our worldwide loss of credibility as a nation. Machiavelli argued that, among one's enemies and potential enemies, it is better to be feared than to be loved, yet under the Bush presidency, we are neither.

The most ironic—and most revealing—aspect of the erosion of America's moral credibility is that the reprehensible policies that caused it were "justified" as necessary steps in a moralistic mission. The president's moral certitude is what enabled, is what spawned, some of the most amoral acts in our country's history.

The Manichean warrior recognizes no limits on the weapons he uses to annihilate the Evil enemies. Those who begin with the premise that they are intrinsically and by divine entitlement on the side of objective Good view any weapons they use as, by definition, just and necessary. Thus, the president who vowed to the world that he would demonstrate the values that have made this country great, thereafter systematically violated those very values to the point where our country is no longer defined by them. The epic challenge in the aftermath of the Bush presidency is the restoration of those national values, a rehabilitation of our national character, so that American morality and credibility are, once again, more than empty slogans in presidential Manichean war speeches. That is the tragic legacy George W. Bush leaves behind for America.

ACKNOWLEDGMENTS

One of the principal advantages of writing a daily political blog is that virtually every aspect of blogging is collaborative. Between one's own readers and other bloggers, every idea is elaborated on and challenged, every error quickly detected and corrected, every undiscovered fact revealed. The views of anyone who spends substantial time reading political blogs—as I do—are the culmination of constant exposure to all of those varied sources. Many of the arguments and observations in this book are the by-product of that collaborative process, even when it is impossible to trace the genesis of a specific idea.

Two individuals—one blog reader and one blogger—were indispensable in my writing this book. Therese Sarah, a longtime reader, volunteered to assist with the research and found even the most obscure information with absurd ease. Mona Holland, a fellow blogger, provided aggressive line-by-line editing that substantially improved and focused the manuscript, and also contributed original ideas that bolstered several of the arguments. Additional thanks to Marilyn Klubenspies, Jennifer Nix, and Werner Achatz.

Sean Desmond, my Crown editor, played a central role in shaping this book from its inception. His suggestions and guidance were uniformly wise, even when I initially resisted them. He oversaw the writing of this book with the ideal mix of encouragement, constructive criticism, and even a little pressure when necessary. Working on a book of this scope is much easier and more fulfilling when one has a smart and insightful editor.

And finally, my infinite and eternal thanks to David Miranda Greenwald, who is the one who makes everything possible.

INDEX

A

Abbas, Mahmoud, 61
ABC News, 1, 14–15
abductions, 231, 251–52
Abdullah, king of Saudi Arabia, 212
Abizaid, John, 90
Abramowitz, Michael, 77
Abrams, Elliot, 100, 173, 195
Abu Ghraib prison, 115, 130, 231, 255
Addington, David, 256
Afghanistan, 98, 137, 206, 215–17, 219.
    See also Taliban
    Al Qaeda in, 3, 215–16, 280
    Iranian cooperation with U.S. in,
        182–83, 184, 185–86
    war in, 2, 6, 105, 119, 166, 169, 175,
        195, 212, 227
Ahmadinejad, Mahmoud, 179, 212, 221
    anti-Israel rhetoric of, 181, 195–96, 207
    equated with Hitler, 156, 168, 170
    Iranian elections and, 142, 208–9, 213
    Iraqi relations with, 211
    nuclear program and, 153
    radical Islamic beliefs of, 196
Albright, David, 222–23
Allison, Jimmy, 87

Allison, Linda, 87
Al Qaeda, 56, 61, 104, 106, 119, 137, 138,
    149, 155, 157, 198, 199, 201, 255, 272
    in Afghanistan, 3, 215–16, 280
    Bush's characterizations of, 6–7
    Iranian stance toward, 182, 199, 200
    Iraqi insurgency blamed on, 165
    Iraqi links ascribed to, 97, 100–101,
        108, 109, 173
    Kerry's strategy against, 131, 133
    in Western Iraq, 3, 146, 215
Al Jazeera, 136
American Enterprise Institute (AEI), 22,
    42–43, 173–74
American Experience, 268–69, 271
American values, 244
    invoked by Bush in days after 9/11,
        103, 104
    Manichean mind-set at odds with,
        232–37, 263
Ammash, Huda Salih Mahdi, 115
Amnesty International, 244
anthrax, 3, 99, 100, 115, 121
anti-Americanism, 2, 35, 92, 135, 175, 180
    Bush's imperial mind-set and, 143
    decline of America's moral credibility
        and, 230–31, 237–38

anti-Americanism *(continued)*:
  of democratically elected leaders,
    142–43, 144
  inflamed by U.S. security impera-
    tives, 141–44, 237
  in Iran, 181
  neoconservatives' views on, 71–72
  spread of Islamic radicalism and,
    136–39
anti-Semitism, 72, 180
antiwar "radicals," 115–29, 136
  American military leaders and,
    122–23
  Manichean mind-set and, 116–19,
    121–22, 124, 128
Anvari, Haleh, 203, 220, 221
appeasement, 73, 106, 197
  Bush supporters' rhetoric and,
    167–69, 171, 177–78, 195, 206–7
Arar, Maher, 251–52
Arbīl, raid on Iranian consulate in, 225
Ashcroft, John, 89, 90
Assad, Bashar, 179
Associated Press (AP), 142, 151, 178, 243,
    247–48, 249, 250
Atlantic Monthly, 137
Augustine, St., 46
"axis of evil," 98–99, 100, 177, 222
  Iran included in, 99, 100, 155, 166,
    182, 187, 191, 197, 202–4, 220, 227

B

Baker, James, 20, 175–76, 179–80
Baker-Hamilton Commission. *See* Iraq
    Study Group
Baldwin, Stanley, 168
Barnes, Fred, 128, 267
Bartlett, Bruce, 68, 83, 270
Bauer, Gary, 195–96
Bayh, Evan, 164
BBC, 143–44, 203
Beinart, Peter, 126–28

Biden, Joe, 76
Bill of Rights, 233–34
bin Laden, Osama, 3, 110, 112, 120, 131,
    136–37, 179, 194, 195, 216
Blair, Tony, 89
Blankley, Tony, 25
Blitzer, Wolf, 114, 126, 127, 128
Bloomberg News, 14
Blum, Léon, 168
Blumenthal, Sidney, 246
Boykin, William G., 193–94, 196
Brazile, Donna, 127
Brinkley, Douglas, 35–36, 37
Brownstein, Ron, 13
Buchanan, Pat, 30–31, 53, 262
Buckley, William, 53
budget deficits. *See* deficit spending
Bumiller, Elisabeth, 113–14
Bush, George H. W., 20, 22, 25, 27,
    30–31, 60–61, 84–87, 179, 184
Bush, George W. *See also specific topics*
  adherence of, to failed policy, 147–51
  advisers' influence on, 44–45, 52
  approval ratings of, 1, 4–5, 6, 8, 12–13,
    14–15, 23, 30, 74, 91, 104, 122, 221,
    272, 277
  cabinet appointments of, 89–90
  collapse of popular support for, x, xi,
    1–18, 64–68, 79
  as conceivably worst U.S. president
    ever, 35–36
  confidence of, 75–82
  conservative principles violated by,
    41–44, 53–54, 61
  conservatives' rejection of, 26–32
  as Decider, 44–45, 89
  domestic failures of, 15–16, 91,
    256–60, 267–71
  entitlement sensibility of, 86–89, 92
  family and upbringing of, 86–87
  federal spending under, 3, 41–43, 217,
    257, 269
  information sources for, 85–86
  legacy of. *See* Bush legacy

loyalty demanded by, 82–86

Manichean moralism of. *See* Manichean mind-set

opposition as viewed by, 64–68, 70–71

religious faith of, 49, 57–66, 68–69, 83, 87–88

2000 presidential campaign and election of, 20, 39, 59–60, 89, 196

2002 State of the Union speech of, 98–100, 202–3

2004 campaign and reelection of, 13–14, 31–32, 39, 90, 122, 130–33, 139, 149–50, 189–90, 196, 236, 265

2004 State of the Union speech of, 143, 149

2005 State of the Union speech of, 221

Washington Establishment's abandonment of, 18–26

Bush, Laura, 148, 151

Bush at War (Woodward), 24–25

Bush Country (Podhoretz), 3–4, 23

Bush Doctrine, 157, 158, 163, 263

Bush legacy, x–xi, 2, 4, 25, 265–84

anti-Americanism and, 35, 230–31, 237–38

destruction of Republican brand and, 32–35

domestic failures and, 267–71

erosion of America's moral credibility and, 283–84

expansion of presidential power and, 2, 5, 92–95, 231–34, 243–46

expectation of historical vindication and, 66, 67

glorifying comparisons of, to Washington, Lincoln, Roosevelt, and Truman, 265–66, 267, 277–78

Iraq invasion and, 10, 267–68

Johnson legacy compared to, xiii–xiv, 268–69, 270–74, 276

political and ideological realignment and, 260–64

C

Canada, 143, 251

Cannon, Lou, 35–36

Carafano, James, 222

Card, Andy, 51, 85–86, 97

Carroll, Kathleen, 249

Carter, Jimmy, 26, 30, 33–34, 41

Casey, George W., Jr., 90, 147, 224

Castro, Fidel, 40, 49

Cato Institute, 41–42, 94

Cavalluzzo, Paul J. J., 251

CBS News, 14, 18–19, 88–89, 107–8, 272

Chamberlain, Neville, 167, 169, 177–78, 179, 197, 206–7

Charen, Mona, 70

Charge to Keep, A (Bush), 59, 69

Chávez, Hugo, 142, 144

Cheney, Dick, 9, 31, 90, 151, 153, 160, 163, 179, 191, 192, 211–12, 234, 262, 270

Cheney, Lynne, 114, 174

China, 3, 145, 217, 269

Chirac, Jacques, 160

Christianity, 46. *See also* evangelical Christians

Bush's evangelical faith and, 49, 57–66, 68–69

Muslims viewed as enemy of, 193–95

religious awakenings and, 63–65

Christians United for Israel, 195

Churchill, Winston, 29, 168, 171, 177

CIA (Central Intelligence Agency), 215, 216, 232, 249, 250, 255

Duelfer Report issued by, 8–12, 13

Civil War, American, 266, 267, 268, 277

Clark, Wesley, 57

Clarke, Richard, 57, 100

Cleland, Max, 57, 112

Clinton, Bill, 57, 85, 169

federal spending under Bush vs., 41–42

Iran policy and, 183–84

Clinton, Hillary, 36, 57, 198

CNN, 10, 106–7, 114, 115, 126–28, 268

Cobra II (Gordon and Trainor), 159–60

Colbert, Stephen, 82

Commentary, 171–73

communism, 40, 49, 66

Congress, U.S., 3, 5, 31, 43, 91, 93, 138,
    183, 198, 215, 250, 257, 258, 267,
    275, 282. *See also* House of Repre-
    sentatives, U.S.; Senate, U.S.
    and authorization of military force
        against Iran, 174–75, 227
    Bush's September 20, 2001, speech to
        Joint Session of, 6–8, 98, 106
    midterm elections and, x, 5–6, 17, 66,
        77–82, 90, 148, 174
    Military Commissions Act of 2006
        and, 2, 231–32, 242, 243–44, 246,
        256
    Republican, conservatives' animus
        toward, 27, 28, 29

Congressional Research Service, 182, 185

Conscience of a Conservative, The (Gold-
    water), 53

conservatism, conservatives:
    Bush rejected by, 26–32
    Bush's deviation from precepts of,
        41–44, 53–54, 61
    Bush's religious convictions at odds
        with, 61–62
    political realignment and, 260, 262
    principles of, 39–40
    Reagan's deviation from precepts of,
        41
    theory vs. practice of, 39–41

Conservative Soul, The (Sullivan), 62,
    68–69

Conservatives Without Conscience
    (Dean), 53, 54, 55, 95

Constitution, U.S., 94, 122, 150, 233–34,
    282

"cowboy diplomacy," 163–64

Crumpton, Henry, 138

Cuba, 162, 250

D

Dallas Morning News, 33

Dallek, Robert, 268

Daniels, Mitch, 85

Daniszewski, John, 248

Darman, Richard, 84, 85

Dean, Howard, 117–22, 125, 128
    demonization of, 118, 121–22
    preinvasion arguments against Iraq
        War made by, 117–21

Dean, John, 53, 54, 55, 57, 95

de Borchgrave, Arnaud, 197, 198

Dedman, Bill, 254–55

Defense Department, U.S., 35

deficit spending, 3, 41, 217, 257,
    269
    conservatives' views on, 27, 30,
        39

DeLay, Tom, 31, 42

democracy, 218, 266
    Bush's imperative for spreading of,
        63, 132, 141–45, 149–50
    election of anti-American leaders
        and, 142–43, 144
    in Iran vs. U.S. allies in region,
        212–13

Democratic Party, Democrats, 8, 11, 26,
    110, 112, 118, 122, 137, 198, 227,
    252–53, 259, 267
    destruction of Republican brand
        and, 33–35
    midterm elections and, x, 6, 17, 65,
        66, 78, 80, 90
    support for war with Iran among, 164

de Rugy, Veronique, 42

detentions, 2, 72, 231–32, 236, 238–46
    of al-Marri, 242–44, 245
    at Guantánamo, 2, 231, 243, 250,
        252–53, 254–56
    of journalists, 247–48, 250
    Military Commissions Act of 2006
        and, 231–32, 239, 242, 243–44,
        246

by other nations, U.S. response to,
245, 246
of Padilla, 92, 231, 238–42, 245, 246
Devlin, Peter, 146
DiIulio, John, 270
Dobson, James, 31–32, 106–7, 195
Doherty, Brian, 50
domestic affairs:
Bush's failures in, 15–16, 91, 256–60,
267–71
Johnson's achievements in, 37,
268–69
domestic surveillance, 30, 93, 232, 235,
236, 248, 253
Dreher, Rod, 33–35
Drudge Report, 14
Drury, Shadia, 50
Duelfer, Charles, 8, 10
Duelfer Report, 8–12, 13
due process, 231–32, 244, 252–53
Durbin, Richard, 66, 267

E

eavesdropping, warrantless, 93, 235, 236,
248, 253
Egypt, 73, 145, 212, 251
elections:
2000 (presidential), 20, 31, 196
2002 (midterm), x, 5–6, 17, 112
2004 (presidential), 13–14, 31–32, 122,
130–33, 139, 149–50, 189–90, 196,
236, 265
2006 (midterm), x, xi, 17, 26, 65, 66,
75, 77–82, 90, 95, 148, 150, 154,
174, 276
Ellis, Joseph, 234
end-of-life issues, 43
enemies, endless need for, 53–57
"enemy combatant" status, 243
English-speaking peoples, alliance
of, 71
Enlightenment, 50–51

evangelical Christians, 192, 193–96
Bush's reelection and, 31–32
Bush's religious faith and, 49, 57–66,
68–69, 87–88
disapproval of Bush among, 74
Iraq War supported by, 69–70, 74
Islam as viewed by, 193–95
Manichean mind-set among, 73–74,
76, 83, 193–95
Evil, 20. *See also* "axis of evil"; Mani-
chean mind-set
Bush's frequent use of word, 101
enemy concept and, 53–57

F

Faith of George W. Bush, The (Mans-
field), 60
Fallows, James, 137
FBI (Federal Bureau of Investigation),
242, 251, 254
Federal Emergency Management
Agency (FEMA), 84–85
federal government:
in battle of Good vs. Evil, 45–46
conservatives' belief in limited power
of, 39–40, 43, 61–62
Reagan's expansion of, 41
Feingold, Russ, 125
Feith, Douglas, 100
Financial Times, 187, 208
Ford, Gerald, 30
Foreign Intelligence Surveillance Act
(FISA), 93–94
Foreign Policy, 91
Foshee, Cuc, 245, 246
Fox News, 9, 25–26, 60, 65, 85–86,
148–49, 151
France, 73, 160, 168
Franks, Tommy, 160
Free Inquiry, 50
Friedman, Tom, 128
Frontline, 184

Front Page Magazine, 22
Froomkin, Dan, 78, 90
Frum, David, 23, 44–45, 61–62, 84, 85, 173, 202, 212
fundamentalism, 68–69, 76, 126. *See also* evangelical Christians

G

Gadhafi, Muammar al-, 189
Gallup polls, 15, 268, 272
Gardner, Sam, 222
Gates, Robert, 124
George, Robert, 127
Gerecht, Reuel Marc, 174, 203
Germany, 159–60, 252. *See also* Nazi Germany
Gerson, Michael, 163–64, 200
Gigot, Paul, 70, 75, 79, 144, 162
Gillespie, Nick, 42
Gingrich, Newt, 28, 29, 128, 167–68, 177
Giuliani, Rudy, 128, 266
Goldberg, Jeffrey, 164
Goldberg, Jonah, 26, 126–28, 169–70
Goldwater, Barry, 53, 54, 76
Gonzales, Alberto, 90, 234, 256, 263
Good and Evil. *See* "axis of evil"; evil; Manichean mind-set
Gorbachev, Mikhail S., 177
Gordon, Michael, 111, 159–60
Gore, Al, 18, 20, 57
Goudreau, Rosemary, 249
governorships, midterm elections of 2002 and 2006 and, 6, 17
Graham, Rev. Billy, 59
Great Britain, 71, 168, 189, 195, 223
    plot by Islamic extremists uncovered in, 134–36
Great Society, 268–69
Guantánamo detainees, 2, 92–93, 231, 243, 250, 252–53, 254–56
Gulf War. *See* Persian Gulf War
gun control, 117

H

Haaretz, 61
habeas corpus, denial of, 253
Hafetz, Jonathan, 244
Hagee, John, 195
Hagel, Chuck, 18, 222, 262
Haj, Sami al-, 250
Hamas, 142, 144, 200, 201, 206
Hamdi, Yaser Esam, 231
Hamilton, Lee, 19
Hammami, Unees, 213
Hannity, Sean, 148–49, 262
Hanson, Victor Davis, 170–71
Hastert, Dennis, 31
Hatch, Orrin, 157
hawks, traditional, 191–92, 193
Hayden, Michael V., 215, 216
Herman, Arthur, 171–73
Hewitt, Hugh, 79–80, 82, 170, 171
Hezbollah, 138, 142, 157, 200–201, 206
    Israeli war with (2006), 89, 134, 195, 205–6
Hill, Julie, 213
Himmelfarb, Gertrude, 70, 71
Hitler, Adolf, 100, 177, 277
    Bush supporters' rhetoric and, 168–71
    Iran's leaders equated with, 154, 156, 161, 168, 170, 208, 209, 227
    Saddam equated with, 105–7, 156, 161
Holocaust, 207, 209
House of Representatives, U.S., 18, 138, 282–83. *See also* Congress, U.S.
    midterm elections and, x, 6, 17, 77, 79, 90
How Would a Patriot Act? (Greenwald), 93
Human Events Magazine, 55, 167–68
human rights abuses, 211–12, 213, 244, 283
Hume, Brit, 60, 85–86
Hurricane Katrina, 15, 23, 84, 258, 268, 269
Hussein, Bilal, 247–48, 250

I

Ignatius, David, 18
Independents, x, 6, 11
India, 214
Inhofe, James, 196
interrogation, coercive, 2, 239, 244,
    254–56. *See also* torture
"intolerance" rhetoric, 91
Iran, 20, 63, 95, 120, 124, 128, 140, 141,
    142, 143–44, 153–227, 250, 258
  Afghanistan issue and, 182–83, 184,
    185–86
  anti-Iraq rhetoric repeated almost
    verbatim with regard to, 156–59
  authorization for use of military force
    against, 174–75, 227
  in "axis of evil," 99, 100, 155, 166, 182,
    187, 191, 197, 202–4, 220, 227
  bellicose language toward, 2, 90,
    154–66, 191, 197, 220–22, 227
  as beneficiary of Iraq War, 145, 146,
    185
  Bush's denial of war plans against,
    160–61
  in Bush's Manichean framework, 154,
    166–67, 191, 197, 202–4, 207, 214,
    221, 227
  Bush supporters eager for war
    against, 163–65, 166–75, 191–96,
    205–7
  Clinton policy toward, 183–84
  conciliatory overture made to U.S. by
    (2003), 187–91
  democratic processes in, 212–13
  destructive effects of Bush's rhetoric
    on, 219–27
  equated with Nazi Germany, 154, 161,
    167–68, 197, 210, 214, 227
  friendly relations of, with other coun-
    tries, 210–11
  gap between reality and Bush's rheto-
    ric on, 181–82, 214
  hostage crisis in (1979), 33–34, 183, 187

  human rights abuses in, 211–12, 213
  Iraqi war with (1980s), 145, 185, 190
  Israeli relations with, 187, 188,
    197–98, 200–205, 207, 209
  Jews in, 213
  lack of U.S. military option against,
    222–23
  leaders of, equated with Hitler, 154,
    156, 161, 168, 170, 208, 209, 227
  newly elected government of Iraq
    and, 182, 210–11, 224
  non-cartoon description of, 207–14
  nuclear program of, 73, 90, 91, 153,
    154–55, 156, 158, 161, 162, 164, 166,
    171–72, 175, 187–88, 190, 198, 214,
    221, 222
  oil assets of, 172, 192
  political life within, 207–9, 211–14,
    219–20
  possibility of diplomatic solution
    with, 158–59, 160, 161, 166, 168,
    175, 179, 180, 181
  preclusion of meaningful policy
    debate on, 214–15
  preparations for U.S. attack in,
    221–22
  rationality of leaders of, 186
  religious pluralism in, 213
  as state sponsor of terrorism, 156,
    157, 158, 161, 162, 163, 199–207,
    221
  U.S. military activity in Persian Gulf
    and, 223–24
  U.S. national emergency declaration
    and, 183–84
  U.S. rapprochement with, in wake of
    9/11 attacks, 181–83, 184–87, 197,
    199, 202–3
  women's status in, 213
Iraq, 6, 183, 206, 212, 222, 223, 250
  Al Qaeda links ascribed to, 97,
    100–101, 108, 109, 173
  Al Qaeda stronghold in, 3, 146,
    215

Iraq *(continued):*
  Bush's denial of war plans against, 159–60
  Bush's rhetoric against, repeated almost verbatim with regard to Iran, 156–59
  equated with Nazi Germany, 105–7, 156, 161
  Iranian relations with newly elected government of, 182, 210–11, 224
  Iranian war with (1980s), 145, 185, 190
  pre-9/11 intentions for invasion of, 51, 100
  terrorism linkage ascribed to, 105, 107–8, 109
  U.N. weapons inspection process in, 105–6, 116, 121
  uniqueness of threat posed by, 155–56, 157
Iraq Study Group (ISG; Baker-Hamilton Commission), 19–21, 66, 147, 148, 151, 224, 227
  Bush and his supporters' reactions to, 175–76, 179–81, 195
Iraq War, 2, 25, 26, 32, 33, 34, 35, 67, 75, 91, 97–151, 154, 168, 169, 170, 174, 192, 195, 205, 215, 217, 219, 221, 227, 282
  Al Qaeda as beneficiary of, 146
  Americans never asked to sacrifice for, 279, 280–81
  anti-Americanism inflamed by, 11, 72, 136–39, 237
  Bush legacy and, 267–68
  Bush's adherence to failed policy in, 147–51
  Bush's December 2006 press conference on, 23–24
  Bush's Manichean mind-set and, 61, 63, 66, 68, 71, 86, 97–151, 155–56, 214, 259–60
  Bush's reliance upon gut instinct and, 76

  Bush's speeches in lead-up to, 98–104, 106, 109–10
  confrontation with Iran in relation to, 163–66, 175
  date for withdrawal from, 72, 181
  decline of popular support for, 11–12, 16, 64–67, 79, 272
  escalation of ("surge" strategy), 18–19, 21, 66, 88–89, 90, 95, 165–66, 174, 225, 276–77, 279–80
  European allies and, 159–60
  evangelicals' support for, 69–70, 74
  exit strategy nonexistent in, 123
  graphic photos of carnage in, 130, 136
  insufficient troop strength and, 279–80
  insurgency and, 139–40, 190, 247, 266–67
  invasion stage of, 8, 259
  Iran as beneficiary of, 145, 146, 185
  Iraqi casualties of, 146
  Islamic radicalism fueled by, 136–39
  journalists' abdication of watchdog role in lead-up to, 108–9, 110–15
  media accused of exaggerating situation in, 147–48
  "Mission Accomplished" declaration in, 266–67
  mistakes made in management of, 16, 90
  normalization of war and, 129–39
  playing cards with pictures of wanted Iraqis in, 114–15
  preinvasion opponents of, 115–29
  rationales for, 5, 51, 97–151, 155–56, 188–90, 198–99, 272–73
  Senate authorization vote for, 107, 110, 112, 119, 131
  supposed linkage to 9/11 attacks and, 51, 97–104, 106–8, 140, 198–99
  U.S. military spending and, 3
  U.S. security harmed by, 140–41
  Vietnam War compared to, 271–77

WMD issue and, 8–12, 16, 99, 105–6, 107, 109, 110, 111, 115–16, 121, 125–28, 146, 155–56, 189, 199
ISG Report, 180
Isikoff, Mike, 138
Islam, Muslims, 6, 7, 16, 103
   evangelical Christians' views on, 193–95
   Israel's right to exist and, 210
Islamic Iran Participation Front, 208–9
Islamic radicalism, 226. *See also* terrorism, terrorists; *specific groups*
   fueled by Iraq War, 136–39
   Manichean approach in, 195, 196
   neoconservatives' views on, 205–6, 261
Israel, 72, 143, 163, 164, 180, 187, 188, 192, 195, 207, 213, 214, 218, 250, 258
   evangelical Christians and, 193, 195–96
   Hezbollah war with (2006), 89, 134, 195, 205–6
   hostility toward, throughout Middle East, 209–10
   neoconservative supporters of, 192, 193, 205–7
   Palestinian peace agreement with, 20, 21, 175, 179
   as target of terrorism, 200–201
   U.S. policy toward Iran influenced by, 197–98, 200–205
Italy, 195

J

Jacoby, Mary, 87
Japan, 143, 195, 266, 277
Jay, John, 282
Jefferson, Thomas, 232
Johndroe, Gordon, 224
Johnson, Lyndon, xiii–xiv, 42, 270–74
   collapse of presidency of, 14, 15, 272, 276, 282

domestic achievements of, 37, 268–69, 270–71
   Manichean rhetoric of, 273–74
   reelection bid declined by, 271–72, 276
   Vietnam War and, 14, 15, 37, 84, 268, 271–74, 276
Jordan (nation), 145, 251
Jordan, Vernon, 20–21
journalists and media pundits, 57, 86, 136, 141, 160
   accused of exaggerating violence in Iraq, 147–48
   adversarial watchdog role abdicated by, 108–9, 110–15
   Bush's abandonment by Washington Establishment and, 18–26
   Kerry's anti-terrorism strategy ridiculed by, 131
   overwhelming respect for Bush among, 114
   preinvasion opponents of war either ignored or pilloried by, 116, 118, 121, 125, 126–29
   press freedoms and, 247–50
Justice Department, U.S., 243

K

Kagan, Fred, 128, 174, 279–80
Kagan, Robert, 54, 159
Kakutani, Michiko, 24–25
Kamiya, Gary, 20–21
Karzai, Hamid, 182, 215, 216
Katrina disaster, 15, 23, 84, 258, 268, 269
Keane, Jack, 279, 280
Keller, Ric, 245
Kennedy, John, 163, 268–69, 275
Kennedy, Ted, 30
Kerry, John, 13–14, 57, 122, 133–34, 135, 141
Kessler, Glenn, 187–88, 190
Khalilzad, Zalmay, 90

Khamenei, Ayatollah Ali, 187, 208, 220

Kharrazi, Kamal, 184

Khatami, Mohammad, 183, 187, 207–8, 220

King, Larry, 106, 195

Klein, Joe, 21–22, 145

Koh, Harold Hongju, 283

Kohut, Andrew, 33

Kondrake, Mort, 25–26

Krauthammer, Charles, 128, 170, 175, 180

Kristol, Bill, 50, 128, 168–69, 174–75, 205–6, 262

Kristol, Irving, 49–51, 174

Kull, Steven, 91

Kurds, 179

L

Langer, Gary, 14–15

LaRouche, Lyndon, 173

Layaz, Saiid, 221

Lears, Jackson, 60

Lebanon, 134, 142, 158, 163, 200, 202. *See also* Hezbollah

Ledeen, Michael, 22, 173, 180, 206–7

Leverett, Flynt, 185–86, 190

Lewis, Bernard, 170

Liberal Fascism (Goldberg), 169

liberalism, liberals, 30, 53, 55, 169, 260, 262

Libya, 189–90

Lichtblau, Eric, 248

Lieberman, Avigdor, 197

Lieberman, Joseph, 122, 128, 140, 165, 200, 262–63

Limbaugh, Rush, 26, 29, 31, 180, 262

Lincoln, Abraham, ix, 13, 64, 265, 266, 267, 268, 277, 281

Lithwick, Dahlia, 92–93, 94

Looming Tower, The (Wright), 135

Los Angeles Times, 13, 33, 56, 128

Lowry, Rich, 28, 29, 32, 63–64, 75, 128, 149, 159

Lyon, Santiago, 248

M

Madison, James, 13

Malaysia, 188, 210

Maliki, Nuri al-, 211

Malkin, Michelle, 247

Manichean, use of term, 46

Manichean mind-set, x–xi, 45–95, 229–64, 281

  appeasement accusations and, 167–69, 171, 177–78, 195, 206–7

  assault on press freedoms and, 246–50

  "axis of evil" designation and, 98–99, 100, 177. *See also* "axis of evil"

  bin Laden's embrace of, 137

  Bush's domestic failures and, 256–59

  Bush's religious faith and, 49, 57–66, 68–69, 87–88

  contrary to core American principles, 232–37

  democracy imperative and, 63, 141–45, 149–50

  demonization of Saddam and, 105–8

  disregard for opposing viewpoints and, 37–38, 64–73

  endless need for enemies and, 53–57

  entitlement sensibility and, 86–89, 92

  among evangelical Christians, 73–74, 76, 83, 193–95

  expansion of presidential power and, 92–95, 231–34, 243–46

  in face of weakness and defeat, 89–95

  faith-based certitude and, 75–82, 148–51

  Hitler or Nazism comparisons and, 167–71. *See also* Hitler, Adolf; Nazi Germany immoral acts resulting from, 229–31, 238–46, 251–56, 283–84

Iran policy and, 153–227

Iraq War and, 61, 63, 66, 68, 71, 86, 97–151, 155–56, 214, 259–60

of Islamic extremists, 195

Johnson's rhetoric on Vietnam War and, 273–74

journalists' abdication of adversarial watchdog role and, 108–9, 110–15

loyalty demands and, 82–86

motives and beliefs leading to, 48–49, 73

neoconservatives and, 49–51, 53–54, 70–73, 260–64

normalization of war and, 129–39

political and ideological realignment and, 260–64

pragmatic vs. moral considerations and, 47–48

preclusion of rational debate and, 214–15, 217–19

preinvasion opponents of war and, 116–19, 121–22, 124, 128

presidential infallibility and, 253–54

prioritizing of physical safety and, 232–37

public opinion manipulated in terms of, 49–51

pure Good and Evil and, 47

religious awakenings and, 63–65

Republican establishment figures at odds with, 175–77

rigid adherence to failed policy and, 147–51

September 11 attacks and, 55–56, 57, 98–104, 140

in supporters' efforts to influence Bush, 166–67, 169, 173, 178, 191, 203–4

Mansfield, Stephen, 60

Mao Tse-tung, 40, 49

Marri, Ali Saleh Kahlah al-, 242–44, 245

Martinez, Mel, 245, 246, 253

Marx, Karl, 40, 50

Masri, Khalid El-, 252

McAuliffe, Terry, 13–14

McCain, John, 31, 124, 128

McConnell, Mitch, 252–53

McKinnon, Mark, 267

McNamara, Robert, 275

media. *See* journalists and media pundits; Washington Establishment

Medoff, Rafael, 105–6

Meet the Press, 21–22, 105–6, 140

Merkel, Angela, 252

Mesbah-Yazdi, Ayatollah Mohammed-Taghi, 208

Meyer, Dick, 18–19

Middle East, 75, 128, 141, 145, 166, 180, 261. *See also specific countries*

anti-American resentment in, 136–39, 142, 175, 180, 181

anti-Israeli sentiments in, 209–10

Bush's Manichean mind-set and, 61, 63, 70–71, 155, 180–81

ISG's recommendations on, 20–21

media in, 136

nuclearization of, 73

oil in, 172, 192, 218

preclusion of meaningful policy debate on, 214–19

spread of Islamic radicalism in, 136–39

U.S. strength in, demonstrated by Iraq invasion, 188–90

U.S. ties with repressive regimes in, 211–12

Miers, Harriet, 15, 90

Military Commissions Act (MCA) (2006), 2, 231–32, 239, 242, 243–44, 246, 256

military spending, 3, 41

Miller, Geoffrey, 255, 256

Miller, Judith, 111

MSNBC, 254–55, 256

Mubarak, Hosni, 212

Murtha, John, 57, 125, 128
Muslim Americans, 7, 103
Muslims. *See* Islam, Muslims
Mylorie, Laurie, 173–74

N

Naím, Moisés, 91
Nasrallah, Sheik Hassan, 201
National Intelligence Estimate (NIE),
　138–39
nationalism, extreme, 48–49
National Public Radio (NPR), 33–35
National Review, 22, 23, 26, 32, 33, 55,
　63–64, 75, 149, 159, 169, 206–7,
　208, 212, 262
National Review Institute Conservative
　Summit (2007), 27–28
National Rifle Association (NRA), 117
National Security Agency (NSA), 93,
　232
National Security Council (NSC), 100
National Strategy for Combating
　Terrorism, 161–62, 201
Nazi Germany, 100, 177, 266, 277
　Bush supporters' rhetoric and,
　　167–71, 195
　Iran equated with, 154, 161, 167–68,
　　197, 210, 214, 227
　Iraq equated with, 105–7, 156, 161
Negroponte, John, 90, 138, 139
neoconservatism, neoconservatives,
　49–51, 53–54, 122–23, 141, 195,
　260–64
　Baker attacked by, 179–80
　Bush's Manichean mind-set and,
　　70–73
　central tenets of, 260–61
　Iran policy and, 171–74, 192, 193, 203,
　　205–7, 208
　Israel-centrism among, 192, 193
Netanyahu, Binyamin, 197, 198
Neuharth, Al, 36

Neumann, Ronald E., 216
Newhouse, John, 184–85
New Republic, 179, 208
Newsweek, 35, 84, 138, 163–64, 200
New Yorker, The, 164
New York Post, 23–24, 175, 180
New York Review of Books, 69–70, 194
New York Sun, 174–75, 211, 262
New York Times, 24–25, 26, 30–31, 60,
　93, 97, 111–12, 113–14, 138–39, 153,
　165–66, 186, 195–96, 197, 216,
　223–24, 225, 234–35, 248, 272
New York Times Magazine, 83–84, 131, 135
Nichols, Terry, 174
Nietzsche, Friedrich, 239
9/11 attacks. *See* September 11 attacks
Nixon, Richard, xi, 13, 14, 26, 27, 31, 36,
　42, 53, 277
Noonan, Peggy, 4, 22–23
Northern Alliance, 182
North Korea, 91, 99, 143–44, 162, 163,
　169, 197, 222, 223–24, 250
Novak, Bob, 26, 32
Novak, Michael, 71
Nuclear Non-Proliferation Treaty
　(NPT), 214
nuclear weapons. *See also* weapons of
　mass destruction
　of Iran, 73, 90, 91, 153, 154–55, 156,
　　158, 161, 162, 164, 166, 171–72, 175,
　　187–88, 190, 198, 214, 221, 222
　Iraq's supposed development of, 99,
　　100, 110, 156
　of North Korea, 162
　U.S. allies proliferation of, 214
　U.S. incentives for, 222
Nunn, Sam, 222

O

Obama, Barack, 125
O'Beirne, Kate, 70, 149
O'Connor, Sandra Day, 20–21

oil, 172, 192, 218
Olmert, Ehud, 197
O'Neill, Paul, 57, 76, 100, 270
Orange County Register, 177
O'Reilly, Bill, 60, 65, 68

P

Padilla, José, 92, 231, 238–42, 245, 246
Paine, Thomas, 232
Painting the Map Red (Hewitt), 79
Pajamas Media, 180
Pakistan, 135, 145, 212, 214, 250
Palestinian Islamic Jihad, 200, 201
Palestinians, 61, 72, 142, 144, 180
  Iranian policy toward, 187, 188, 200,
    202, 203
Parsi, Trita, 188, 190, 191
Patriot Act, 121, 235
PBS, 184, 268–69, 271
Pelosi, Nancy, 79, 88–89, 125, 128
Peretz, Marty, 179–80
Perle, Richard, 105–6, 173, 174
Persian Gulf War (1991), 10, 123, 129–30,
    179, 186
Peters, Ralph, 180
Pew Research Center for the People &
    the Press, 12–13, 30, 33, 74
Phelps, Fred, 173
Phillips, Howard, 177
Pickering, Thomas, 184–85
Plan of Attack (Woodward), 67
Podhoretz, John, 3–4, 23–24, 173, 175,
    180, 206
Podhoretz, Norman, 70, 71, 172–73
Politico, 266
Popper, Sir Karl, 229
port deal controversy, 258–59
port operations, 15–16, 280
Powell, Colin, 76, 90, 121, 184
pragmatism, 74, 83
presidential power, Bush's expansion of,
    2, 5, 92–95, 231–34, 243–46

press freedoms, assault on, 247–50
Price of Loyalty, The (Suskind), 100
Priest, Dana, 248–49
pundits. *See* journalists and media
    pundits

Q

Qahtani, Mohammed al-, 254–55

R

Rafsanjani, Hashemi, 208
Rahn, Richard, 270
Rasmussen Reports, 80–81, 259
Reagan, Ronald, 26–27, 29, 30, 31, 32, 34,
    61, 62, 84, 129, 176–78, 184, 200
  appeasement of Soviet Union
    ascribed to, 177–78
  as embodiment of political conser-
    vatism, 41
Real Clear Politics, 81
Reason, 50
Rebel in Chief (Barnes), 267
religion, 48, 55. *See also* Christianity;
    evangelical Christians; Islam,
    Muslims
  Bush's Manichean mind-set and, 49,
    57–66, 68
  fundamentalism and, 68–69
religious awakenings, 63–65
rendition, 230–31, 232, 236, 251–52
Reporters Without Borders (RSF),
    249–50
Republican National Convention
    (RNC) (2004), 131–33, 150, 183,
    236
Republican Party, Republicans, 18,
    26–27, 28, 83, 110, 118, 196, 246,
    257, 258, 259
  Buchanan's primary challenge to
    Bush 41 and, 30–31

Republican Party, Republicans
    (continued):
  Bush's destruction of Republican
    brand and, 32–35
  federal spending increases under,
    41–43
  midterm elections and, x, 6, 17,
    77–82, 90, 148, 150, 174, 276
Reuters, 153
Revolutionary War, 265–66
Rice, Condoleezza, 18, 85–86, 90, 97,
    108, 225, 252
Ricks, Thomas, 146
Right Man, The (Frum), 23, 44–45,
    61–62, 84
Risen, James, 216, 248
Ritter, Scott, 57, 125–28, 128
Roberts, Andrew, 70, 71–72, 73
Robertson, Pat, 60, 177
Robinson, James, 60
Rohde, David, 216
Romney, Mitt, 31
Roosevelt, Franklin, 6, 13, 266, 268,
    278, 281
Rove, Karl, 77, 78, 85, 265, 270
Rubin, Michael, 169
Rumsfeld, Donald, 50, 85, 89–90, 92,
    100, 148, 153, 160, 163, 177–78,
    179, 191, 194, 254, 277
Russert, Tim, 21
Ryan, Robert, 275

S

Saddam Hussein, 5, 21, 22, 61, 112,
    114–15, 119, 123, 132–33, 136, 139,
    160, 173, 179, 194, 211, 222, 248, 259
  Al Qaeda contacts ascribed to, 97
  equated with Hitler, 105–7, 156, 161
  execution of, 130, 170–71
  Iranian cooperation in ouster of, 185
  links to international terrorism
    ascribed to, 97, 109, 199

  Manichean rhetoric against, 105–8,
    109, 145, 214
  9/11 connection ascribed to, 51, 99,
    107–8, 109, 116, 199
  pre-9/11 desire for overthrow of, 100
  purported weapons programs of,
    8–12, 107, 109, 110, 111, 115–16, 121,
    125–28, 155–56, 189, 199
  uniqueness of threat posed by, 155–56
Safire, William, 31
St. Louis Post-Dispatch, 177
Salon, 20–21, 87, 203, 220
SALT treaty, 177–78
San Francisco Chronicle, 221–22
San Jose Mercury News, 222–23
Santorum, Rick, 31
Saudi Arabia, 73, 145, 188, 192, 210, 212,
    250
Schiavo, Terri, 43
Schier, Steven, 267–68
Senate, U.S., 18, 196. *See also* Congress,
    U.S.
  Armed Services Committee, 215, 216
  authorization vote for Iraq War in,
    107, 110, 112, 119, 131
  Foreign Relations Committee, 18,
    124, 170
  midterm elections and, x, 6, 17, 79,
    80–81, 90
September 11 attacks (2001), 2, 4–5, 34,
    47, 93, 126, 132, 137, 165, 196, 210,
    221, 235, 236, 256, 258. *See also*
    terrorism, terrorists
  Americans' faith in Bush in wake of,
    ix–x, 68
  Bush's explanation for motives
    behind, 144
  Bush's rhetoric in days after, 6–8,
    98–104, 106
  law enforcement efforts and, 135
  Manichean mind-set and, 55–56, 57,
    98–104, 106, 107, 140
  manipulation of American public
    opinion and, 198–99

rationale for Iraq War and, 51, 97–104,
106–8, 109, 116, 140, 198–99
U.S. rapprochement with Iran in
wake of, 181–83, 184–87
SERE (Survival, Evasion, Resistance,
and Escape), 255
Shiites, 140, 145, 146, 155, 157, 179, 182,
185, 199, 210–11
signing statements, 92
Simpson, Alan, 20–21
60 Minutes, 100, 150
Smith, Jeffrey, 91
Smith, Mary, 87
Snow, Tony, 266–67
Social Security, 15, 23, 79, 257, 267, 269
Soviet Union, 123, 177–78, 186
Spiegel, Der, 250
State Department, U.S., 182–83, 187, 245
State of Denial (Woodward), 24–25
states rights, 40, 43, 117
Stelzer, Irwin, 70–73
Stevens, John Paul, 57
Stoll, Richard, 15
Strauss, Leo, 50–51
Sudan, 91, 162
Sullivan, Andrew, 31, 62, 68–69, 262
Sunnis, 139–40, 145, 155, 157, 182, 185,
199, 212, 215
Supreme Court, U.S., 15, 56–57, 89,
238, 268
Suskind, Ron, 76, 83–84, 85, 100, 250,
270
Syria, 89, 141, 212
Bush supporters' bellicose rhetoric
toward, 170, 171, 205, 206
ISG recommendations on, 20, 175
rendition in, 251
as state sponsor of terrorism, 157, 162

T

Taha, Rihab Rashid, 115
Taheri, Amir, 208

Takeyh, Ray, 221
Talabani, Jalal, 224
Taliban, 3, 6, 106, 137, 169, 182–83,
185–86, 194, 199, 215, 216, 255,
280
tax cuts, 217, 257, 268, 269
Tenet, George, 250
terrorism, terrorists, 54, 55, 63, 123,
220, 268, 272–73, 280. *See also*
September 11 attacks; *specific
terrorist groups*
abductions, detentions, rendition,
and torture as responses to threat
of, 230–32, 236, 238–46, 251–56
assault on press freedoms and,
247–50
democracy as antidote for, 132, 141–45
expansion of presidential power and,
92–94, 231–34, 243–46
heightened fear of, 110–11
inflamed by Bush policies, 136–46
Iraqi insurgents labeled as, 139–40
Kerry's strategy against, 131, 133–34,
135, 141
Manichean mind-set and, 51, 52,
105–8, 130–39, 229–64
manipulative uses of term, 139
National Strategy for Combating
Terrorism and, 161–62, 201
opponents of Bush policy accused of
siding with, 105, 107, 112, 114,
116–17
political realignment in U.S. and,
262
port deal controversy and, 258–59
prioritizing of physical safety and,
232–37
"state sponsors of," 156, 157, 158, 161,
162, 163, 198–207, 221
U.K. bomb conspiracy and, 134–36
War on, 161, 193, 194, 196, 263, 279
Thatcher, Margaret, 62
Third Great Awakening, 63–65
Thomas, Evan, 84

Time, 21, 128, 145, 170

Tira, Oded, 198

Tonkin Gulf Resolution (1964), 276

torture, 2, 146, 230–31, 232, 236, 239, 244, 251–52, 253, 254–56

Trainor, Bernard, 159–60

Truman, Harry S., 13, 65–66, 226, 265, 267, 277, 281

Turkey, 120

U

"unacceptable," presidential use of term, 161

United Arab Emirates (UAE), 15–16, 145, 209–10
   port deal and, 258–59

United Nations (U.N.), 106, 121, 131, 142, 183, 223, 244
   Iran's nuclear program and, 153, 156, 158, 171
   weapons inspection process and, 105–6, 116, 121, 125, 126, 127, 128, 158, 189

UPI, 177, 197, 198

U.S. News & World Report, 77–78

USA Today, 36, 107, 267–68

V

values. *See* American values

Venezuela, 142, 144

Vietnam, detention of U.S. citizen in, 245, 246

Vietnam War, 34, 37, 84, 129, 268
   collapse of Johnson presidency and, 14, 15
   Iraq War compared to, 271–77
   Johnson's Manichean rhetoric on, 273–74
   origins of, 274–75

Voinovich, George, 170

W

Wallace, Mike, 150

Wall Street Journal, 4, 22, 23, 75, 79, 144, 162

Walsh, Kenneth, 77–78

wars. *See also specific wars*
   constitutional provisions on declaration of, 281–82
   normalization of, 129–39
   presidential legacies and, 268

Washington, George, 265–66, 267

Washington Establishment:
   Bush abandoned by, 18–26
   findings of Iraq Study Group and, 19–21
   initial support for Iraq War denied by, 21–22
   reversals of opinion in, 22–26

Washington Monthly, 30, 173–74

Washington Post, 1, 10, 16, 18, 24, 35–36, 54, 59–60, 77, 78, 90, 91, 92–93, 122–23, 128, 146, 156–57, 161, 165, 170, 175, 184–85, 187–88, 190, 200, 211–12, 215, 216, 222, 248–49, 252, 270, 280

Washington Times, 25, 270

weapons of mass destruction (WMDs):
   Iranian nuclear program and, 73, 90, 91, 153, 154–55, 156, 158, 161, 162, 164, 166, 171–72, 175, 187–88, 190, 198, 214, 221, 222
   Iraq's purported development of, 8–12, 16, 99, 105–6, 107, 109, 110, 111, 115–16, 121, 125–28, 146, 155–56, 189, 199
   Ritter's antiwar views on, 125–28
   U.N. weapons inspection process and, 105–6, 116, 121, 125, 126, 127, 128, 158, 189

Webb, Jim, 122–24

Weekly Standard, 70, 71, 168–69, 203, 205–6

Westmoreland, William, 276

White House Correspondents Dinner
(2006), 82
Whitman, Christine Todd, 76, 85
Wilkerson, Lawrence, 246
Will, George, 53–54, 133–34, 135, 141,
262
Wills, Garry, 69–70, 194, 196
Wilson, Joe, 57
Wilson, Woodrow, 268
Wolf, Josh, 250
Wolfowitz, Paul, 50, 100, 174
Wolfson, Charles, 222
Woodward, Bob, 24–25, 60–61, 63, 67,
150
Woolsey, James, 163
World Trade Center. *See also* September
11 attacks
first bombing of, 173
World War I, 123, 268

World War II, 72, 178, 195, 266, 268,
277–78. *See also* appeasement;
Nazi Germany
Wright, Lawrence, 135

Y

Ynet, 198
Yoo, John, 173, 256

Z

Zakaria, Fareed, 35
Zawahiri, Ayman al-, 216
Zeeck, David, 248
Zelizer, Julian, 151
Zinsmeister, Karl, 174